Markets against Modernity

Capitalist Thought: Studies in Philosophy, Politics, and Economics

Series Editor: Edward W. Younkins, Wheeling Jesuit University

Mission Statement

This book series is devoted to studying the foundations of capitalism from a number of academic disciplines including, but not limited to, philosophy, political science, economics, law, literature, and history. Recognizing the expansion of the boundaries of economics, this series particularly welcomes proposals for monographs and edited collections that focus on topics from transdisciplinary, interdisciplinary, and multidisciplinary perspectives. Lexington Books will consider a wide range of conceptual, empirical, and methodological submissions. Works in this series will tend to synthesize and integrate knowledge and to build bridges within and between disciplines. They will be of vital concern to academicians, business people, and others in the debate about the proper role of capitalism, business, and business people in economic society.

Advisory Board

Books in Series

On the Private and Public Virtues of an Honorable Entrepreneur by Felix R. Livingston

The Ontology and Function of Money: The Philosophical Fundamentals of Monetary Institutions by Leonidas Zelmanovitz

Andrew Carnegie: An Economic Biography by Samuel Bostaph

Water Capitalism: Privatize Oceans, Rivers, Lakes, and Aquifers Too by Walter E. Block and Peter Lothian Nelson

Capitalism and Commerce in Imaginative Literature: Perspectives on Business from Novels and Plays edited by Edward W. Younkins

Pride and Profit: The Intersection of Jane Austen and Adam Smith by Cecil E. Bohanon and Michelle Albert Vachris

The Seen, the Unseen, and the Unrealized: How Regulations Affect Our Everyday Lives by Per L. Bylund

Global Economics: A Holistic Approach by Clifford F. Thies

On the Private and Public Virtues of an Honorable Entrepreneur: Preventing a Separation of the Honorable and the Useful by Felix R. Livingston

Perspectives on Ayn Rand's Contributions to Economic and Business Thought by Edward W. Younkins.

The Dialectics of Liberty: Exploring the Context of Human Freedom by Roger E. Bissell, Chris Matthew Sciabarra and Edward W. Younkins

Markets against Modernity: Ecological Irrationality, Public and Private by Ryan H. Murphy

Markets against Modernity

Ecological Irrationality, Public and Private

Ryan H. Murphy

LEXINGTON BOOKS
Lanham • Boulder • New York • London

Published by Lexington Books
An imprint of The Rowman & Littlefield Publishing Group, Inc.
4501 Forbes Boulevard, Suite 200, Lanham, Maryland 20706
www.rowman.com

6 Tinworth Street, London SE11 5AL, United Kingdom

British Library Cataloguing in Publication Information Available

Library of Congress Control Number: 2019950448

To populists of all parties,

Contents

List of Figures, Tables, and Text Boxes

FIGURES

TABLES

TEXT BOXES

Preface

American homebrewers brewed about 1 percent of total U.S. beer production in 2017,[1] thereby participating in the cultural fad of "doing-it-yourself" (DIY) instead of just buying the beer. The snarky economist reaction is: why would you homebrew at all? Is there something wrong with what you can find at the store? Introductory economics textbooks, contrary to how they are often portrayed, are replete with instances of the free market failing to live up to some model of perfection. These textbooks then follow with a series of public policies to potentially rectify each of the market's imperfections. But outside some distant fringes of the profession, you will rarely see it suggested that DIY is a serious solution to the imperfections of the market.

I *don't* think markets work perfectly and I *do* think there are plenty of times where doing it yourself makes sense. But when and where that is has nothing to do with the claims of DIY evangelists, who seem to think that avoiding engagement with the global economy is somehow the prudential gateway to affluence. An internet search of "save money diy" will yield hundreds of millions of results in your browser, with lists upon lists of instructions teaching you how to make, build, or fix pretty much anything on your own.

And it's not just DIY. There are many attitudes that, upon cursory consideration, do not make any sense from an economic or analytical perspective. Why do people think that buying local is good for the local economy and the environment? Why are people terrified by vaccines, and even relatively intelligent people will use any excuse they can unearth to maintain their belief that vaccines are somehow sinister? Why do people attach a sense of morality to "Buy American"? Why are people willing to put in place onerous restrictions on their diet to reduce their carbon footprint, only to later purchase a plane ticket with a carbon footprint that singlehandedly wipes away a year's worth of the environmental benefits of the diet? Why buy fair trade coffee to help the global poor instead of giving them the money directly? Why spend good money on the anti-establishment health fad of the week, whether that is Vitamin C, GMO-free, or homeopathic medicine? I will argue that every one of these has the same basic root cause. There is a fundamental mismatch between our minds and the institutional environment of modernity.

To those who have studied it, the mismatched, counterintuitive, modern institutional environment is supportive and essential for the relative comfort, health, and ease of today's world. The institutions of modernity include science, pluralistic democracy, markets, globalization, civil rights, and the rule of law. You can find intellectual support for the wonders of the modern world and today's modern institutional environment spanning almost the entirety of the political spectrum: on the right, in *In Defense of Openness* by Bas van der Vossen and Jason Brennan and *The Rational Optimist* by Matt Ridley, in the center with *The Age of Abundance* by Brink Lindsey and *Enlightenment Now* by Steven Pinker, and on the left with *Factfulness* by Hans Rosling, and *Open* by Kimberly Clausing.[2] While in the remainder of this book, I will most emphasize *Enlightenment Now* by Pinker, my intellectual presuppositions lie at the intersection of all these works. However, you can find enemies, not just friends, of modernity spanning the political spectrum as well.

Why is there such a mismatch between our modern institutional environment and our brains? Economist Bryan Caplan has already given half of the answer to the question. He was able to disentangle and distill a series of differences in opinion on public policy between the public and the consensus among economists into a set of four biases. These four biases do most of the work in explaining what economists think about the economy and what everyone else thinks about the economy. However, as originally presented, Caplan describes these four biases as arising in public policy, not in the private sphere. What I will do is to generalize Caplan's point in two ways—to the private sphere (e.g., DIY and homeopathy), and applying it to our overall institutional environment, not "just" markets and the economy.

In some of the following chapters, we will observe situations where people freely and consciously make choices that are contrary to their stated intention. Given these observations, it might seem natural to read my hypothesis in light of the proliferating field of behavioral economics. But both my approach and conclusions strongly differ from behavioral economics. The field is preoccupied with finding anomalies to rational behavior, while only occasionally explaining why the anomaly arose in the first place. One of my first tasks for this book is to provide firmer theoretical foundations for the biases described by Caplan. It is only after I identify these theoretical foundations do I apply them to the real world. While here and there I will cite work by behavioral economists, little of my approach or conclusions would sit comfortably within the scope of the behavioral economics research program.

In the first chapter, I take a step back to justify the most basic claim about the advantages of the modern institutional environment—that Trade Is Good. Subsequently in the first chapter, I will give an outline for the rest of the book. I will not defend the institutional environment in its entirety—you have van der Vossen & Brennan, Ridley, Lindsey, Pinker, Rosling, and Clausing for that. My task, rather, is to explain *why* the human mind is so resistant to rule-bound, pluralistic, science-driven, liberal, global capitalism, and the implications of all that. But I'd have problems convincing you of much of anything if you are hostile to the idea that Trade Is Good, as I can't say much about anything without assuming that.

NOTES

1. This is according to the American Homebrewers Association statistics page as of June 25, 2019.

2. Bas van der Vossen and Jason Brennan, *In Defense of Openness: Why Global Freedom Is the Humane Solution to Global Poverty* (New York: Oxford University Press, 2018); Matt Ridley, *The Rational Optimist: How Prosperity Evolves* (New York: HarperCollins, 2010); Brink Lindsey, *The Age of Abundance: How Prosperity Transformed America's Politics and Culture* (New York: HarperCollins, 2007); Steven Pinker, *Enlightenment Now: The Case for Reason, Science, Humanism, and Progress* (New York: Viking, 2018); Hans Rosling, *Factfulness: Ten Reasons We're Wrong About the World – and Why Things Are Better Than You Think* (New York: Flatiron Books, 2018); Kimberly Clausing, *Open: The Progressive Case for Free Trade, Immigration, and Global Capital* (Cambridge: Harvard University Press, 2019).

Acknowledgments

This project grew slowly out of a part of my dissertation, which eventually formed the basis for the chapter, "Ecological Irrationality in the Wild." To say that my dissertation was unorthodox is a bit of an understatement, and I ought to start by thanking my dissertation committee of David Tuerck, Benjamin Powell, and Roger Koppl for channeling my sometimes combative contrarianism towards productive uses.

But most of all, I must thank my wife, Jiawen, for her patience and support for me as I developed these ideas first as academic papers and then as I synthesized them into a book. She has been a constant sanity check and discussant as I have gone through the many drafts of the manuscript.

My boss at the O'Neil Center, Bob Lawson, has been supportive of this project throughout, even as it has strayed from our primary academic research goal of measuring economic institutions. In addition to providing comments for the manuscript, he facilitated a workshop for the book which led to several important additions to it. Participating in the workshop and providing me comments after having read it in full were Nathaniel Bechhofer, Dan D'Amico, Adam Martin, Colin O'Reilly, Ben Southwood, and Nick Whitaker.

Others who have read the manuscript in full and gave me helpful comments are Sam Dumitriu and William Peden. Bryan Caplan read a portion of the manuscript and offered several criticisms that led to tightening and strengthening core aspects of my argument. My O'Neil Center colleagues who read and gave feedback for chapters of the book were Richard Alm, Liz Chow, Michael Davis, Dean Stansel, and Meg Tuszynski. Others who have read chapters and given me feedback at different points of the development of the manuscript are Frank Conte, Eric Li, Jonathan Lindbloom, David Mitchell, Kelly Murphy, Alex Nowrasteh, Jamil Ragland, Alex Salter, Brad Taylor, and Luke Yeom.

Chapter 1

Trade is Good

Thomas Thwaites decided to build a toaster from scratch. He bought the cheapest toaster he could find (costing under £4) and disassembled it as his starting place. Thwaites immediately realized that the sheer complexity of the shoddy little toaster he chose would be impossible to match, no matter how much time he spent on it. He instead chose five materials to acquire himself from their original sources as cheaply and reasonably as possible. He went to an iron mine to make steel out of iron ore, gathered a small amount of copper from water which had leeched the metal from an old mine, chipped off mica from the side of a mountain, scavenged plastic from a recycling plant, and melted down Canadian coins for their nickel. The result was a functioning, but horrifically ugly gadget you would never voluntarily choose to use for yourself.[1]

In 2015, Andy George took recent food fads to their logical conclusion by sourcing literally everything himself to make a chicken sandwich. He traveled cross-country to turn saltwater into salt, milked a cow, made his own cheese and butter, harvested grain and turned it into bread, collected honey with the help of beekeepers, and dispatched a chicken. It took six months and he spent $1,500. The result? "It's not bad," he said. "That's about it."[2]

The age of information and bored millennials has allowed the world to test the hypothesis proposed by Leonard E. Read in his 1958 essay, *I, Pencil*.[3] Read makes the claim that no one in the world actually knows how to make a pencil from scratch—the knowledge to fabricate just one is dispersed across thousands of individuals via the impersonal, and as we will see, *unnatural* exchange of markets. The wood, the metal, the paint, the rubber, and the lead (or graphite) of the pencil all require specialized knowledge to gather, process, transport, and assemble them, and more specialized knowledge is needed to then distribute and retail the final good. Each individual step requires operational, financial, and managerial support that is itself subject

1

to high degrees of specialization. This specialization drives down the price of writing utensils to such an extent that you get a free pen when you check into your hotel room. If you were to try and make your own pen—for real, that is—it would quickly devolve into an expensive setup for a documentary film, not something you would ever want to do practically in your daily life. If you want to coordinate the actions of all those workers to make use of their dispersed knowledge without putting the knowledge into a single mind (as was attempted by Thomas Thwaites and Andy George above, as well as by Vladimir Lenin and Mao Zedong historically), you need markets and trade.

Let me pose a different question: can you grow a banana in North Dakota? The answer is, literally, yes—if you were to use expensive greenhouses and cared little about the cost. Most, though not all, trade skeptics intuitively understand that differences in agriculture and climate mean that we probably shouldn't grow very many bananas in America, or at least North Dakotans shouldn't only demand bananas grown in North Dakota. But what causes us to trade both with our neighbors and people across the globe is ultimately driven by similar, although less tangible, factors. Besides nature's endowments of soil, sun, and minerals, our capabilities to cheaply produce different goods or services are also determined by variations in cultures and skills across the world, which are quite vast.[4] For example, some cultures are much more capable to cooperate at the scale necessary to build a large corporation, which is necessary to efficiently manufacture certain goods like automobiles.[5]

Even if cultures, skills, and the environment are similar across two regions, there are other reasons why we would expect specialization across the globe to be desirable. The clustering of knowledge and skills allows for the rapid evolution of many industries in particular places. This is familiar to Americans regarding the development of high tech in Silicon Valley or the entertainment industry in Hollywood, but as a point of comparison, entire cities in China are devoted to specializing in manufacturing umbrellas or zippers.[6] This relentless specialization makes what would have been luxury goods a few generations ago clock in around the rounding error from your weekly trip to the supermarket. To take part in this miracle, one must do no more than simply perform work for pay at a for-profit firm.

There is a standard script that countries across the world have followed on their path to economic development. A traditional society (that is, in contrast to an industrial or modern society) devotes an overwhelming proportion of its workforce to agriculture simply so it can feed itself, with any surplus used to feed the aristocracy, government officials, clerics, and maybe a few extra morsels for the peasants during festivals. When markets and technology develop and free up (also known as "layoff") workers from tasks related to agriculture, these workers enter into basic manufacturing industries, often textiles (i.e., sweatshops). As the manufacturing sector of the economy increases in scale and workers become more educated, the accumulation of knowledge and skills, over time, allows workers to carry out more sophisticated manufacturing tasks efficiently, with some workers shifting focus to the theoretical design of new products. Lower-level manufacturing work is outsourced to other countries. The descendants of many of the factory workers in the first country, now educated, enter the service sector, where they work in fields such as finance, medicine, or law, or they work on basic science. Meanwhile, those who are not as well-educated find themselves in the parts of the service sector that require fewer skills.

This process has occurred in the United States, Western Europe, Japan, South Korea, and Taiwan, as well as many other developed countries—and countries such as China are undergoing the process as we speak. Objections to this process are like a record on repeat; the recent complaints about China's misuse of U.S. intellectual property, for instance, closely mirror the ways in which the United States itself was criticized for appropriating British technology in the nineteenth century.[7] The changes we see in trade patterns over time are merely what happens as countries enter the global marketplace in the course of economic history over the last two centuries.

Shifts from agriculture to manufacturing to services should be regarded as inevitable so long as something resembling economic growth is desired, because employing fewer people in agriculture and manufacturing while getting the same or more output is largely what "economic growth" means. Economic growth and getting more stuff aren't all there is to life, and growth will always coincide with hardship for some, but failing to appreciate the essential humane character of what growth facilitates evinces insularity. And as recently argued by economist Tyler Cowen, economic growth solves a variety of philosophical problems that dominate public and academic discourse.[8] All the while, the less aesthetically pleasing dimensions of growth, including offshoring, outsourcing, and layoffs, are a crucial part of the story of how we went from using monks as scribes as our only means of producing books to giving away free pens and pads of paper to whoever shows up.[9]

All that is to say is that there is a direct analogy between trade and technology in a deep, fundamental sense. A stylized fable illustrating this fact has been suggested by James Ingram.[10] Suppose a farmer in Iowa invents a miraculous manufacturing process which can convert a large amount of corn into a full-functioning automobile. This farmer would appear on the cover of *Scientific American* and *Discover Magazine* and would be lauded as the new Edison (or if you want to get all hipster about it, the new Nikola Tesla). The re-arrangement of matter from corn to horseless carriage would be understood as a supreme advancement in human well-being.

But what if we find out the farmer is a fraud and had invented no such innovation? Suppose instead he had simply shipped corn to Japan each night in exchange for a car—what has changed? Did the number of jobs lost in the U.S. automobile industry change? Was there any effect on the finances of the U.S. government? Should you have any reason to be more suspicious of the quality or safety of a car melded out of corn via alchemy than a car assembled in Japan? Absolutely not.[11] The first, though not final, approximation of trade must be that it is akin to any other form of technology. It is first to be thought of as an apparent source of economic growth which *may* happen to have negative secondary effects. *Any* source of economic growth may ultimately have secondary negative effects. Why in the world are we focused on hypothetical negative effects of specifically trade, and not the other sources of economic growth with identical effects?

Maybe I should point out that this is not quite the conventional narrative as to why Trade Is Good. That concept is, fundamentally, comparative advantage. If you specialize in what you are most effective at, and the people you work with specialize in what they are most effective at, and you all trade, overall economic output (the "size of the pie") is maximized. Suppose a worker who is not very economically productive, perhaps one from a developing country, joins global markets and specializes. Due to that entry, workers in developed nations will, overall, become more productive. Meanwhile, the ability of the low-skilled worker to participate in a global market radically increases the worker's own productivity and wages.[12] Everything else is second order, just as is true for the secondary effects of more conventional technological growth.

If you are skeptical that this is "just theory," here is some very basic data analysis. I am a coauthor of the *Economic Freedom of the World* report.[13] We collect data from a few dozen sources to construct a single number summarizing the freedom of each country's economic institutions and policies. You do not need to accept it as a statement of how the world "should" look like in order to use it. One-fifth of the index is concerned with measuring the freedom to trade internationally. It starts with measures of tariffs, but it also includes measures of the regulation of trade, capital controls, discrepancies in exchange rates, and whatever else that is relevant and we can find for a large number of countries.

We can compare this free trade number, which runs zero to ten, with higher index scores corresponding to freer trade, to whatever definition of good social outcomes you would like. I collected eight: real gross domestic product per capita (PPP adjusted), the Human Development Index, infant mortality rates, life expectancy, happiness, inequality, and two definitions of poverty (the percentage of the population living on less than $1.90 and the percentage of the population living on less than $5.50 per day). For all of these measures, descriptively, more free trade either has a "good" relationship or a flat relationship with the data. These appear as figures 1.1–1.8. There are

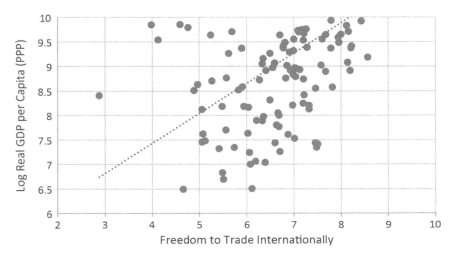

Figure 1.1   Freedom to Trade and Logged RGDP per Capita (PPP adjusted). *Source*: Generated by Author Based on Gwartney et al., Economic Freedom of the World; World Development Indicators.

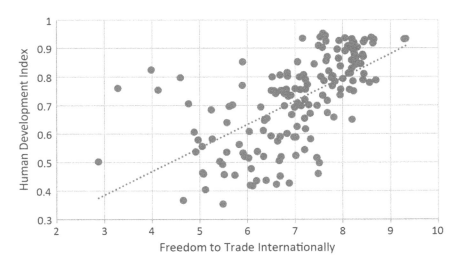

Figure 1.2   Freedom to Trade and the Human Development Index. *Source*: Generated by Author Based on Gwartney et al., Economic Freedom of the World; United Nations.

more sophisticated ways of doing this, but if all you want to do is look at the data, there isn't much to suggest that Trade Is Bad. If you wish to dig more deeply into the literature, please feel free—I suggest Jagdish Bhagwati's *In Defense of Global Capitalism*, Douglas Irwin's *Clashing Over Commerce* or Donald Boudreaux's *Globalization* as starting points.[14] But the consensus that

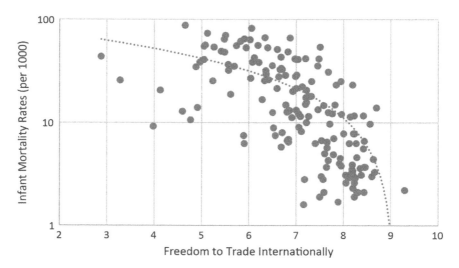

Figure 1.3   Freedom to Trade and Infant Mortality Rates (Per 1,000 Births). *Source*: Generated by Author Based on Gwartney et al., Economic Freedom of the World; World Development Indicators.

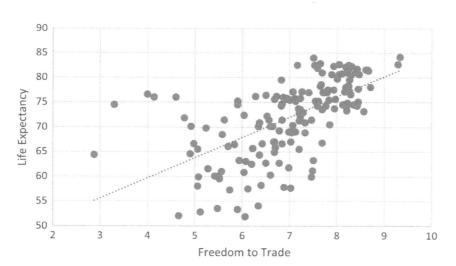

Figure 1.4   Freedom to Trade and Life Expectancy. *Source*: Generated by Author Based on Gwartney et al., Economic Freedom of the World; World Development Indicators.

"Trade Is Good" is deeply accepted among economists across the political spectrum. Those trying to argue to the contrary simply misconstrue published research.[15] We will return to objections to Trade Is Good in the appendix of chapter 10.

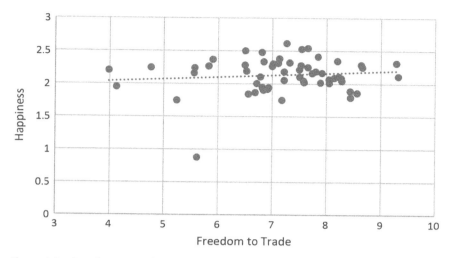

Figure 1.5 Freedom to Trade and Happiness. *Source*: Generated by Author Based on Gwartney et al., Economic Freedom of the World; Question V10 of Wave 6 of the World Values Survey.

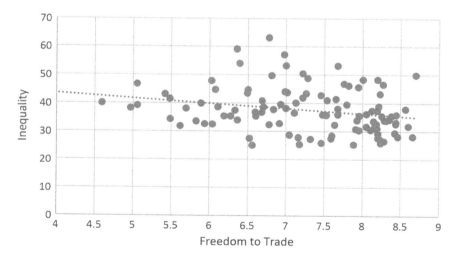

Figure 1.6 Freedom to Trade and Inequality. *Source*: Generated by Author Based on Gwartney et al., Economic Freedom of the World; World Development Indicators.

While the notion that Trade Is Good is, or should be, an uncontroversial position, it is simply impossible for me to go any further without taking Trade Is Good as a given. Yet nearly all countries have some protectionism, and those barriers were much larger historically. To explain why protectionism persists, economists have long viewed protection as a subversion of

Figure 1.7   Freedom to Trade and Extreme Poverty. *Source*: Generated by Author Based on Gwartney et al., Economic Freedom of the World; World Development Indicators.

Figure 1.8   Freedom to Trade and Poverty. *Source*: Generated by Author Based on Gwartney et al., Economic Freedom of the World; World Development Indicators.

democracy—the result of certain favored industries hijacking the state for their own interests at the expense of society as a whole. But Bryan Caplan, an economist at George Mason University, has argued that this framing is incorrect. The world gets as much protectionism as it does because protectionism is popular and its supporters believe it will bring prosperity, despite the consensus to the contrary among those who have studied the issue. The intuition for Trade Is Good is not the natural starting place for the human mind.

The public systematically errs not only with respect to trade, but with respect to many other policies. You do not need to take my word for it—I will be discussing the evidence Caplan offers in favor of this conclusion in the chapter that follows. But in contrast to Caplan, I will not confine my discussion to public opinion or to questions of public policy. I will argue that if you accept his findings, the argument is generalizable. Our errors cluster around specific questions concerning social and economic relationships, and they are not limited to public policy. We are innately skeptical of the concept of economic progress—the idea of growing the size of the pie for everyone—and skeptical that cooperation with people we've never met can be mutually beneficial. We are militantly skeptical of the idea that economic growth is a thing for *us*: we assume that what others call "economic growth" will always be at the expense of us and those whom we identify with.

These intuitions, I contend, we carry with us in conducting the ordinary business of our lives, not just as part of politics. This is because the human mind is not built to work well within the institutions of the modern world—institutions like the rule of law, capitalism, globalism, pluralistic democracy, and science—all the while these institutions support the standard of living and relative peace found in the developed world. It is only with effort to train our minds in counterintuitive modes of thought that we are capable of understanding these institutions, and we often end up rejecting them as evil. Since individuals readily act on these intuitions in the private sphere—not just the public sphere, I have titled this book, *Markets against Modernity*. We use markets to express our hostility toward the institutions of modernity, including the market itself.

The book will use the power and virtue of our modern institutional environment as a running theme, even though that theme is not itself one of my hypotheses. Rather, it is something we will continually return to as an important, central fact. The word "institutions" in the scholarly context is loosely defined, but institutions are generally thought of as the "rules of the game" by which a society conducts itself.[16] This includes those listed above, like democratic political institutions and market economies. Economists are split among those who believe that institutions are *the* key to understanding the rise of economic growth, or if they "merely" play an intermediate or supporting role.[17] Many recent books have celebrated the benefits of our modern institutional environment, namely, for example, *Enlightenment Now* by Steven Pinker, with premises similar to my own. Having already argued that Trade Is Good, however, I will take it as a given that our modern bundle of institutions is desirable and important, while following in the broad tradition of countless others who already have made the argument.

I will spend the first half of the book explicating the intellectual backdrop of my work and developing a complete statement of my own position. Following the present introductory chapter, the subsequent three chapters consist of, first, the intellectual history of Bryan Caplan's argument, second, a more detailed exposition of how our natural intuitions conflict with the institutions of the modern world, and third, the evidence supporting my hypothesis that individuals are willing to perform costly, irrational actions in the private sphere. I will then develop connections between these behaviors and a new form of conspicuous consumption, which has been described at length by urban planning scholar Elizabeth Currid-Halkett and several predecessors. The second half of the book consists of applications of my argument to issues across the social sciences.

My first application is to investigate the implications of my argument for political institutions. While Caplan presents the free market implications of his position as if they are self-evident, I am less sanguine about the solution lying in markets themselves, since I believe similar issues arise when decisions are made privately. To do so, I will discuss others' earlier extensions to Caplan's argument with respect to political institutions. Some of these extensions are outgrowths of how Caplan originally made his argument, which in part demonstrated the low quality of public opinion. Those extending Caplan's paradigm, most notably political philosopher Jason Brennan, have argued that we should reconstruct political institutions in a way that places more power in the hands of the informed. There may be something to this, and in the United States there are already explicit checks on the power of majorities in place, whether that means the First Amendment, the Second Amendment, or *Roe v. Wade*. However, my own research cautions against the more strongly stated versions of this argument which seek to actively curb democratic political institutions. In this chapter, I will examine the arguments of others as well as those of Brennan.

Following that analysis of political institutions, I will discuss social capital, that is, the ability of members of a society to cooperate, the density of social networks within a society, and the general cohesiveness of a society. Most social scientists across the political spectrum see social capital as a societal good; I suggest it can be something we can have "too much" of. There is a growing body of evidence suggesting that too much social capital begins making people act inappropriately in markets and politics, and if high levels of social capital are not mediated appropriately, it may create hostile attitudes toward outsiders. What this means, in practice, is that social capital may detrimentally interact with the human brain's mismatch with the modern institutional environment. The market functions effectively when the norms of the market are applied to them. They work less well when you apply to the market the norms for interacting with close friends and family.

I subsequently explore the implications of my argument for the individual consumer, through the lens of the do-it-yourself movement. Think of the examples that opened the chapter—the toaster and the chicken sandwich. Dogmatic do-it-yourself is the antithesis of Trade Is Good, writ small. In saying that, I do not mean there is no situation where you would want to do something yourself (like a household task), but that the general mantra that doing it yourself is more financially responsible or cost-effective is utterly ridiculous. The primary—although not only—reason for doing it yourself is the cost and hassle involved in hiring someone to do the task for you. The intuition fueling the belief that doing it yourself saves money, as a general rule, is simply resentment for markets and globalization, bereft of any reasonable assessment of the true costs and benefits of doing it yourself.

Often, those who promulgate "do-it-yourself" are also those who went through the trouble of acquiring the skills to do-it-yourself in the first place. Suppose I am correct and that doing it yourself is actually wasteful. If so, learning the skills to do-it-yourself (DIY) was a mistake. In response, those who took the time to gain those skills will go through great lengths to socially sanction whoever questions the value of their skill. This point generalizes. For a concrete example, wine connoisseurs cannot show any discernable ability when their abilities are tested, so they viciously malign attempts at testing them. This is socially wasteful, in the same way that lobbying the government for your own private benefit is wasteful. "Luddism" is a general term for anyone seeking to hold up social progress for their own narrow benefit. The attempts by DIY advocates, wine connoisseurs, and many others to hold up social progress to protect their own interest through social sanctions I call "Social Luddism." Examples of Social Luddism, we will find, cluster around implicit hostility for the institutions of modernity.

Finally, I point out a central tension or even irony within my argument. Expert opinion suggests that laissez-faire in trade and elsewhere is generally the way to go. In politics, it is populism (regardless of any jingoistic American rhetoric to the contrary) that pushes us in the direction away from laissez-faire. At various points in this book, I argue that people in their private lives may act against their own interests, with the canonical example being the failure to vaccinate children. Here, expert opinion is unambiguously correct—like with trade. But there are numerous examples of experts betraying our trust, including elsewhere in medicine. Among the worst offenders of Social Luddism are experts, whether wine connoisseurs or, sometimes, medical doctors. Ultimately, there is no clear institutional mechanism of determining how we should delegate authority to experts. We face a tradeoff when delegating authority to experts: on average, experts do know more, but it can be hard for the public to discern expertise from snake oil salesmen like Social Luddites. And even genuine experts often betray our trust.

If I've successfully convinced you that Trade Is Good and that these other ideas sound interesting, we first have a brief detour to make. To best convey how my argument is a twist or inversion to existing scholarship, I will give you a brief intellectual history of how we got here, beginning with work that would yield the 1986 Nobel Memorial Prize in economics and ending with the work of Bryan Caplan. This is the history of an analytical framework—the controversial idea that we should use the same assumptions about human motivation in politics as we do in the analysis of human motivation in markets. This is known as Public Choice Theory, and it forms the basis for the next chapter.

NOTES

1. Thomas Thwaites, *The Toaster Project: Or a Heroic Attempt to Build a Simple Electric Appliance from Scratch* (New York, NY: Princeton Architectural Press, 2011).

2. Andy George, "How to Make a $1500 Sandwich in Only 6 Months," *How To Make Everything*, September 15, 2015, https://www.youtube.com/watch?v=URv WSsAgtJE.

3. Leonard Read, *I, Pencil* (Irvington-on-Hudson: Foundation for Economic Education, 1958). The essay is available in many forms online, including here: http://www.econlib.org/library/Essays/rdPncl1.html.

4. Thomas Sowell, *Migrations and Cultures* (New York: Basic Books, 1996).

5. Francis Fukuyama, *Trust: The Social Virtues and the Creation of Prosperity* (New York: The Free Press, 1995).

6. David Muir, "Reporter's Notebook: Inside a Chinese Factory Town," *ABC News*, November 10, 2010, http://abcnews.go.com/Business/chinas-booming-fact ory-towns-specialize-zippers-umbrellas-santa/story?id=12150627.

7. Charles R. Morris, "We Were Pirates, Too," *Foreign Policy*, December 6, 2012, https://foreignpolicy.com/2012/12/06/we-were-pirates-too/.

8. Tyler Cowen, *Stubborn Attachments* (San Francisco: Stripe Press, 2018).

9. The description of how trade has continually evolved and outsourced in this matter here is uncontroversial and conventional among economists, even if it may be controversial among laypeople. For one description of this historical process and its intertwinement with growth, see Alan S. Blinder, "Offshoring: The Next Industrial Revolution?" *Foreign Affairs* 85, no. 2 (March 2006): 113–128.

10. The argument originates in James C. Ingram, *International Economics*, 2nd ed. (New York: Wiley and Sons, 1986), 356–357, but a closer exposition to the one found here is in David D. Friedman, *Price Theory: An Intermediate Text* (Cincinnati: South-Western Publishing Co., 1996), 123–124.

11. The only difference I can think of here is that shipping the car across the globe may have more carbon emissions, but to be honest I do not know how to measure the carbon emissions from a hypothetical transformation of corn to an automobile via alchemy.

12. The size of these effects is the most arresting when considering worker wages when a worker from a less-developed country is able to migrate. Immigration and international trade are very different policies from the standpoint of politics, but their effects on productivity operate through identical mechanisms. See, Michael Clemens, Claudio Montenegro, and Lant Pritchett, "The Place Premium: Bounding the Price Equivalent of Migration Barriers," *Review of Economics and Statistics* 101, no. 2 (May 2019): 201–213.

13. James Gwartney, Robert Lawson, Joshua Hall, and Ryan H. Murphy, *Economic Freedom of the World* (Vancouver: Fraser Institute, 2018).

14. If you wish to dive straight into the data, a formal literature review can be found in Douglas Irwin, "Does Trade Reform Promote Economic Growth? A Review of Recent Evidence" (*NBER Working Paper* no. 25927, Cambridge: National Bureau of Economic Research, 2019).

15. See Paul Krugman, *Pop Internationalism* (Cambridge: MIT Press, 1996). We will return to the economic arguments against trade just before the conclusion of this book.

16. Douglass C. North, *Institutions, Institutional Change, and Economic Performance* (Cambridge: Cambridge University Press, 1990).

17. Rafael La Porta, Florencio Lopez-de-Silanes, and Andre Shleifer, "The Economic Consequences of Legal Origins," *Journal of Economic Literature* 46, no. 2 (June 2008): 285–322; Stephen Knack and Philip Keefer, "Institutions and Economic Performance: Cross-Country Tests Using Alternative Institutional Measures," *Economics & Politics* 7, no. 3 (November 1995): 207–227; William Easterly and Ross Levine, "Tropics, Germs, and Crops: How Endowments Influence Economic Development," *Journal of Monetary Economics* 50, no. 1 (January 2003): 3–39; James Gwartney, Randall Holcombe, and Robert Lawson, "Institutions and the Impact of Investment on Growth," *Kyklos* 59, no. 2 (May 2006): 255–273; Daniel Bennett, Hugo Faria, James Gwartney, and Daniel Morales, "Economic Institutions and Comparative Economic Development: A Post-Colonial Perspective," *World Development* 96 (August 2017): 503–519.

Chapter 2

"Extreme Voter Stupidity"

With the exception of Hong Kong, all countries in the world have some degree of protectionism. Tariffs are, overall, much lower on average than they were a half century ago across the world. But since 2000, various free trade indicators have deteriorated in many countries. This preceded all the recent rumblings of trade wars. The World Economic Forum's *Global Competitiveness Report* tells us that business people in the United States have experienced higher non-tariff barriers to international trade, and that there is now greater difficulty for foreigners to invest.[1] According to the IMF's *Annual Report on Exchange Arrangments and Exchange Restrictions*, as of 2000, the United States had four of the possible thirteen capital controls. As of 2016, it had eight of the thirteen.[2] Similar developments have occurred elsewhere.[3] There is no shortage of bad policies, even in countries with the world's most effective governance.

But *why* do we get bad policies? In democracies, policies are created by politicians, and sometimes politics seems hopeless. More often than not, both candidates are slimeballs, and you end up voting by party affiliation, or by your careful assessment regarding which candidate appears less slimy at the moment. And no, I am not just referring to the 2016 presidential election. Tricky Dick resigned less than a half century ago, and his predecessor, Lyndon Johnson, may too have been a crook.[4] In a 2004 episode, *South Park* satirizes the despair of American politics by presenting its main characters forced with making a decision to vote for either a "giant douche" or "turd sandwich" for the new school mascot. Not everyone felt that way about choosing between George W. Bush and John Kerry during that particular election cycle, but as a rule, democracies aren't putting angels in places of high power.

So why do we end up with such dissatisfactory outcomes in our democratic institutions? One field of study emerging in the twentieth century seeking to answer this question is Public Choice Theory. A way of describing Public Choice more formally is that it applies the tools and assumptions of mainstream ("neoclassical") economics to political behavior. If we assume that individuals are rationally trying to attain their ends through whatever means they have at their disposal—in politics and not just "in the economy"—what does that imply about politics and the workings of government?

While it did have forerunners, most see the founding of the approach as coinciding with the publication of *The Calculus of Consent* by James Buchanan and Gordon Tullock in 1962.[5] Buchanan would go on to win the 1986 Nobel Memorial Prize in economics for his work in Public Choice. In 2009, Elinor Ostrom became the first female winner of the Nobel Memorial Prize in economics for her own work in Public Choice. All this was achieved despite a great deal of hostility toward the project from much of academia,[6] which to some extent, persists.[7]

To explain findings in Public Choice, we need to define some terms. Conceptually, we need to distinguish between *profit-seeking* and *rent-seeking* behavior. In a narrow sense, "profit-seeking" means that my actions add more to society than they take away. For example, I could transport bananas to a market where they were in demand but none were to be had. My reward is the profit, which does not come at the expense of society overall, though there still may be losers: perhaps I ended up eating into an apple merchant's business. Rent-seeking, on the other hand, means that the benefits of my actions for me are, in fact, at the expense of society overall. Rent-seeking is analogous to me hitting you in the kneecap with a baseball bat and making off with your wallet.[8]

Many problems with the public sector can be interpreted as rent-seeking behavior. A business can concoct some rationale why it should get money from the government for doing whatever it does. But why do some businesses or other interest groups successfully use the government to seek rent, and some do not? One political scientist using the tools of Public Choice, Mancur Olson, gave a rather satisfactory explanation, which is known as the Logic of Collective Action.[9] According to Olson, when groups are small, they have a lot to gain by passing a law that taxes everyone in the country for the benefit of the group. But large groups are tough to organize and it only helps them by a small amount individually if they lobby, perhaps to prevent such a tax. In most such cases, the bill ultimately passes. This mechanism, the logic of concentrated benefits and dispersed costs, means that the small group gets the concentrated benefits, and the costs are dispersed among the larger group.

This has been the standard public choice interpretation of why we have trade barriers.[10] Among the most significant trade barriers remaining in the United States is its quota on sugar. Sugar prices in the United States are much higher than they are elsewhere in the world, essentially because, if you want to buy sugar, you must purchase it from the very politically organized U.S. sugar industry, led by Jose "Pepe" Fanjul and who the press has dubbed the "First Family of corporate welfare."[11] If you want to see how this can affect your everyday life, these restrictions are why soda in the United States contains high fructose corn syrup instead of sugar.[12] The corporate welfare persists because the benefits of these restrictions on trade are largely concentrated among a small number of families, while the costs are felt in small amounts across hundreds of millions of people in the United States.

Another thing to consider is, were you even aware of these quotas? Most Americans are not, but I do not blame you. It is difficult to get informed and figure out which sources of information you can trust and which you cannot. Unless you get pleasure from reading policy studies, you are likely to be rationally unaware of the corporate welfare in the sugar industry. Why take the time to learn it only so you can save a nickel each time you buy a pack of gum in the very unlikely event that your voting power sways the relevant election? Because the personal benefits to you would be so small, it is perfectly reasonable to remain in the dark about the sugar industry's political activities. Public Choice theorists call this *rational ignorance*, which remains important in the formal analysis of politics.[13]

Scholarship in Public Choice rapidly flowered throughout the second half of the twentieth century, with different styles of analysis developed in different academic institutions across the country. Reflecting where Buchanan and Tullock worked, first University of Virginia and then Virginia Polytechnic Institute, what is known as the Virginia School of Political Economy blossomed while emphasizing the importance of constitutions.[14] Scholars of this school describe how constitutions create the rules of the political process, analyzing how different sets of rules or meta-rules yield better or worse outcomes in politics. Second, Elinor Ostrom founded the Bloomington School of Political Economy, which investigates how local communities solve public good problems (like managing the rules for catching fish so overfishing does not occur) more effectively than solutions formulated by a central authority.[15] Another group of scholars, adherents of what is known as the Rochester School, creates formal mathematical models of political processes, such as voting.[16] Finally, the flavor of Public Choice analysis that most concerns us here, the Chicago School of Political Economy, exemplified by economists such as George Stigler, Gary Becker, and Sam Peltzman, uses a relentless focus on rationality, maximization, and efficiency to understand political phenomena.[17]

We should step back to discuss what economists mean by the word "rational." In reality, what it means depends on who you ask.[18] The baseline model in economics, *homo economicus*, is that people are hyper-rational, are able to calculate optimal responses instantaneously, and care only about themselves. This model is very easy to work with and yields precise predictions, but to its detriment, it is generally wrong. At the other end of the spectrum there are economic models of rationality that are consistent with any behavior but make no predictions; in this framework, the fact that people are trying to achieve something when acting is what makes the action rational.[19]

The better models are somewhere in between, most notably the more subtle viewpoint of the Chicago School and specifically Gary Becker.[20] Informally speaking, we can take *homo economicus*, allow it to care about other people, or hold other values, and put certain constraints on its hyper-rationality.[21] This model of human behavior is what you can keep in the back of your mind when confronting the following arguments made by the Chicago School. I will make use of other definitions of rationality later in this book, and will define them as appropriate. However, note upfront that what I am claiming does not necessitate the caricature of *homo economicus*.

Exemplifying Chicago thinking as applied to politics is the theory of economic regulation developed by George Stigler[22] (another Nobel Laureate) and formalized carefully by Sam Peltzman.[23] This theory considers why it is that economic regulation occurs in some industries but not others. The conventional thinking had been that voters seek to regulate the prices monopolists may charge when and where monopolists are able to reap extra-normal profits. However, it's also possible for firms in very *competitive* industries to lobby governments to regulate prices and drive them *upwards*. Therefore, there is a political incentive for voters to seek regulation when monopoly power is especially strong, and for an industry to seek regulation when an industry is especially competitive. Among the conclusions of Stigler and Peltzman were that, counterintuitively, the two sets of industries most likely to be regulated were monopolies *and* extremely competitive industries.

Peltzman's formal mathematical model found that the regulated price chosen by a successful politician would balance the demands of the voters with the political sway of the industry. The regulated price would neither be the full monopoly price nor the competitive price, but somewhere in between. *Where* exactly in between would be determined by the relative strength of the voters and the industry. Successful politicians are those who would favor the regulation of prices with these factors in mind. In this sense, perversely, the regulated price as chosen by the successful politician is "efficient," in the sense that the successful politician is acting optimally given his or her constraints. Similar analysis can show how politicians may balance different interest groups when determining policy.[24] This analysis presents an underlying economic logic as to which policies become adopted, how, and why, seamlessly integrated within the economic structure of rationality, maximization, and equilibrium.

Historically, the Chicago School has been interested in understanding the efficiency of markets.[25] Chicago School adherents subsequently translated their style of analysis beyond narrow economics into fields such as sociology, law, and here, politics,[26] all with the focus of efficiency in mind. But this raises the question—if all other fields of human endeavor are rational or efficient, well outside the ordinary business of consumers and firms, how is it still the case that government is the solitary beast still clinging to its inefficiency? Enter Donald Wittman, author of *The Myth of Democratic Failure*.[27]

Wittman offers a compelling argument. Hiding in the background of claims of government failure, especially democratic failure, are assumptions that economists, especially the adherents of the Chicago School, are loathe to make elsewhere. For the Public Choice explanations to hold analytically, one must assume (a) voters are extremely stupid, (b) there is a serious lack of competition to hold office, or (c) negotiating in politics is extremely costly. Wittman marshals a wide array of supporting arguments and evidence including, for example, why the political power of regulated industries described by Stigler and Peltzman may not be particularly important. But is this argument compelling? Bryan Caplan, one Public Choice theorist, thought so.

> Future historians of thought will be puzzled by the transformation of the Chicago School. How does one get from Milton Friedman to Donald Wittman? My answer: Step by step, and myopically. More than anyone else, Friedman cemented the Chicago view that the free market is under-rated. Since many market failure arguments assume that consumers or workers are irrational, Chicago economists eagerly joined the rational expectations revolution. Initially, the outlook made their defense of free markets more truculent; government intervention seemed even more pointless than previously believed. But this position was unstable. If people have rational expectations, how can the free market be "under-rated"? And if the free market is *not* under-rated, then what reason is there to second-guess democratically chosen policies? The pointed question gnawed away at the intellectual conscience of Chicago economists until enough were ready to hear Wittman's unconflicted answer: There *is* no reason to second-guess democratically chosen policies.[28]

Caplan's innovation was that we should relax the assumption that voters are *not* extremely stupid.

By "extreme voter stupidity" what is meant by Wittman and Caplan is something actually *worse* than rational ignorance, which we mentioned earlier. Rational ignorance, by itself, is a surmountable flaw in democracy. By the "miracle of aggregation," it need not actually be a problem. Imagine if only 2 percent of the population is informed and 98 percent of the population is ignorant. What "rational ignorance" implies, as it is typically formulated, is that people vote *randomly*. If you are ignorant and just don't know whether some bank regulation is desirable, and you barely know anything about the financial system in the first place, how do you know whether or not to support it? For both complex financial regulations and sugar quotas in America, someone who is truly ignorant does not have anything more than a coin flip to inform them with.

The rationally ignorant voters therefore vote randomly, with, on average, half of the 98 percent voting for the correct choice. This 49 percent is joined by the 2 percent that is informed, and democracy has chosen correctly, 51–49 percent. So, in many cases, rational ignorance is an insufficient basis for democratic failure. What you need for democratic failure to arise reliably is what Caplan calls "systematically biased beliefs." Uninformed voters must sometimes default to the *wrong* direction on many issues. Then, the small set of informed voters cannot outweigh the majorities who defaulted to the wrong position. Such a situation would imply that, contrary to Wittman, that voters are extremely stupid.

This raises a few objections. How do we determine what constitutes good policy? On economics, you could ask economists, but what if economists are biased by something like ideology? Before I go into how Caplan addressed such concerns, I should get more specific about his model, which he presented to the public in his 2007 book, *The Myth of the Rational Voter*.[29] Caplan argues that forcing yourself to be rational is an annoying, costly experience. Changing your mind is difficult. You can literally watch people feel negative emotions, regardless of where they are on the political spectrum, when you present them with evidence contrary to their beliefs. At the same time, at least according to Caplan, people are more or less rational when they feel the costs of their irrationality. You do not jump off a cliff waving your arms believing you can fly.

Caplan used this collection of facts to keep his theory of irrationality somehow within the framework of rationality and economics. We want to avoid changing our beliefs, but will respond by changing our beliefs (or at least how we behave) when we are given sufficient incentives to do so. You are properly incentivized not to jump of a cliff waving your arms. So, Caplan claims, when the cost of being irrational is low, you are irrational. When the cost is high, you act rationally. Now suddenly we have derived the economist's demand curve, the demand for irrationality. If you only act on your irrationalities when its cost is low, you are being rationally irrational. Hence, Caplan's term for it: *Rational Irrationality*.

There are few circumstances where being rational is less important *for you as an individual* than when you vote. One analysis, which focused on the absolute best case for an individual's vote to sway a presidential election, found that such a voter had a one-in-ten million chance of determining the outcome.[30] Texas, where I currently call home, is said to be trending purple, but most U.S. states remain either safely red or blue, with few states plausibly swinging an election. You can in principle construct situations where your vote is in some sense meaningful in specific instances. But if people are going to express their irrationality, the voting booth is a good place to look.

It's around this time that others describing these issues with voting may try to explain to you that this is why you shouldn't vote. I would just point out that one person's vote does not matter, but if you have a platform for your ideas, like a book, you are not impacting whether one person votes. If you are effective, you are impacting far more than one person's vote. Telling large numbers of people who are inclined to agree with you *not* to vote might be the most counterproductive take I can imagine. If you are reading this, I encourage you to vote. I will leave it unclear whether I vote.

To show that voters are systematically biased, Caplan uses data from the Survey of Americans and Economists on the Economy, which poses questions to randomly selected members of the public as well as individuals with PhDs in economics.[31] These questions pertain to a wide array of topics like international trade, economic growth, and gas prices. Caplan then statistically measures what would happen if, controlling for other characteristics, you were to force members of the public through the harrowing process of getting a PhD in economics.

When you do that, suddenly the public starts to sound a whole lot more like economists. Contrary to their previous beliefs, the public when statistically adjusted to "get a PhD," believes it's fine if companies downsize. Immigration is not harming the economy. Trade agreements are good. Gas prices are set by the laws of supply and demand. If you take the gap between economists and the public and try to explain it away by claiming that it follows from economists largely being conservative and wealthy, you do not get very far. Ideology and self-serving beliefs, together, explain only about 20 percent of the gap. (It's notable that, despite their reputations, the median economist is a moderate Democrat.[32]) The remainder, Caplan argues, is the result of training in economics. Moreover, economists and the public, the latter now traumatized by being forced to learn the calculus of variations and Shephard's lemma for no reason, actually skew to "the left" on some issues. For instance, the economists and those statistically forced to get a PhD do not see the negative effects of welfare or high tax rates as being a very big deal, at least compared to the public's perceptions.

Caplan later studied the determinants of that gap more closely. He and Stephen Miller found that education, and especially raw intelligence, are what primarily drive it.[33] Elsewhere, the two found that questions relating to *facts* about the economy are highly correlated with *opinions* about what economic policies should be pursued, and that knowing those facts and holdings those opinions both have a close relationship with education.[34] Empirically, the data do seem to indicate that members of the public systematically differ from the views of the economists, and those differences would greatly diminish were they to take the time to get educated. I would supplement the findings of Caplan and Miller with the small social scientific literature on intelligence and political beliefs. This literature does not find that intelligence predicts where you would fall on a simple left-right political spectrum. But intelligence does predict both free market and socially progressive policy opinions.[35]

What are the dimensions of these systematic differences in beliefs? Caplan enumerates "anti-market bias," "anti-foreign bias," "make-work bias," and "pessimistic bias." Anti-market bias refers to the degree to which the public underrates the effectiveness of markets. Anti-foreign bias is our particular wariness toward international trade and other interaction with foreigners (like immigration). Make-work bias refers to our tendency to frame too many economic policy questions in terms of the impact on the number of jobs available, which is small potatoes compared to the essential importance economic growth. Finally, pessimistic bias is the public's perpetual gloomy sentiments about the possibilities of the future, as well as its nostalgia for the past. Economists have typically been the only ones in the room willing to point out that the world has gotten a whole lot better over the last two centuries.

So where does that leave us? Most academics working in Public Choice, especially those in the under-forty crowd, see room for both conventional explanations regarding self-interest and "rational irrationality" to be important and relevant. The analysis of government failure on the conventional grounds has not died out, though one may say that the more fervently Chicagoan approach has been marginalized, relatively speaking. But it's still hard to argue that the public is aware of those restrictions on sugar imports, or that theories of self-interest do not do a lot to help explain why these kinds of restrictions exist.

Among the responses to Caplan, the most prominent criticism of "rational irrationality" is to claim that it is a fundamentally incoherent concept, and squaring it with human psychology requires ludicrous, or literally impossible, assumptions. It is there where we will visit next chapter, where I will also develop what I think is really going on "underneath the hood" of rational irrationality.

NOTES

1. Klaus Schwab, ed., *The Global Competitiveness Report 2015–2016* (Geneva: World Economic Forum, 2015).

2. International Monetary Fund, *Annual Report on Exchange Arrangements and Exchange Restrictions* (Washington, DC: International Monetary Fund, 2015).

3. Ryan H. Murphy, "What Do Recent Trends in *Economic Freedom of the World* Really Tell Us?" *Economic Affairs* 35, no. 1 (February 2015): 138–150.

4. See the volumes of Robert Caro's *The Years of Lyndon Johnson*, for example, Robert Caro, *The Means of Ascent* (New York: Knopf, 1990).

5. James M. Buchanan and Gordon Tullock, *The Calculus of Consent* (Ann Arbor: University of Michigan Press 1962).

6. David M. Levy and Sandra J. Peart, "'Almost Wholly Negative': The Ford Foundation's Appraisal of the Virginia School," *Working Paper*, Fairfax: George Mason University, 2014), https://papers.ssrn.com/sol3/papers.cfm?abstract_id=248 5695; Charles K. Rowley and Daniel Houser, "The Life and Times of Gordon Tullock," *Public Choice* 152, no. 1 (July 2012): 3–27.

7. For the broader statements which attack this style of applying economics, James Kwak, *Economism: Bad Economics and the Rise of Inequality* (New York: Pantheon, 2017); John Quiggan, *Zombie Economics: How Dead Ideas Still Walk among Us* (Princeton: Princeton University Press, 2010); Steve Keen, *Debunking Economics: The Naked Emperor of the Social Sciences* (New York: St. Martin's Press 2002).

8. For a more complete and technical explanation, see Gordon Tullock, "The Welfare Costs of Tariffs, Monopolies and Theft," *Western Economic Journal* 5, no. 3 (June 1967): 224–232.

9. Mancur Olson, *The Logic of Collective Action: Public Goods and the Theory of Groups* (Cambridge: Harvard University Press, 1965).

10. Anne O. Krueger, "The Political Economy of the Rent-Seeking Society," *American Economic Review* 64, no. 3 (June 1974): 291–303.

11. Elaina Plott, "Marco Rubio's Billion Dollar Sugar Addiction," *National Review*, November 13, 2015, http://www.nationalreview.com/article/427001/marco -rubios-billion-dollar-sugar-addiction-elaina-plott. For a less narrowly political discussion of the issues, see Chris Edwards, "The Sugar Racket," *Cato Institute Tax & Budget Bulletin* no. 46 (June 2007), https://object.cato.org/sites/cato.org/files/pubs/ pdf/tbb_0607_46.pdf

12. Benjamin Powell, "A Taste for Protectionism: Coca-Cola in the Classroom," *Journal of Private Enterprise* 23, no. 1 (Fall 2007): 154–158.

13. Ilya Somin, *Democracy and Political Ignorance: Why Smaller Government Is Smarter* (Stanford: Stanford University Press, 2013).

14. Peter Boettke and Alain Marciano, "The Past, Present, and Future of Virginia Political Economy," *Public Choice* 163, no. 1 (April 2015): 53–65.

15. See Vlad Tarko, *Elinor Ostrom: An Intellectual Biography* (London: Rowman & Littlefield, 2016). Ostrom's most influential work can be found in Elinor Ostrom, *Governing the Commons: The Evolution of Institutions for Collective Action* (New York: Cambridge University Press, 1990).

16. S.M. Amadae and Bruce Bueno de Mesquita, "The Rochester School: The Origins of Positive Political Theory," *Annual Review of Political Science* 2 (June 1999): 269–295.

17. See William C. Mitchell, "Chicago Political Economy: A Public Choice Perspective," *Public Choice* 63, no. 3 (December 1989): 283–292.

18. Richard B. McKenzie, *Predictably Rational? In Search of Defenses for Rational Behavior in Economics* (Berlin: Springer, 2010).

19. Ludwig von Mises, *Human Action: A Treatise on Economics* (New Haven: Yale University Press, 1949).

20. Gary S. Becker, *The Economic Approach to Human Behavior* (Chicago: University of Chicago Press, 1976).

21. Many of the Chicago School models will make use of *homo economicus* assumptions as a simplifying device. The reasonableness of this approach would quickly bring us to questions of economic methodology and philosophy of science that are far beyond the scope of this discussion. Gary Becker, certainly, saw the need for a more thoughtful portrayal of human motivation than the desire for more money. Whether the complications to *homo economicus* ought to be brought in the fold is guided, methodologically speaking, by whether they improve the predictive accuracy of the model.

22. George Stigler, "The Theory of Economic Regulation," *The Bell Journal of Economics and Management Science* 2, no. 1 (Spring 1971): 3–21.

23. Sam Peltzman, "Toward a More General Theory of Regulation," *Journal of Law & Economics* 19, no. 2 (August 1976): 211–240.

24. Gary S. Becker, "A Theory of Competition among Pressure Groups for Political Influence," *Quarterly Journal of Economics* 98, no. 3 (August 1983): 371–400; Gary S. Becker, "Public Policies, Pressure Groups, and Dead Weight Costs," *Journal of Public Economics* 28, no. 3 (December 1985): 329–347; Pablo T. Spiller, "Politicians, Interest Groups, and Regulators: A Multiple-Principals Agency Theory of Regulation, or 'Let Them Be Bribed'," *Journal of Law & Economics* 33, no. 1 (April 1990): 65–101.

25. For a broad statement on the Chicago School, see Melvin W. Reder, "Chicago Economics: Permanence and Change," *Journal of Economic Literature* 20, no. 1 (March, 1982): 1–38.

26. See, for example, Richard Posner, *Economic Analysis of Law*, 2nd ed. (Boston: Little-Brown, 1977); Gary S. Becker, *A Treatise on the Family* (Cambridge: Harvard University Press 1993); Douglass C. North, "Institutions, Transaction Costs and Economic Growth," *Economic Inquiry* 25, no. 3 (July 1987): 419–428.

27. Donald Wittman, *The Myth of Democratic Failure: Why Political Institutions Are Efficient* (Chicago: University of Chicago Press, 1995). See also his earlier article, Donald Wittman, "Why Democracies Produce Efficient Results," *Journal of Political Economy* 97, no. 6 (December 1989): 1395–1424.

28. Bryan Caplan, "From Friedman to Wittman: The Transformation of Chicago Political Economy," *Econ Journal Watch* 2, no. 1 (April 2005), 15.

29. Bryan Caplan, *The Myth of the Rational Voter* (Princeton: Princeton University Press, 2007).

30. Andrew Gelman, Nate Silver, and Aaron Edlin, "What Is the Probability Your Vote Will Make a Difference?" *Economic Inquiry* 50, no. 2 (April 2012): 321–326.

31. Bryan Caplan, "Systematically Biased Beliefs about Economics: Robust Evidence of Judgmental Anomalies from the Survey of Americans and Economists on the Economy," *The Economic Journal* 112, no. 479 (April 2002): 433–458.

32. Stephen C. Miller, "Economic Bias and Ideology: Evidence from the General Social Survey," *Journal of Private Enterprise* 25, no. 1 (Fall 2009): 31–49; Daniel B. Klein and Charlotta Stern, "Professors and their Politics: The Policy Views of Social Scientists," *Critical Review* 17, no. 3–4 (2005): 257–303; c.f. Daniel B. Klein, "The Ideological Migration of Economics Laureates: Introduction and Overview," *Econ Journal Watch* 10, no. 3 (September 2013): 218–239.

33. Bryan Caplan and Stephen C. Miller, "Intelligence Makes People Think More Like Economists: Evidence from the General Social Survey," *Intelligence* 38, no. 6 (November–December 2010): 636–647.

34. Bryan Caplan and Stephen C. Miller, "Positive versus Normative Economics: What's the Connection? Evidence from the *Survey of Americans and Economists on the Economy* and the *General Social Survey*," *Public Choice* 150, no. 1 (January 2012): 241–261.

35. This is a standard finding. Headlines claiming that progressive political opinions are associated with higher IQ focus on social attitudes. See for instance, Steven G. Ludeke and Stig H. R. Rasmussen, "Different Political Systems Suppress or Facilitate the Impact of Intelligence on How You Vote: A Comparison of the U.S. and Denmark," *Intelligence* 70 (September–October 2018): 1–6; Yoav Ganzach, "Intelligence and the Rationality of Political Preferences," *Intelligence* 69 (July–August 2018): 59–70; Noah Carl, "Cognitive Ability and Political Beliefs in the United States," *Personality and Individual Differences* 83 (September 2015): 245–248; Arthur Nilsson, Arvid Erlandsson, and Daniel Vastfjall, "The Complex Relation Between Receptivity to Pseudo-Profound Bullshit and Political Ideology," *Personality and Social Psychology Bulletin*, forthcoming.

Chapter 3

The Obvious and Simple System of *Unnatural* Liberty

The Myth of the Rational Voter was well-received by academia and the public, especially considering that it challenged the received orthodoxy of those most familiar with its subject. However, one political science journal, *Critical Review*, released an issue dedicated to criticizing it. Two of the articles in the issue, including the lead article co-authored by the editor of the journal, make the argument that the basic concept of rational irrationality, and therefore the entire book *The Myth of the Rational Voter*, is nonsensical.[1] These concerns have been echoed elsewhere.[2] Caplan, in his allotted reply in the issue, referred to this criticism as "sophistical."[3] For the most part, Caplan was right.

The gist of the criticism is this. Caplan treats the question of "Should I be irrational?" as an issue of rational choice. In *some* sense,[4] the model assumes that people wake up in the morning, calculate how many *utils* (the imaginary unit of economic utility that economists will reference when looking to troll people) they will receive by being rational, and how many *utils* they will receive by being irrational. But you cannot really do that. If you know one of the choices is irrational, in what sense can choosing it be rational? Once you reach that conundrum, the carefully ordered system of Caplan comes crashing down and we are back to square one. This is why, according to some of the critics, you cannot use economic theory as an explanation for public opinion diverging from appropriate and effective policy.

In my mind, Caplan was absolutely right for calling this sophistry. One of my personal annoyances in academia is the attempt by other academics to play word games on an *a priori* basis regarding questions that should be answerable by data. Instead of challenging whether some relationship in the world exists, you parse words and argue about definitions. This is not a productive use of time, even though many accord these methods status. Caplan's critics, from my vantage point, were not disputing the substance of his claims, instead choosing to argue that what he described did not conform to the definitions of words as preferred by his critics, and therefore, his hypothesis doesn't count.

But, the systematic divergences between public and expert opinion are empirical facts to be explained, and they remain after controlling for socio-economic differences between the public and the experts. The presentation of the divergences as "rational" was a statement on Caplan's expectation that the public would be responsive to incentives if incentivized to hold rational opinions on the issues. That there is a negative relationship between incentives to holding rational opinions and actually holding them, as shown in voting behavior, is an empirical stylization that deserves an explanation, not something to be whisked away because of an objection to the word "rational."

Moreover, "rational irrationality" isn't some weird outlier position; it actually holds a middle ground between conventional neoclassical economics, which assumes that irrationality does not exist, and behavioral economics, which sometimes holds that individuals become even more irrational when stakes are higher.[5] Ultimately, if the empirical relationships Caplan argues are true and expert opinion is more accurate than public opinion, just about every conclusion from *The Myth of the Rational Voter* holds, and the *a priori* academic word games played by Caplan's critics are utterly irrelevant.

An acquaintance of mine changed my mind—to some extent. Brad Taylor, now a lecturer at University of Southern Queensland in Australia, wrote one of his dissertation chapters arguing that, no, rational irrationality is not incoherent, but the psychology of what is going on in rational irrationality is lacking, and may be lacking in such a way that matters.[6] Taylor and I would ultimately conclude that the way we preferred this solved differed, but it was upon reflection of my discussions with him that I came to accept that there was a small point to the criticism.

Caplan does discuss the issue of psychological plausibility,[7] ultimately outlining the following steps of how rational irrationality plays out psychologically.

Step 1: Be rational on topics where you have no emotional attachment to a particular answer.

Step 2: On topics where you have an emotional attachment to a particular answer, keep a "lookout" for questions where false beliefs imply a substantial material cost for you.

Step 3: If you pay no substantial material costs of error, go with the flow; believe whatever makes you feel best.

Step 4: If there are substantial material costs of error, raise your level of intellectual self-discipline in order to become more objective.

Step 5: Balance the emotional trauma of heightened objectivity—the progressive shattering of your comforting illusions—against the material costs of
error.

There is no need to posit that people start with a clear perception of the truth,
then throw it away. The only requirement is that rationality remain on
"standby," ready to engage when error is dangerous.

Yet even with this very careful explication, what Caplan calls "Step 5" still
requires people to wake up in the morning, count how many utils they will
receive by being rational versus by being irrational. It's not sufficient that
people merely do not already have "a clear perception of the truth;" "Step 5"
*still requires people to tacitly know they are on some level wrong and irra-
tional.* This assumption, while not impossible, is implausible.

To be clear, I do not find this ultimately damning of *The Myth of the
Rational Voter.* These steps are all that is needed to "derive a demand curve
for irrationality" and provide an apt description of the empirical question we
seek to address (that is, why do voters choose bad policies?). But it points
to the theory being incomplete. The point of emphasis from his critics,
that something akin to rational irrationality could not be stated coherently,
remains sophistical. Caplan, moreover, already touches on the points that I
think completes the theory more satisfactorily.[8] So, let's develop those ideas.

One counterargument to the recently fashionable fields of cognitive psychology and behavioral economics, which claim to find a new human "bias"
anytime they turn over a rock,[9] is that many such "biases" are actually useful rules-of-thumb, or heuristics, that allow people to make reasonably good
decisions without expending a tremendous amount of conscious brainpower.
Thinking isn't cheap and it takes time. When our ancestors evolved on the
savannah in Africa, they didn't have the opportunity to metaphorically take
out a pencil and paper to solve for *x*, because doing so would result in getting
eaten by a cheetah. Instead, evolution gave us a set of rapid ways of thinking
that work pretty well for most tasks. In fact, at times, these decision-making
methods *outperform* deliberately "rational" tactics espoused by the behavioral economists.[10] When a way of thinking is suited for efficiently dealing
with the constraints of the environment (time, brainpower, social constraints,
cheetahs, etc.), it is defined as *ecologically rational.*[11]

Being afraid of the dark, snakes, or spiders makes sense as being ecologically rational.[12] Instead of being taught, whether through elders or experience,
that snakes should be treated with caution, simply "building it in" to the
human mind likely confers greater benefits than costs. Even if a snake in
the grass is harmless, your response to jump and take several steps back is

ecologically rational, despite the behavioral economist correcting you ten minutes later that the snake was harmless after looking up the species of snake on Wikipedia. On average, acting cautiously around a snake is better than not acting cautiously. (The behavioral economist, by the way, was later eaten by a pack of hyenas while trying to solve for x).

The evolution of these behaviors overwhelming occurred tens, or even hundreds, of thousands of years ago. The mental tool we know as "being afraid of snakes" pre-dates humanity; you can observe the same behavior in primates. A number of videos online show that the sight of a cucumber can freak out a housecat, as the cucumber just enters the cat's vision. Evolution trained the poor animal to jump two feet in the air upon seeing anything that looks *vaguely* like a snake. Our minds, therefore, are a by-product of the constraints faced by early humans. And do you know what was absolutely rational for humans to be afraid of during this period? Humans from outside your own group.

The social milieu of early modern humans was that of a group of around 25–150 in number. You could reasonably trust this group to cooperate with you and not to cause you harm. The human brain actually struggles to keep track of social dynamics of groups larger than 150 people; this is "Dunbar's number" that creeps up periodically in psychology and sociology. Outside your own group, it was another story. The equivalent of "war" between the groups was commonplace, with the victor killing any remaining males, while taking women as slaves or concubines. If you had not been born with a deeply seated suspicion of those outside who you perceived as part of your group, you were at a severe disadvantage and prone to getting yourself killed.[13] Natural selection accounts for this.

Over time, in the process of the development of civilization, these small groups grew into tribes, often via the use of a common heroic ancestor as a means of securing cooperation among people who may not all know one another closely. Later, religion and ethnic identity helped spur the process of securing cooperation or preventing harm within larger groups, often promoted by states and rulers who found such order to be useful.[14] Philosopher Peter Singer has called the historical expansion of the number of people individuals in societies accord the status of personhood "The Expanding Circle."[15]

Anti-foreign bias isn't so much a "bias" as it is the mental heuristic labeled "hostility for outsiders" getting flipped on. For conservatives in the United States, this heuristic is flipped on when they think about immigration or see an unfamiliar ethnic restaurant displace a traditional American diner. But this isn't just about conservatives; people throughout the political spectrum view corporations as outsiders and the same heuristic is flipped on in dealings with them.[16] This is not to morally equate migrant workers and multinational corporations, but to emphasize that hostility is applied to whoever is perceived to be outside the broader moral community. And in recent decades, the West has been trending toward thinking of your political opponents as outsiders, with this logic holding equally for either end of the political spectrum.[17]

Similarly, the long run per capita economic growth rate of those living in prehistory was zero. Under these circumstances, the nature of trade differed, with negative or zero sum a more frequent result of social interaction. For those living in prehistory, an individual having a lot of stuff was evidence of exploitation of the group overall. If you did not focus like a laser on making sure trades were "fair," the less scrupulous among you will start accumulating all the quality clothing, tools, and protein at the expense of everyone else.[18]

In fact, the circumstances underlying early humanity's situation are even worse than this sounds. There were periods of technological improvement and subsequent prosperity, but these periods would later lead to more population in the same geographical area. More population would consume the new surplus of resources until the surplus disappeared, and per capita consumption would fall back where it was to begin with. This is the model of "Malthusian growth" that accurately described the world up until growth *per person* took off at the end of the eighteenth century.[19] Reflexive pessimism toward any claims of future prosperity was the appropriate human response for a very, very long time.

There was some amount of exchange and specialization,[20] yes, but to ensure your own standard of living, carefully tracking the "fairness" of trades was absolutely necessary. Today, where the institutional environment is radically different, we do not have the mental tool needed for readily grasping the positive sum nature of our world. In today's world, trading with someone who has more than you can easily leave you *better* off. In the zero sum world, there is no presumption that this is true, and the zero sum presumption is what we are built with. As such, this comes along with a hefty skepticism of both markets and economic progress.

Here are some things that did not exist on the savannah 50,000 years ago:[21] Pluralistic democracy, capitalism, science, technology, and the rule of law. This is our modern bundle of institutions. We never developed the mental tools for using these things. When we apply the mental tools we developed in the social environment of prehistory to modern day societies, politics, and economics, we are not being ecologically rational. We are being *ecologically irrational*.[22] This is contrary to Adam Smith, who described the modern liberal order as "The Obvious and Simple System of Natural Liberty." Our world of pluralism, civil liberties, global capitalism, and science is a profoundly *unnatural* way of living for us as humans, and it's no wonder we err so much when issues relating to them arise. The very unnatural-ness of our institutions—that is, what makes the nature of life differ from life in prehistory—simultaneously enriches humanity and causes hostile attitudes toward them.[23]

Think of how people react to and criticize modern institutions of pluralism, international organizations, global capitalism, and yes, even to science
and technology. They are *unnatural*. See *The Great Transformation*,[24] *The
Alchemy of Finance, Gattaca*, or even *Jurassic Park*. "Oh what's so great
about discovery? It's a violent, penetrative act that scars what is observes.
What you call discovery, I call the rape of the natural world," declared Ian
Malcolm, played by the dashingly awkward Jeff Goldblum, who voices the
pre-modern quasi-wisdom that new ways of doing things are bad. Without
discovery, there are no human rights, no literacy, and no collapses in infant
mortality rates. Or consider the angsty British TV show, *Black Mirror*, whose
premise is to feed off of the "informed" Westerner's anxiety toward innovation, science, and technology, or for that matter, the technophobic message of
Pixar's celebrated *WALL-E*.[25]

We fear our world, the wealthiest, richest, and happiest one that has yet
existed because it feels unnatural. But as pointed out by Steven Pinker, "natural" does not have any scientific meaning in the sense its proponents use it.
Did you know that "natural" almond extract contains trace amounts of arse-
nic, while artificial almond extract does not? Or that peanut butter is relatively
carcinogenic? Most people do not, because the perception of "natural" gives
things like them a pass, when in reality their "naturalness" is irrelevant.[26]
Forty tablespoons of peanut butter carry the same actuarial risk of cancer as
does living 150 years within 20 miles of a nuclear power plant, living two
months with a smoker, or getting a chest x-ray.[27]

On a similar note, today there is widespread fear of genetically modified
organisms (GMOs), as can readily be observed in pop culture like *Resident
Evil, The Island of Dr. Moreau*, and the first *Pokémon* movie, although at the
moment, the scientifically informed have control of the policy levers (at least
in the United States; in Europe, GMOs are grossly overregulated). Besides
outright fabrications, GMO skeptics are generally reduced to pretentious ges-
turing dressed up as analytics.[28] A recent study in *Nature Human Behaviour*
found that the extreme opponents of GMOs believe that they know the facts
about GMOs the best, when, among all groups, they actually know the least
about them.[29] Humanity has genetically modified other species for centuries,
and the only difference today is the means by which we do it. This much is
generally well-known.

Less well-known is the extent and efficacy of conventional methods in
transforming an organism. A single species, Brassica oleracea, was transformed using traditional breeding techniques into kale, broccoli, Brussels
sprouts, cabbage, kohlrabi, and cauliflower, with many of these innovations
occurring since the seventeenth century.[30] The many kinds of squash (including acorn and pattypan), ornamental gourds, pumpkins, and zucchini are also

the same species, Curcurbita pepo.[31] If you are worried about Frankenfood, then you should probably swear off kale too, just to be safe.

Another criticism of modern institutions is that they are *inauthentic*. This is an off-the-shelf epithet routinely thrown at global corporations. In response, all firms, from Walmart to Mom-and-Pop, are obsessed with marketing their products in such a way that minimizes the perception that are unnatural or inauthentic. But good luck defining "authentic" in such a way that is not circular. Authenticity tends to boil down to what or who can pretend to be uncorrupted by global supply chains, which are deemed evil by definition. Firms, at least those that can get away with it, will use "authenticity" as a marketing ploy so as to increase demand for their products, which the public credulously accepts as evidence that they offer a good value.

Journalist Andrew Potter has compiled a list of goods marketed as authentic, found below. The dots connecting the "authenticity" are the ways in which they are presented as being apart from the corruption of pluralistic democracy, global capitalism, science, or technology even though in many cases they are inherent to them. Potter's list, which is slightly outdated (because of how these things operate as a moving target), is:

> Italian cuisine, Chinese cuisine, Ethiopian cuisine, American cuisine, Canadian cuisine, Coca-Cola, Bailey's Irish Cream, distressed jeans, skateboards, skateboarding shoes, books, independent bookstores, typewriters, chainsaws, Twitter, crowdsourcing, blogs, comments on blogs, ecotourism, communist tourism, slum tourism, Al Gore, John McCain, Sarah Palin, Barack Obama, Susan Boyle, Michael Phelps' mom, the Mini Cooper, the Volkswagen Beetle, botox, baseball, Samuel Adams beer, Russian vodka, English gin, French Wine, Cuban chocolate, Cuba, Bhutan, organic coffee, organic produce, locally grown produce, locally grown organic produce, the 100-mile diet, the 100-mile suit, urban lofts, urban lofts with no-flush toilets, and mud floors in suburban homes.[32]

Is there *anything* possibly more "authentic" than Thomas Thwaites' barely functional toaster or Andy George's $1,500 chicken sandwich? Elsewhere, language, which is now reserved for lambasting the inauthentic architectural style of McMansions, was once used to describe the beloved brownstone homes in New York City by critics when they first appeared—because now they are *authentic*,[33] due to what they represent today. The architecture itself doesn't have a damned thing to do with how they are described. In 2019, Kombucha and cold brew coffee are the two most recent products to have fallen off the authenticity treadmill and onto the shelves of Walmart, because "authentic" is defined, effectively, as "not on sale at Walmart."

Similar themes are pervasive within our culture. *The Dark Side of the Moon* spent 741 consecutive weeks on the *Billboard* album chart; one of its two singles is "Money," with trite, empty criticisms of modern institutions scattered across the rest of the album. If that feels like cherry-picking, remember that similar criticisms are the central themes of most of the remainder of Pink Floyd's oeuvre, including roughly all of *Animals, The Wall*, and *Wish You Were Here*.[34] And *No Logo*, the opus of the world's most celebrated sommelier of ignorance, Naomi Klein, was an important influence on Radiohead's *Kid A*.[35] Or consider the themes of movies like *They Live, Falling Down*, or *Office Space*. In contrast, opposition to global capitalism was the outward identity of U2 frontman Bono until he became sufficiently invested in the importance of economic development that he accidentally learned that business and globalism are both enriching, not impoverishing, the developing world.[36]

The idea of humans possessing mental heuristics or tools specialized for certain tasks, known as mental modules, was popularized by Steven Pinker in the context of language and early childhood psychology.[37] We are remarkably good as a species at learning language, but often in very specific ways the brain was built for. We could, alternatively, imagine a very intrinsically foreign means of communicating. We could, in principle, communicate and process information in binary code, as computers do. It would be extremely difficult to do so, and it would take a ton of brainpower because our mental module isn't built for that. But we could.

Communicating economics and thinking as an economist does about issues relating to markets, or other strange modern institutions, is akin to forcing yourself to think in binary code. Alternatively, it's akin to calmly petting a scary looking snake or spider. Because the mental modules in question also overlap with our sense of morality, economics frequently sounds deeply immoral to many people. And all this holds for getting people to think appropriately about science and technology as well. "Natural" and "authentic" are synonymous with moral or goodness for many people. The modern institutions I have emphasized are neither.

That is my proposed psychological mechanism for "rational irrationality." For certain economic, political, or social concerns, it is human nature to use mental modules or heuristics that were developed tens of thousands of years under institutional arrangements quite different from the ones we live under today. When you ask people to contradict what these modules suggest, you are asking them to cast aside what evolution has taught us is wise. The overlap between the mental modules and morality means that people find it upsetting and painful to think in these ways. Costly incentives are necessary to kick people into thinking in models of the world that reflect reality.

This does not require people to tacitly know that they are wrong when engaging in ecological irrationality. It is a broad finding in moral psychology that moral (and political) intuitions about what *should* be true come first, prior to reasoning.[38] Reasoning, if it happens at all, occurs afterwards; David Hume was correct when he claimed that reason is the slave to passions. When opponents of trade are confronted with the correct arguments that Trade Is Good, I do not think it is appropriate to interpret them as tacitly understanding such arguments for trade to be correct.[39] They believe their interlocutors are devious or foolish. They don't tacitly think that they themselves are actually wrong, but changing their minds isn't worth their while. And if the argument reaches a point that they must switch over to using the human mind's crappy general-purpose reasoning device, subsequent reasoning will frequently remain a slave to what people already want to believe.

In low cost environments for ecological irrationality, humans stick with mental modules and heuristics like anti-foreign bias because evolutionary history gives them to us as a default. For most of human history, *people telling you to override your anti-foreign bias were wrong.* You could describe the inner logic of Trade Is Good all day to early humans, and nothing you say would make it applicable to the institutional environment of pre-history. In the modern context and when ecological irrationality is of higher cost, people may become more open minded to learning alternative heuristics like "Trade is Good," or doing the hard work of "thinking in binary code"-style of reasoning. None of this involves an implicit understanding that the instinctive belief was actually wrong before you consciously changed your mind.

On these points, I mentioned in chapter 2 that there is a connection between intelligence and thinking like an economist.[40] I wish to emphasize that this connection is only in part because people who are more intelligent are better able to perform conscious, explicit reasoning. Important aspects of human intelligence are merely capabilities to reason by analogy,[41] which is less about carefully applied logical or mathematical thinking and more about an ability to learn and apply models (i.e., simplifications) of reality to specific cases. Even "Trade Is Good" can itself be thought of as one of these models. (Making use of many different models of reality—these models at times possibly contradicting one another—actually correlates with higher predictive accuracy.[42]) All this is to say that I do not wish to overplay the importance of the mind's ability to reason and calculate, in a narrow sense, relative to other ways by which intelligence reduces ecological irrationality. We will return to what else might further reduce ecological irrationality in the conclusion of this book.

My conceptualization of ecological irrationality neatly applies in general to anti-foreign bias, anti-market bias, and pessimistic bias. It only weakly applies to "make-work bias." I have some points to raise regarding this problem. One, "make-work bias" was always a bit of the odd duck among the four. Second, it may be less that people are in favor of "make-work" as it is their belief that economic growth is not something to take seriously at a conceptual level. If this is the case, "make-work bias" is simply the other side of the coin of pessimistic bias. Lastly, events since the 2007 publication of *The Myth of the Rational Voter* suggest that economists are not nearly as united on the issue of "make-work bias" as it may have appeared. With all that in play, my preference is to subsume some of "make-work bias" into pessimistic bias and drop the rest from ecological irrationality.

I wish to address the frequent criticism of evolutionary explanations such as the explanation given in this chapter: that evolutionary explanations are (or can be) "just-so" stories. What this criticism means is that my explanation makes no predictions about the world and cannot be tested. While this criticism may pertain to certain evolutionary explanations, there have been instances of evolutionary explanations tested by data and shown to be false.[43] Meaning, they are falsifiable. I would point to two predictions implied by my description of ecological irrationality, meaning it is not a just-so story. First, the conceptualization of ecological irrationality as a mental module implies that the biases described by Caplan are Human Universals.[44] This means we would expect them to appear in every society. Second, Caplan's biases are things we must "unlearn;" people start with these views of the world and only begrudgingly come to acknowledge that Trade Is Good, not the other way around. Neither of these points would be predicted by the bare "Rational Irrationality" model, and I would argue that both of them to are true, although I can imagine the existence of certain caveats.

Another point one could raise is that other modern institutions do not elicit the same hostility as do markets, science, and others. Namely, most people don't have the same kind of negative response toward centralized government and organized religions, even though both of these institutions are also relatively new to the scene in the scope of human history. I would first point out that on many margins, people do in fact have these negative responses toward central government or organized religion that fall on similar lines to their hostility for our other institutions—think about complaining about the DMV or the New Atheist[45] response to religion. Whatever the merits of complaining about the DMV or New Atheism, hostility to centralized governments or organized religion is certainly something that exists in the world.

However, what distinguishes government and religion is that people see them to reflect explicit collective action, the celebration of which is a core aspect of the human experience (per Emile Durkheim).[46] Dan Klein, an economist, has even expressed frustration at the celebration of collective action as blinding people to the dangers of government.[47] But this ultimately cuts both ways. At times we could be giving excuses to government because it is romanticized collective action, while at others we may be hostile to it because bureaucracy feels unnatural and stupid. The proper role for the size and scope of government is obviously itself a question for social science. It isn't best answered by either intuitive model. To reiterate: first, it isn't correct to say that there is no analogous hostility toward governmental and religious institutions, and second, the reason the skepticism or suspicion is muted is a rather obvious application of a longstanding sociological explanation of religion.

F. A. Hayek spoke of how our ability to work within our modern institutional framework relied on a commitment to institutions that stood somewhere "between instincts and reason," meaning, as part of a tradition, norm, or more. Ecological irrationality arises either when you make decision on raw instinct and when you apply "reason" too simplistically. I do not wish however, to draw too close attention to the parallels between Hayek's argument to my own, and I believe that modern acolytes of Hayek may do so a bit too readily. Hayek's focuses differ from mine, and his commentary on evolution and psychology are somewhat inchoate. My closest predecessor in advancing these arguments is not Hayek, but the economist Paul Rubin, who created the concept of "Folk Economics."[48] Folk Economics essentially is the groundwork for the preceding discussion on the clash between how the human brain wishes to view economic and social relationships and the modern institutional environment. (Caplan cites and quotes Rubin briefly in passing but does not fully develop the argument as I have done here.[49]) There are many other predecessors I could point to who run closer to my argument than does Hayek,[50] and there is no lack of general scholarship exploring the implications of evolution for public policy and social science.[51] Hence, I do not wish to overemphasize Hayek.

I should also underline that none of these remarks contradict that there is a "demand curve for irrationality." At the level of where this could be modeled in economics, it didn't really matter how exactly the psychology played out. The empirical facts remained the empirical facts. On the other hand, it does matter for when we want to explore rational irrationality in untraversed territory, for example under alternative institutional arrangements, as I consider in chapter 6. But when speaking about rational irrationality in liberal Western democracies, little ultimately changes.

All that said, this presents a problem. If I am correct, there is little reason to believe that rational irrationality, or as I will now refer to it, ecological irrationality, is something specific to the analysis of democratic governance. We still may expect ecological irrationality to be less important the more individually costly it is to express it, but we should expect it to be widespread in markets as well. Those are the titular markets against modernity and the empirical examination which is the topic of the next chapter.

NOTES

1. Stephen E. Bennett and Jeffrey Friedman, "The Irrelevance of Economic Theory to Understanding Economic Ignorance," *Critical Review* 20, no. 3 (2008): 195–258; Jon Elster and Helene Landemore, "Ideology and Dystopia," *Critical Review* 20, no. 3 (2008): 273–289.

2. Anthony J. Evans and Jeffrey Friedman, "'Search' vs. 'Browse': A Theory of Error Grounded in Radical (Not Rational) Ignorance," *Critical Review* 23, no. 1–2 (2011): 73–104; Gerry Mackie, "Rational Ignorance and Beyond," in *Collective Wisdom: Principles and Mechanisms*, ed. Helene Landmore and Jon Elster (Cambridge, UK: Cambridge University Press, 2012), 290–319.

3. Bryan Caplan, "Reply to My Critics," *Critical Review* 20, no. 3 (2008): 377–413.

4. My description here is a bit theatrical and should not be taken too literally.

5. Bryan Caplan, "Rational Irrationality: A Framework for the Neoclassical-Behavioral Debate," *Eastern Economic Journal* 26, no. 2 (Spring 2000): 191–211.

6. Brad Taylor, "Rational Irrationality as Dual Process Theory," in *Exit and Voice: Papers from a Revisionist Public Choice Perspective* (PhD diss., Canberra, Australia: Australian National University, 2014), 40–57.

7. Caplan, *The Myth of the Rational Voter*, 125–131.

8. Caplan, *The Myth of the Rational Voter*, 24, 178.

9. Gerd Gigerenzer, "The Bias Bias in Economics," *Review of Behavioral Economics* 5, no. 3–4 (2018): 303–336.

10. Gerd Gigerenzer and Daniel G. Goldstein, "Reasoning the Fast and Frugal Way: Models of Bounded Rationality," *Psychological Review* 103, no. 4 (October 1996): 650–659; Gerd Gigerenzer and Henry Brighton, "Homo Heuristicus: Why Biased Minds Make Better Inferences," *Topics in Cognitive Science* 1, no. 1 (January 2009): 107–143.

11. See, for example, Gerd Gigerenzer, Peter M. Todd, and the ABC Research Group, *Simple Heuristics that Make Us Smart* (Oxford: Oxford University Press, 2000); Gerd Gigerenzer, *Rationality for Mortals: How People Cope with Uncertainty* (Oxford: Oxford University Press, 2010). "Ecological rationality" has separately defined as a characteristic of institutions, not people. There is overlap between the two approaches, but mine will hew far more closely to the definition and approach of Gigerenzer. See Vernon L. Smith, "Constructivist and Ecological Rationality in Economics," *American Economic Review* 93, no. 3 (June 2003): 465–508. Broadly speaking, another argument similar that of Gigerenzer is Douglas T. Kenrick and Vladas Griskevicius, *The Rational Animal: How Evolution Made Us Smarter Than We Think* (New York: Basic Books, 2013), a work we will return to in chapter 5.

12. Arne Ohman and Susan Mineka, "Fears, Phobias, and Preparedness: Toward an Evolved Module of Fear and Fear Learning," *Psychological Review* 108, no. 3 (July 2001): 483–522; Arne Ohman and Susan Mineka, "The Malicious Serpent: Snakes as Prototypical Stimulus for an Evolved Module of Fear," *Current Directions in Psychological Science* 12, no. 1 (February 2003): 5–9.

13. For the nature and scale of violence among early humans, see Steven Pinker, *The Better Angels of Our Nature: Why Violence Has Declined* (New York: Viking, 2011).

14. Francis Fukuyama, *The Origins of Political Order: From Prehuman Times to the French Revolution* (New York: Farrar, Straus and Giroux, 2011).

15. Peter Singer, *The Expanding Circle: Ethics and Sociobiology* (New York: Farrar, Straus and Giroux, 1981).

16. See Ryan H. Murphy, "Corporations as the Outgroup?" *Working Paper* (Dallas: Southern Methodist University, 2018), https://papers.ssrn.com/sol3/papers.cfm?abstract_id=3279828; Tyler Cowen, *Big Business: A Love Letter to an American Anti-Hero* (New York: St. Martin's Press, 2019), 183–206; c.f. Leda Cosmides and John Tooby, "Cognitive Adaptations for Social Exchange," in *The Adapted Mind: Evolutionary Psychology and the Generation of Culture*, ed. Jerome H. Barkow, Leda Cosmides, and John Tooby (New York: Oxford University Press, 1992), 163–228.

17. Lynn Vavreck, "A Measure of Identity: Are You Wedded to Your Party?" *The New York Times*, January 31, 2017, https://www.nytimes.com/2017/01/31/upshot/are-you-married-to-your-party.html.

18. This may be the underlying intuition for why inequality is objected to, but I emphasize fairness since it, and not inequality, seems to be what drives moral sentiments. See Christina Starmans, Mark Shaskin, and Paul Bloom, "Why People Prefer Unequal Societies," *Nature Human Behaviour* 1 (April 2017), no. 0082.

19. Gary D. Hansen and Edward C. Prescott, "Malthus to Solow," *American Economic Review* 92, no. 4 (September 2002): 1205–1217; Oded Galor and David N. Weil, "From Malthusian Stagnation to Modern Growth," *American Economic Review* 89, no. 2: 150–154.

20. Some intragroup trade may have been especially important – I share my food with you when times are lean for me, and you pay me back later. But while favor trading was and is important, these kinds of social exchanges do not work along the same logic of market exchange. Consider, for example, how you may buy your neighbor a case of beer as thanks for helping with some task, but it would be a norm violation to hand your neighbor $20 instead. Intragroup trade likely functioned similarly. See Alan P. Fiske, "The Four Elementary Forms of Sociality: Framework for a Unified Theory of Social Relations," *Psychological Review* 99 (October 1992), no. 4: 689–723; c.f. Alan P. Fiske and Philip E. Tetlock, "Taboo Trade-offs: Reactions to Transactions that Transgress the Spheres of Justice," *Political Psychology* 18, no. 2 (June 1997): 255–297. We will return to somewhat similar issues in chapter 7.

21. It is a slight exaggeration to assert that there have been *no* changes to the human genome since this period. Tolerance for lactose is the most famous counterexample. But it is one thing to point to humans evolving to cope with the rise of something like agriculture, and quite another to argue that we as a species have already evolved to make effective use of the modern bundle of institutions, all of which are recent inventions.

22. In the cases of both ecological rationality and ecological irrationality, they can be thought of as a form in terms of bounded rationality. See Herbert A. Simon, "A Behavioral Model of Rational Choice," *Quarterly Journal of Economics* 69, no. 1

(February 1955): 99–118; conceptually, see also Nabil L. Al-Najjar and Jonathan Weinstein, "The Ambiguity Aversion Literature: A Critical Assessment," *Economics and Philosophy* 25, no. 3 (November 2009): 249–284.

23. For a presentation of this theme, see Jonah Goldberg, *Suicide of the West: How the Rebirth of Tribalism, Populism, Nationalism, and Identity Politics is Destroying American Democracy* (New York: Crown Forum, 2018).

24. Arguably, I should emphasize the pernicious influence of Karl Polanyi's claims in *The Great Transformation*, but simultaneously it may seem like I am echoing him, as he claims markets are an historical outlier and therefore "unnatural." See Karl Polanyi, *The Great Transformation* (New York: Farrar & Rinehart, 1944). However, I do not deny that for a considerable period of human history, there was *some* amount of market activity. But people historically treated the market with contempt, just they do now. On the a-historical character of Polanyi's claims, see Alex Nowrasteh, "Karl Polanyi's Battle with Economic History," *Libertarianism.org*, September 12, 2013, https://www.libertarianism.org/blog/karl-polanyis-battle-economic-history.

25. On *WALL-E* in particular, I recommend Emergent Order, "EconPop – The Economics of WALL-E," June 6, 2014, https://www.youtube.com/watch?v=g9O g4qkn67o.

26. Steven Pinker, *The Blank Slate: The Modern Denial of Human Nature* (New York: Penguin, 2002), 162–165, 229–233.

27. W. Kip Viscusi, John M. Vernon, and Joseph E. Harrington, Jr., *The Economics of Regulation and Antitrust*, 4th ed. (Cambridge, MA: MIT Press, 2006), 696.

28. For an example of the latter, see Mark Spitznagel and Nassim Nicholas Taleb, "Another 'Too Big to Fail' System in G.M.O.s," *The New York Times*, July 13, 2015, https://www.nytimes.com/2015/07/14/business/dealbook/another-too-big-to-fail-sys tem-in-gmos.html.

29. Philip M. Fernbach, Nicholas Light, Sydney E. Scott, Yoel Inbar, and Paul Rozin, "Extreme Opponents of Genetically Modified Foods Know the Least But Think They Know the Most," *Nature Human Behaviour* 3 (January 2019): 251–256.

30. Joseph Stromberg, "Kale, Brussels Sprouts, Cauliflower, and Cabbage Are All Varieties of the Same Magical Species," *Vox*, February 10, 2015, https://www.vox .com/xpress/2014/8/6/5974989/kale-cauliflower-cabbage-broccoli-same-plant.

31. R. Lira Saade and S. Montes Hernandez, "Cucurbits (*Cucurbita* spp.)," in *Neglected Crops: 1492 from a Different Perspective*, ed. J. E. Hernandez Bermejo and J. Leon (Rome: Food and Agriculture of the United Nations, 1994), 67–68.

32. Andrew Potter, *The Authenticity Hoax: How We Get Lost Finding Ourselves* (New York: HarperCollins, 2010), 103.

33. Suleiman Osman, *The Invention of Brownstone Brooklyn: Gentrification and the Search for Authenticity in Postwar New York* (New York: Oxford University Press, 2011), 29–30.

34. A description of pop culture as expressing disdain toward our institutional environment, although with a different emphasis, can be found in Jonah Goldberg, *The Suicide of the West*, 242–261.

35. David Cavanagh, "I Can See the Monsters," *Q Magazine*, October 2000, 102–103.

36. Mark Hendrickson, "U2's Bono Courageously Embraces Capitalism," *Forbes*, November 8, 2013, https://www.forbes.com/sites/markhendrickson/2013/11/08/u2s-bono-courageously-embraces-capitalism/#5225baa7575a.

37. Steven Pinker, *The Language Instinct: How Minds Create Language* (New York: W. Morrow 1994). See also Steven Pinker and Paul Bloom, "Natural Language and Natural Selection," *Behavioral and Brain Sciences* 13, no. 4 (December 1990): 707–727.

38. Jonathan Haidt, *The Righteous Mind: Why Good People Are Divided by Politics and Religion* (New York: Pantheon, 2012), 27–71; c.f. Kevin Simler and Robin Hanson, *The Elephant in the Brain: Hidden Motives in Everyday Life* (New York: Oxford University Press, 2018).

39. Caplan at times enthusiastically presents betting as a way of demonstrating that people do not believe what they claim to believe, as they are unwilling to bet on their stated beliefs. I believe that creating the norm of more frequent bets on beliefs is good, but I do not take peoples' unwillingness to bet as evidence that they implicitly understand that they are wrong. Asking people to bet is frequently a norm violation, and more importantly, the viewpoint that beliefs should map into a willingness to bet requires certain metaphysical or philosophical positions that not everyone shares, even though they may well be true. In any case, I suspect that betting moderates positions rather than causing beliefs to move stridently in one direction or another, for the reasons developed in Barbara Mellers, Philip Tetlock, and Hal R. Arkes, "Forecasting Tournaments, Epistemic Humility, and Attitude Depolarization," *Cognition* 188 (July 2019): 19–26.

40. On certain specific margins, intelligence can actually make ecological irrationality *worse*. Jason Brennan, whose work we will explore thoroughly in chapter 6, argues that those who are below average in intelligence are simply unengaged with political modes of thought. More intelligence or knowledge simply leads to partisanship and emphasis on winning political arguments. I acknowledge this argument but my framing does not emphasize those who are simply politically unengaged.

41. Dedre Gentner and Keith J. Holyoak, "Reasoning and Learning by Analogy: Introduction," *American Psychologist* 52, no. 1 (January 1997): 32–34; Dan Chiappe and Kevin MacDonald, "The Evolution of Doman-General Mechanisms in Intelligence and Learning," *The Journal of General Psychology* 132, no. 1 (January 2005): 5–40.

42. Philip Tetlock, *Expert Political Judgment: How Good Is It? How Can We Know?* (Princeton: Princeton University Press, 2005).

43. Jaime C. Confer, Judith A. Easton, Diana S. Fleischman, Cari D. Goetz, David M. G. Lewis, Carin Perilloux, and David M. Buss, "Evolutionary Psychology: Controversies, Questions, Prospects, and Limitations," *American Psychologist* 65, no. 2 (February-March 2010): 110–126.

44. In their connection to evolutionary psychology, see Pinker, *The Blank Slate*, 51–58; Donald E. Brown, *Human Universals* (New York: McGraw-Hill, 1991).

45. I am giving New Atheism as an example for primarily rhetorical reasons. A broader example would be the disconnect between the natural religions humanity evolved with and modern organized religions. A provocative instance of this is that,

in Early Modern Europe, the peasantry was actually much more enthusiastic for prosecuting women for witchcraft than were the clerics. See Peter T. Leeson and Jacob W. Russ, "Witch Trials," *The Economic Journal* 128, no. 613 (August 2018): 2066–2105. No position is taken here as to whether natural religions are "better" than organized religions, from the utilitarian standpoint. The issues I am raising are also orthogonal to the truth or falsehood of any given religion. The existence of hostility for organized religion is the pertinent point.

46. Jonathan Haidt, *The Righteous Mind*, 221–245.

47. Daniel B. Klein, "The People's Romance: Why People Love Government (As Much as They Do)," *The Independent Review* 10, no. 1 (Summer 2005): 5–37.

48. Paul H. Rubin, "Folk Economics," *Southern Economic Journal* 70, no. 1 (July 2003): 157–171. See also Paul H. Rubin, *Darwinian Politics: The Evolutionary Origin of Freedom* (Piscataway: Rutgers University Press, 2002); Pascal Boyer and Michael Bang Peterson, "Folk-Economic Beliefs: An Evolutionary Cognitive Model," *Behavioral and Brain Sciences* 41, E158 (2018). Rubin cites Hayek with a quotation that gives the impression, in my opinion, that Hayek's position is close to Rubin's (and mine) than it actually is.

49. Caplan, *The Myth of the Rational Voter*, 178.

50. One author who comes very close to my position on the issues can be found in Jonah Goldberg, *Suicide of the West*, 239–242. See also for example, Toban Wiebe, "Evolutionary Psychology and Anti-Market Bias," *Mises Daily*, September 15, 2010, https://mises.org/library/evolutionary-psychology-and-antimarket-bias; J. R. Clark and Dwight Lee, "Econ 101 Morality: The Amiable, the Mundane, and the Market," *Econ Journal Watch* 14, no. 1 (January 2017): 61–76; c.f. Larry Arnhart, "The Evolution of Darwinian Liberalism," *Journal of Bioeconomics* 17, no. 1 (April 2015): 3–15; Hans Rosling, *Factfulness*. Making broader points that can be construed in terms of ecological irrationality is Rick Shenkman, *Political Animals: How Our Stone-Age Brain Gets in the Way of Smart Politics* (New York, Basic Books, 2016).

51. Steven Pinker, *The Blank Slate*; Matt Ridley, *The Origins of Virtue: Human Instincts and the Evolution of Cooperation* (New York: Penguin, 1996); Charles Darwin, *The Descent of Man, and the Selection in Relation to Sex* (London: John Murray, 1871); Peter Singer, *A Darwinian Left* (New Haven: Yale University Press, 2000); Avi Tuschman, *Our Political Nature: The Evolutionary Origins of What Divides Us* (Amherst: Prometheus Books, 2013).

Chapter 4

Ecological Irrationality in the Wild

In Colonial America, the Townshend Acts were instituted as a demonstration by the British Parliament that it could tax the colonies, as a matter of principle. The American colonies were already legally forced to buy goods from Britain. This was not the straw that broke the camel's back—that would be the Intolerable Acts—but the Townshend Acts led to boycotts of British products. The boycotts, by nature, imposed hardships on the boycotters. While the proximate causes of upheaval in the colonies were taxation and colonial representation in parliament, these issues also reflected the hardships imposed by the mercantilist system.

In modern day, Quincy, a city south of Boston and named for the son of the American revolutionary and later president, is home to a hip New American restaurant called The Townshend. The restaurant explains itself as,

> The Townshend Acts were laws imposed by Britain in the 1760's that increased duties on imported goods like glass, paper and tea in the American colonies. This was viewed as an abuse of power by the colonists, leading them to limit imports from Britain, making a stand for economic and political self-determination. Our restaurant, The Townshend, was founded in the spirit of this refreshing independent sensibility.[1]

A story run on local Boston-area television further clarifies this, stating, "So instead of revolting, the colonists simply learned how to farm and manufacture things themselves. Jumping forward to the present day, and that's pretty much the philosophy in the kitchen. All the sauces, pastas, doughs, and dressings are crafted in the kitchen,"[2] thereby missing the entire point of the story behind the boycotts of the Townshend Acts. Even as many restaurants obviously produce better sauces than what they could get off-the-shelf from their restaurant supplier, the colonists were imposing *hardships* on themselves by boycotting their coerced economic arrangement with the British. While they would be better off with free access to international markets (contra the Navigation Acts), buying imports from Britain was still better than producing everything in the colonies. The boycott impoverished them. Today, the local and do-it-yourself ethos permeates our hip, "enlightened" restaurant culture, exemplified in how the ownership of The Townshend gets the story of the Townshend Acts precisely backward. We are now what economist Steve Horwitz has described as being "rich enough to play at being poor"[3](see figure 4.1).

In *The Myth of the Rational Voter*, Caplan's most highly emphasized presentation of "the demand for irrationality" is the "near neoclassical demand" for irrationality.[4] What a "near neoclassical demand curve for irrationality" means is that an individual is fully rational unless the negative repercussions of being irrationality are almost zero. One such example is voting. I have drawn the near neoclassical demand curve on figure 4.2 as D_{Caplan}. If the relationship between how much irrationality is expressed and how much it costs is as it is drawn, there is little-to-no room for irrationality in the private sphere.

Here is one possible intuition for what this curve means. People rarely change their minds substantively in politics. But when they do, it is described as a painful, grueling process. They must admit that their moral convictions were backward and they must see their longtime allies as new adversaries. If you are able to avoid confronting where your beliefs contradict reality, you are able to live a happier, simpler life. In the context of the near neoclassical demand curve for irrationality, you will do away with irrationality whenever there is any real personal cost to yourself. You remain irrational only where it costless for you to be irrational.

While Caplan notes the private demand for irrationality, he does so only briefly. It arises in the book in an aside on betting,[5] and later in a blog post.[6] For the most part, the "demand for irrationality" in *The Myth of the Rational Voter* is outlined narrowly in order to justify carving out a minor divergence from the assumptions of the Chicago School of Economics (see chapter 2). As support, Caplan appeals to two respected figures in the history of economic thought, Frederic Bastiat and Joseph Schumpeter, as having made verbal arguments similar to a near neoclassical demand curve for irrationality, so as to defend the position that this small perturbation from the conventional rational choice model is reasonable.[7]

In comparison to other demand curves, the depiction of demand is idiosyncratic. Drawn next to it is a more conventional demand curve, $D_{Conventional}$. When I recast rational irrationality as ecological irrationality and gave the concept firmer psychological foundations, there was little suggesting that the implicit demand curve would be shaped anything like the near neoclassical

TEXTBOX 4.1 SUPPLY AND DEMAND

The cornerstones of microeconomics are demand and supply. They appear graphed in Figure 4.1. Demand is how much the purchaser of a good will buy at a given price. Supply is how much the seller of a good will sell, at a given price. Graphically, what is important to remember is that ~~that~~ demand slopes downwards and supply slopes upwards. All that means is that participants in the market will want to buy more of something when its price is lower, and sellers in the market will want to sell more of something when its price is higher. The point at which the two curves intersect is the market clearing price, and the corresponding price and amount of goods sold being the "equilibrium" of the market.

While this is simple enough, it resolves what is known as the Diamond-Water paradox. Why is water cheaper than diamonds, even though you need water to live? The answer is that, given the constraints of the world we live in, water is very abundant. If there were less supply of water, the supply curve would shift upwards, the price of water would be higher, and we would use water much less on its less essential uses. For example, with less water, we would use less on things like keeping yards green or recreation, while still using it to keep us hydrated and healthy.

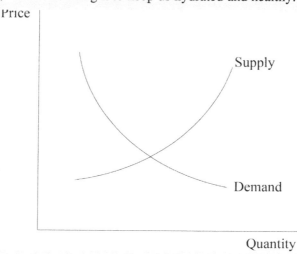

Figure 4.1   Demand and Supply, Drawn Conventionally. *Source*: Author.

demand curve. Our impulses against modern institutions are deeply embedded within us. The impulses are how we're wired. Contradicting the way we were built to think requires thought processes that are alien to us. All that

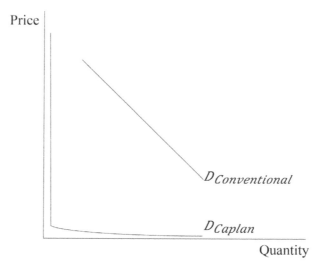

Figure 4.2 Near Neoclassical Demand and Conventional Demand Curves. *Source:* Author.

would strongly suggest we are willing to incur some costs to hold on to our irrationality. Generalizing Caplan's argument to the private sphere will: (1) allow us to observe the same phenomena in other social contexts and (2) yield different implications for the comparison between markets and political institutions, as will be discussed in chapter 6. Further implications will be expanded upon in the remainder of the book.

To show that a conventionally drawn demand curve is a closer approximation to reality than the near neoclassical demand curve, we would first need to specify what it would even look like when people express a willingness-to-pay greater than zero for ecological irrationality. "Willingness-to-pay" is economics jargon for the most you are willing and able to pay for a given unit of a good. For example, perhaps an apple at a supermarket costs $0.50 and you are willing to pay for the apple at this price. You are also willing to pay for the apple when it is $0.51 and $0.52, all the way up to, say, $1.10. A dollar-ten is your willingness-to-pay, in this case.

But there are far more exotic examples of willingness-to-pay, which will be relevant much later in this chapter. For example, Texas weather sucks. I need to be paid extra to work in Texas instead of California, even after controlling for the higher cost of living in California, to compensate me for the relentless summers. (In August and September, I often find myself jealously looking up the summer weather of Northern European cities. This is known as Stockholm syndrome.) The extra cash I require is a willingness-to-accept—that is, I accept and agree to supply my labor while living in the brutal heat in exchange for more compensation. Willingness-to-accept is the other side of the coin of willingness-to-pay. You may express a willingness-to-pay when choosing a restaurant not only for its food, service, and vibe, but also its convenience, your sentiments, or your mood. Even though I believe that the sandwich chain Subway is so bad that it is the single greatest piece of empirical evidence that maybe we should return to the hunter-gatherer lifestyle, I still exhibit a positive willingness-to-pay for their products because of Subway's ubiquity and convenience.

The Myth of the Rational Voter presented voters as having a positive but very, very small willingness-to-pay for irrationality. This is what the "near neoclassical demand" curve for irrationality entails. Caplan's emphasis was on the rejection of free market capitalism (or something approximating it). As I have argued, it is not so much capitalism alone as it is modern institutions that do not have a close analogue for early humanity, including globalism, science, and pluralistic democracy.[8] An implicit willingness-to-pay to aggress against any of these institutions should be seen to reflect the same underlying mechanism as those leading voters to make poor choices at the voting booth.

Before delving any further, I want to discuss a problematic issue for ecological irrationality, whether it is in the public sphere or private sphere. Years before *The Myth of the Rational Voter*, philosophers Geoffrey Brennan and Loren Lomasky tried to solve many puzzles in political science by explaining voting behavior as *expressive voting*.[9] This theory states that voters make their decisions not to achieve any particular goals, but to express the type of person they are: for instance, their beliefs, ideology or identity. "Rational irrationality" has been criticized on the grounds that little differs between it and expressive voting.[10] My own position is that these theories complement one another. Certain consumer behaviors we will discuss can be interpreted in terms of the expression of values.[11] But sometimes these expressions of values are empirically testable statements of cause and effect. "Buy American" may be an expression of patriotism, but it is intertwined with empirically false beliefs about the welfare of those living in the United States and international trade. The extent to which this is an issue for private ecological irrationality, it is an issue parallel to the comparison between *The Myth of the Rational Voter* and expressive voting.

But what should we look for to find ecological irrationality in the wild, so we can actually observe it in consumer behavior? There are four mechanisms or "signposts" that point to ecological irrationality, which I will make use of to help us observe it. The first three signposts we have mentioned already in chapter 3—authenticity, naturalness, and Folk Economics. All three of these concepts appear to signal that the good or service or concept or what have you is uncorrupted by the modern world and its institutions. "Naturalness" in particular relates to the concept of Folk Biology,[12] which is the intuitive sense of how organic life functions. Folk Biology has its benefits—we are born with some idea of which plants are safe to consume and how to avoid contaminated food. But in the modern world, it also gives us many misleading intuitions, generally via equating the natural with the good, that is, the naturalistic fallacy. Folk Economics and "authenticity" were each broadly covered last chapter. The fourth signpost is interpreting many of these kinds of consumer behavior through the lens of conspicuous consumption and status signaling. Because that argument is a bit more complicated, it will be the topic of chapter 5. It will provide additional support for the position I take in this chapter, but it is not strictly necessary and will otherwise weigh down the narrative I wish to convey.

With the first three signposts in hand, we have an idea of what private ecological irrationality may look like, but we need to first lay some additional ground rules. I am looking for goods, services, or practices that fail the test of instrumental rationality. Meaning, suppose that the stated reason for using a good is to achieve better health. Suppose we also have no reason to doubt the stated reason. If the good does not achieve better health, then the means do not fit the ends. In part, I do so to focus on issues which are not purely related to the expression of values, or they at least are not at first glance.

This definition of rationality is more meaningful than the definition employed by scholars who attempt to rationalize any behavior,[13] but weaker than claiming that rationality requires hewing perfectly to the predictions of an abstract economic model.[14] To this end, I am leaving out situations where the "science may be settled," but where divergence from "science" persists for reasons relating to value judgments. For specific examples, I am not considering value-laden divergences related to the implications of evolutionary theory, dietary restrictions, and proscriptions against various medical procedures. What this means is that I am eliminating many possible examples from consideration in order to minimize ambiguities of interpretation as much as possible.

That is to say, the claims I am making are actually weaker than would be made by those imposing a secular utilitarian framework as a guide for rational human decision-making;[15] I am evaluating individuals' decisions on their own terms.[16] For instance, I am not evaluating whether ethical vegetarianism or keeping Kosher is actually good for your health or has some other secondary benefit, as the given reasons for the diets are "normative," not instrumental. But I would consider a diet whose intent it was to improve health, if there were clear evidence that it does not. The attitudes expressed by The Townshend restaurant were stated to be useful and effective for producing good food, so it would also be a candidate. But if this focus were relaxed, it would drastically increase the potential magnitude of private ecological irrationality, not reduce it.

For example, one may wish to take an action to help the environment, but it is relevant whether that action actually improves the environment. There are many reasonable avenues to reduce your own carbon footprint, and there are reasonable policy choices one could advocate for to reduce carbon output. In your personal life, one reasonable suggestion is to reduce the number of miles you fly each year, simply because flying is so carbon-intensive.[17]

But there are many methods that really do not add up. One notable example is buying local to reduce your carbon footprint. There have been attempts at measuring your food in terms of "food miles," but the results of calculating the complete environmental impact of your daily actions can be very counterintuitive. On average, the per-person fuel economy of buses is actually worse than personal cars.[18] Or, as described by economist Tim Harford, an entire day of obsessively re-ordering your life to make it as environmentally friendly as possible can be wiped out by the negative environmental impact of forgetting to turn off your computer at night.[19] The fact is that global supply chains are incredibly efficient in minimizing energy output. You should not at all assume that "farm-to-table" via a ten mile excursion to a farmer's market is better for the environment than "farm-to-table" shipped across the country, or even the world, using the efficiencies of the world's supply chain. Numerous economists and other social scientists have come to agreement on this point.[20]

James E. McWilliams, a Professor of History at Texas State University, summarizes the attraction to food miles that should call back immediately to our signposts for ecological irrationality.

> When we survey the expansive literature supporting the food-miles approach, one thing becomes evident: the prevailing arguments for stressing food miles is driven less by concrete evidence than by a vague quest to condemn globalization. In this respect, buying local is a political act with ideological implications.[21]

With the caveat that the buy local movement has metastasized into a doctrine with numerous rationales (one more of which will be discussed in chapter 7), we can at least assess how much consumers are willing to pay as a premium for locally produced goods. One study places the willingness-to-pay for a package of a local product over a non-local product at between $0.48 and $1.18,[22] depending on the context and modeling assumptions. Another, which combines a meta-review with other results, yields a price premium of 22.4 percent.[23] For the sake of "ballparking" the magnitude of what a consumer who buys all food locally will end up paying for the sake of it being local, we will use 20 percent.

To work out how much this corresponds to in terms of cash, again roughly speaking, you can make an assumption for the percentage of income the individual spends on food, and what an individual's income is. The Bureau of Labor Statistics assigns weights to all classifications of consumer goods for urban consumers when it builds the Consumer Price Index (from which the primary method of measuring inflation is derived). As of April 2019, the weight was 13.2 percent.[24] If you wish to apply these two assumptions (20% price premium for local and 13.2% of income spent on food) to a given level of income, simply multiply the income by (20%)*(13.2%). Using a nice, even number of $50,000 per year, this implies $1,320 per year. This amount of money is not in any sense debilitating, but even if we divide that number by ten, it is non-negligible.

Another example of ecological irrationality is Fair Trade coffee. Fair Trade coffee is intended to raise the wages of the global poor by requiring higher wages for the workers producing the coffee. Raising wages of the global poor is truly a noble goal. But making sure this gets translated into higher wages for the poor is considerably more difficult than it may first appear,[25] although at the time of this writing, the most recent high quality paper has found it to increase wages.[26] However, the biggest economic challenge to fair trade isn't for the actual workers to receive higher wages. The problem with Fair Trade is that it creates the incentive to move production from the poorest countries producing coffee to countries producing coffee that are already part of the global middle class, where labor productivity is already higher and it is easier to achieve Fair Trade compliance. Via this mechanism, Fair Trade systematically shifts labor demand away from the truly destitute and toward those living in comparative comfort.

Estimates of willingness-to-pay for fair trade vary from an 11 percent premium in Britain[27] to 38 percent in Sweden.[28] A study focusing on the United States found the number to be roughly $0.20 per pound of coffee.[29] According to the most recently available data from U.S. Department of Agriculture Economic Research, Americans consume 7.8 pounds of coffee per year.[30] This would imply that the willingness-to-pay is less than $2 per year, although this would quickly be eclipsed for those willing to spend an extra quarter for fair trade as part of their morning routine. Two dollars per person is an average of everyone, including those who do not consume coffee. An extra quarter for each cup, three cups of coffee per week, and fifty weeks per year corresponds to $37.50, for example.

But while fair trade coffee may be small, what is not is the willingness-to-pay implicit in failing to vaccinate children. Incredibly specious reasoning, reflecting distrust of modern medicine and science, persists predominantly because vaccines are perceived not to be "natural."[31] In the words of satirist Christian Lander regarding the anti-vaxx movement, "[The logic of affluent Westerners] follows a number of paths. The first is a need to get back to a natural state, specifically the one that is vulnerable to the diseases that killed off many of our ancestors."[32] I do not feel the need to justify the point that vaccines are safe, confer health benefits, and do not cause autism, and if you are educated and still insist on their danger, I offer no response except to shame you. The most prominent public intellectual in this sphere, if you are curious, is the pediatrician Paul Offit, who has written a number of accessible books on this and related topics.

Research elsewhere has measured the differential increase in the likelihood to catch various diseases in the absence of getting vaccinated, conditional on living in the developed world (not a developing country, where presumably failing to get vaccinated is even costlier), as well as the baseline morbidity (the rate of infection) of each disease. Data is also readily available for this differential for the baseline morbidity of pertussis (whooping cough),[33] invasive pneumococcal disease,[34] and varicella (chicken pox).[35] These data are what you want to know to assess how much *additional* risk of getting these diseases is incurred because you did not get vaccinated. What I do here is to estimate the willingness-to-accept associated with incurring these risks, with that willingness-to-accept interpreted as expressed demand for irrationality.

In order to put those risks in an economic context, I will make use of something akin to "the statistical value of a human life," which for the non-economist readers may sound creepy. "We can't put a dollar value on an individual life," is the common refrain.[36] But think about it this way. According to how most people think about public policy, public safety is an important role of government. Suppose that, according to our best guesses, one policy could save a life for $10,000,000, while a more cost-effective one could save a life for $1,000,000. Maybe we want to save both lives and incur both costs, but the pertinent question is *where we should be drawing the line*. If there's a policy on the table that could save a life for $5,000,000, we should be doing that, first, before considering the policy that costs $10,000,000. If you don't follow this logic, implicitly or explicitly, it means that you are saving fewer lives, on average, for a given amount of money.

If you do not employ the statistical value of human life in some way, you are literally unable to make safety or health decisions coherently. Whether or not you want to believe it, you must employ this kind of thinking when you decide, for instance, which car seat to buy for your child. The number isn't infinity, because otherwise you won't drive your child anywhere. You can argue for moving the line upward or downward, that is, assume a higher or lower statistical value of a human life, certainly. But in the realm of public policy, on average, people will needlessly die if you do not ruthlessly apply the logic of the statistical value of a human life. When economists provide their own number for where to set the line, they are looking into the world, running the numbers, and trying to estimate where people themselves set the line when taking on risks in markets, for instance, when working in risky professions.

The Environmental Protection Agency uses an estimate of $7.4 million in 2006 dollars as its statistical value of a human life.[37] Inflated to 2019 dollars, this is $9.4 million. Elsewhere, the Federal Aviation Administration has developed numbers which attempt to compare the costliness of different classifications of injuries to the statistical value of a human life.[38] These range from "Minor" (examples being "Superficial abrasion or laceration of skin; digit sprain; first-degree burn; head trauma with headache or dizziness (no other neurological signs)") to "Critical" (examples being "Spinal cord injury (with cord transection); extensive second or third degree burns; cerebral concussion with severe neurological signs (unconscious more than 24 hours).") "Minor" is counted as 0.20 percent of the statistical value of a human life, and "Critical" is counted as 76.25 percent of a human life.

For all three diseases, I use the value for a "Serious" injury, which is 5.75 percent of the statistical value of a human life. This is $540,500. A more granular analysis would attempt to categorize different outcomes for each disease, but data this detailed is not available, to my knowledge. Finally, I must address the fact that the decision to vaccinate is not adults deciding for themselves, but parents deciding for their children. Following findings elsewhere, I provide estimates assuming that parents put equal value on themselves and their children, estimates assuming that they put 50 percent more value on their children than themselves, and estimates assuming that they put 100 percent more value on their children.[39]

I report my findings in table 4.1. These estimates range from less than $100 per child per failure to vaccinate to over $1,000 per child per failure to vaccinate. Childhood vaccination has even more expert consensus behind it than perhaps free trade, and the size of these numbers loudly reflect that consensus that it is incredibly consequential and important that children should be vaccinated. The anti-scientific, anti-modern, "natural" worldview is worth thousands upon thousands of dollars for any parent with more than one child. Another way of interpreting these numbers is that, in a more typical context, parents would be willing to *pay* these amounts in exchange for reductions in risk as significant as reductions in risk implicit in children vaccination. These are systematically biased beliefs, implicitly costing the risk equivalent of thousands of dollars for each person acting on them, because

Table 4.1 Willingness-to-Pay Implicit in Refusing Vaccinations of Children

Ratio of Willingness-to Pay of Parent-to-Child to Parent-to-Self	Pertussis ($)	Invasive Pneumococcal Disease ($)	Varicella ($)
1:1	497	696	56
1.5:1	745	1,043	84
2:1	994	1,391	113

human beings are ecologically irrational in the context of scary, unnatural science.

Using the midrange estimate of the three diseases and a recent study finding 1.3 percent of young children in America are entirely unvaccinated,[40] and applying it to the roughly 74 million children currently living in the United States, we arrive at a cost of $1.8 billion.[41] This number is somewhat high because the earlier cohorts were vaccinated at a higher rate, but on the other hand, failing to vaccinate is presently trending upward. Note that this is all the personal, *internal* cost of failing to vaccinate for these three particular diseases, and entirely sets aside the external costs of not vaccinating. If you care about harming others, then the numbers should be higher.

In my previous exploration of this topic, I also provided a willingness-to-pay for ecological irrationality implicit in the use of local currencies. My methodology for backing out willingness-to-pay was even more convoluted than the methodology I just described, so I will spare you a lengthy description of it. Local currencies are, effectively, voluntary tokens (e.g., the Berkshares in the Berkshire region of Massachusetts) which locally owned businesses use to "keep money in the community," which from the perspective of an economist, is a word salad.[42] The wealth of a community depends on their assets and productivity, not whether cash is somehow leaking out. As established, Trade Is Good. These currencies exist ultimately as a simple reaction to globalization and capitalism,[43] while entirely misinterpreting what globalization and capitalism mean.

In my willingness-to-pay estimate, I used a result from development economist James Feyrer that an increase in a given amount of trade will be accompanied by an increase overall income by half that amount.[44] If you want a guess for how economically counterproductive local currencies are, take a guess of how much they reduce trade with those outside the community by, and cut whatever number you come up with in half. That is how much the private initiative is destroying local income, approximately. For instance, Feyrer's estimation implies that a 10 percent reduction in trade is associated with a 5 percent reduction in income.

There are many other examples of private ecological irrationality that are more difficult to develop in-depth, and are more speculative on my part. But they are all along these same lines. One of these, do-it-yourself, is discussed at length in chapter 8 because the reasons why it is ecologically irrational are a bit more complicated. Another example is the pointlessness of re-usable shopping bags. One study has found that you need to re-use a cotton shopping bag 7,100 times until it has a lower total environmental impact than a normal plastic shopping bag.[45] That would mean, if you re-use it twice a week, it would be 68 years until it would be "worth it." That "worth it," by the way, is in reference to Mother Nature, not you, personally. Before you reach that point, the cotton shopping bag is actively counterproductive for the environment.

Some other examples include GMO-free products (using only GMO-free products would cost a family roughly $3,000 per year[46]), homeopathic medicine (a billion dollar industry[47]), detox diets, and most acupuncture. Examples which I believe are similar, but for various reasons I am less comfortable stating in quite as strong terms, are consuming raw milk, the use of Vitamin C to protect against and combat the common cold, and the fear of high fructose corn syrup. And I have not yet mentioned organic food, the sales of which account for four percent of the total U.S. food market,[48] and which, to phrase this as provocatively as possible, is "natural on steroids." Many of these issues are small in comparison to, say, the total size of U.S. GDP, but as they say, a few billion here, a few billion there, pretty soon, you're talking real money.

This is also not yet mentioning schadenfreude involving the Dihydrogen Monoxide Hoax—it is surprisingly easy to get environmentalists to sign a petition calling for banning water—or that you can now purchase GMO-free salt and GMO-free water, or that a majority of Americans are willing to sign a petition requiring firms to disclose whether food contains DNA on their packaging.[49]

Perhaps even more speculatively, I conjecture that the entirety of the U.S. automobile industry is still alive only through a combination of bailouts from the U.S. taxpayer and ecological irrationality. According to those who are paid to evaluate automobiles dispassionately, foreign vehicles are simply superior.[50] It is just not America's comparative advantage, and no amount of kicking and screaming is going to change that; it is the comparative advantage of Japan, Korea, and Germany. "Everyone" knows that foreign cars are better constructed, cheaper, or both, with American automobile enthusiasts appealing to their much celebrated "intangibles" (read: things that do not exist) as the reason why they prefer unreliable, inefficient vehicles. To re-capitulate, I believe that outside of small niches, the entirety of the U.S. automobile industry only exists because of ecological irrationality.

Caplan's informal response to the presence of private ecological irrationality is that markets allow participants to exit and not engage in foolish behaviors.[51] In politics, a sufficiently foolish voting bloc could ban childhood vaccination for everyone. But this is an unsatisfing response, for a number of reasons. One is that a more conventionally drawn demand curve may have considerably different implications in the comparison of political institutions (see chapter 6). The other is that an important goal of social science, as I understand it, is to go much further than the narrow solution Caplan presents. If ecological irrationality is bad, an interesting and important social scientific question is how to reduce it for society overall, not just for those who are smart enough to see through it.

That is the punctuation on my own conceptualization of ecological irrationality. But before we enter the applications and implications of ecological irrationality, I will discuss the one final signpost for ecological irrationality that I skipped over before: the interpretation of it as a new form of conspicuous consumption. This will require significantly more explanation than did the other signposts. But if this interpretation is correct, it will turn all previous discussions of the public policy implications of conspicuous consumption on their head.

NOTES

1. The Townshend, "About," accessed June 27, 2019, http://www.thetownshend. com/about.

2. Phantom Gourmet, "The Townshend – Quincy (Phantom Gourmet)," May 2, 2016, https://www.youtube.com/watch?v=qNy6dFPxk3w.

3. Steve Horwitz, "The Calling: In Defense of Complex, Global, Fast Living." *FFF Articles*, May 2, 2013, https://www.fff.org/explore-freedom/article/the-calling -in-defense-of-complex-global-fast-living/.

4. Caplan, *The Myth of the Rational Voter*, 131–135. An earlier version of my argument in this chapter, overall, can be found in Ryan H. Murphy, "The Willingness-to-Pay for Caplanian Irrationality," *Rationality and Society* 28, no. 1 (2016): 52–82.

5. Caplan, *The Myth of the Rational Voter*, 130–131.

6. Bryan Caplan, "Market Failure: The Case of Organic Food," *Econlog*, May 21, 2012, https://www.econlib.org/archives/2012/05/market_failure_6.html.

7. Caplan, *The Myth of the Rational Voter*, 134–135.

8. My caveats from chapter 3 about governments and religion remain in place— humans at times express similar attitudes toward them, but their nature as explicit collective action is a tempering, countervailing force.

9. Geoffrey Brennan and Loren Lomasky, *Democracy and Decision: The Pure Theory of Electoral Preference* (Cambridge: Cambridge University Press 1993).

10. Loren Lomasky, "Swing and a Myth: A Review of Caplan's 'The Myth of the Rational Voter'," *Public Choice* 135, no. 3–4 (June 2008): 469–484.

11. C.f. J. S. Johar and M. Joseph Sirgy, "Value-Expressive versus Utilitarian Advertising Appeals: When and Why to Use Which Approach," *Journal of Advertising* 20, no. 3 (1991): 23–33.

12. Scott Atran, "Folk Biology and the Anthropology of Sciences: Cognitive Universals and Cultural Particulars," *Behavioral and Brain Sciences* 2, no. 4 (August 1998)1: 547–609.

13. See Jon Elster, "Economic Order and Social Norms," *Journal of Institutional and Theoretical Economics* 144, no. 2 (April 1998): 357–366.

14. See Peter J. Boettke and Rosolino Candela, "Rational Choice as If the Choosers Were Human," in *Handbook of Behavioral Economics and Smart Decision-Making:*

Rational Decision within the Bounds of Reason, ed. Morris Altman (Northampton: Edward Elgar, 2017), 68–85.

15. For example, Sam Harris, *The Moral Landscape: How Science Can Determine Human Values* (New York: Free Press, 2010).

16. Some of the following examples will relate to the environmental movement. In some corners, the environmental movement may have taken on religious elements (such as New Age). If one wishes to argue that this accounts for the majority of environmentalism, such examples should be either considered "edge cases" or phenomena similar to value-laden examples that were previously excluded. On the other hand, to the extent that certain religious beliefs have false empirical content, such as Christian Science, modern Flat Earth societies, or prosperity theology, they *should* be included. Questions of evolutionary theory may have empirical content in the scientific sense, but they are not as practically consequential as the examples explored here.

17. Tatiana Schlossberg, "Flying Is Bad for the Planet. You Can Make it Better," *The New York Times*, June 27, 2017, https://www.nytimes.com/2017/07/27/climate/airplane-pollution-global-warming.html.

18. Alternative Fuels Data Center, "Average Per-Passenger Fuel Economy of Various Travel Modes," last updated November, 2018, https://afdc.energy.gov/data/10311.

19. Tim Harford, *Adapt: Why Success Always Starts with Failure* (New York: Picador, 2011), 167–177.

20. Kelly Rai Chi, James MacGregor, and Richard King, *Fair Miles: Recharting the Food Miles Map* (London: IIED, 2009); Tyler Cowen, *An Economist Gets Lunch: New Rules for Everyday Foodies* (New York: Dutton Adult, 2012), 167–186; Pierre Desrochers and Hiroko Shimizu, *The Locavore's Dilemma: In Praise of the 10,000-Mile Diet* (New York: Public Affairs, 2012); Edward Glaeser, "The Locavore's Dilemma: Urban Farms Do More Harm than Good to the Environment," *Boston.com*, June 16, 2011, http://archive.boston.com/bostonglobe/editorial_opinion/oped/articles/2011/06/16/the_locavores_dilemma/; Jayson L. Lusk and F. Norwood Bailey, "The Locavore's Dilemma: Why Pineapples Shouldn't be Grown in North Dakota," *Library of Economics and Liberty*, January 3, 2011, http://www.econlib.org/library/Columns/y2011/LuskNorwoodlocavore.html; James E. McWilliams, *Just Food: Where Locavores Get it Wrong and How We Can Eat Truly Responsibly* (New York: Little, Brown and Company, 2009); Steven Sexton, "Does Local Production Improve Environmental and Health Outcomes?" *Agricultural and Resource Economics Update* 13, no. 2 (November-December 2009): 5–8.

21. James E. McWilliams, *Just Food*, 30.

22. Kim Darby, Marvin T. Battle, Stan Ernst, and Brian Roe, "Decomposing Local: A Conjoint Analysis of Locally Produced Foods," *American Journal of Agricultural Economics* 90, no. 2 (May 2008): 476–486.

23. Kristen Park and Miguel I. Gomez, "Do Price Premiums Exist for Local Products?" *Journal of Food Distribution Research* 43, no. 1 (March 2012): 145–152.

24. The current version of this data can be found at Bureau of Labor Statistics, "Consumer Price Index for All Urban Consumers (CPI-U): U.S. City Average, by Expenditure Category)," last updated June 12, 2019, https://www.bls.gov/news.release/cpi.t01.htm.

25. Victor Claar and Colleen Haight, "Fair Trade Coffee: Correspondence," *Journal of Economic Perspectives* 29, no. 1 (Winter 2015): 215–216.

26. Raluca Dragusanu and Nathan Nunn, "The Effects of Fair Trade Certification: Evidence from Coffee Producers in Costa Rica," *NBER Working Paper* no. 24260 (Cambridge: National Bureau for Economic Research, June 2019).

27. Ibon Galarraga and Anil Markandya, "Economic Techniques to Estimate the Demand for Sustainable Products: A Case Study for Fair Trade and Organic Coffee in the United Kingdom," *Economia Agaria y Recursos Naturales* 4, no. 7 (2004): 109–134.

28. Linda Schollenberg, "Estimating the Hedonic Price for Fair Trade in Sweden," *British Food Journal* 114, no. 3 (2012): 428–446.

29. Maria L. Loureiro and Justus Lotade, "Do Fair Trade and Eco-Labels in Coffee Wake Up the Consumer Conscience?" *Ecological Economics* 53, no. 1 (April 2005): 129–138.

30. The data was found at "https://www.ers.usda.gov/webdocs/DataFiles/50472/ctcsp.xls?v=42942" under the title, "Coffee, tea, cocoa: Per capita availability – USDA ERS."

31. Paul Offit, *Deadly Choices: How the Anti-Vaccine Movement Threatens Us All* (New York: Basic Books, 2011), 116–117; Gregory A. Poland and Robert M. Jacobson, "Understanding Those Who Do Not Understand: A Brief Review of the Anti-Vaccine Movement," *Vaccine* 19, no. 17–19 (March 21, 2001): 2440–2445.

32. Christian Lander, *Whiter Shades of Pale*, New York: Random House, 2010), 139.

33. Baseline morbidity for pertussis is found in CDC, "Summary of Notifiable Diseases – United States, 2008" *MMWR* 57, no. 54 (June 25, 2010), 13–14. Increase in morbidity is found in Jason M. Glanz, David L. McClure, David J. Magid, Matthew F. Daley, Eric K. France, Daniel A. Salmon, and Simon J. Hambridge, "Parental Refusal of Pertussis Vaccination is Associated with an Increased Risk of Pertussis Infection in Children," *Pediatrics* 123, no. 6 (June 2009): 1446–1451.

34. Baseline morbidity for invasive pneumococcal disease is found in CDC, "Invasive Pneumococcal Disease in Children 5 Years after Conjugate Vaccine Introduction – Eight States, 1998–2005," *MMWR* 57, no. 6 (February 15, 2008): 144–148. Increase in morbidity is found in Jason M. Glanz, David L. McClure, Sean T. O'Leary, Komal J. Narwaney, David J. Magid, Matthew F. Daley, and Simon J. Hambridge, "Parental Decline of Pneumococcal Vaccination and Risk of Pneumococcal Related Disease in Children," *Vaccine* 29, no. 5 (January 29, 2011): 994–999.

35. Baseline morbidity for varicella is found in Matthew M. Davis, Mitesh S. Patel, and Achamyeleh Gebremariam, "Decline in Varicella-Related Hospitalizations and Expenditures for Children and Adults after Introduction of Varicella Vaccine in the United States," *Pediatrics* 114, no. 3 (September 2004): 786–792. Increase in morbidity is found in Jason M. Glanz, David L. McClure, and David J. Magid, "Parental Refusal of Varicella Vaccination and the Associated Risk of Varicella Infection in Children," *Archives of Pediatrics & Adolescent Medicine* 164, no. 1 (January 2010): 66–70.

36. For an accessible defense of the concept, see Jo Craven McGinty, "Why the Government Puts a Dollar Value on Life," *Wall Street Journal*, March 25, 2016,

https://www.wsj.com/articles/why-the-government-puts-a-dollar-value-on-life-1458 911310. For an in-depth history of the concept, see H. Spencer Banzhaf, "The Cold War Origins of the Value of Statistical Life," *Journal of Economic Perspectives* 28, no. 4 (Fall 2004): 213–226.

37. See United States Environmental Protection Agency, "Morality Risk Valuation," accessed June 27, 2019, https://www.epa.gov/environmental-economics/m ortality-risk-valuation. I should note that this number has been questioned as being too *large* and that better statistical methodologies find a lower number of around $1.5 million. This would reduce the numbers I report in this chapter. See John P. A. Ioannidis, T. D. Stanley, and Hristos Doucouliagos, "The Power of Bias in Economics Research," *The Economic Journal* 127, no. 605 (October 2017), F250.

38. GRA, Incorporated. *Economic Values for FAA Investment and Regulatory Decisions, A Guide* (FAA Office of Aviation Policy and Plans, U.S. Federal Aviation Administration. Washington, D.C, 2007), 2.2–2.4. https://www.faa.gov/regul ations_policies/policy_guidance/benefit_cost/media/ECONOMICVALUESFORFA AINVESTMENTANDREGULATORYDECISIONS10032007.pdf.

39. Alistair Hunt and Ramon Arigoni Ortiz, "Review of Revealed Preference Studies on Children's Environmental Health," report prepared for OECD Project on the "Valuation of Environment-Related Health Impacts, with a Particular Focus on Children," (Unpublished manuscript, Bath: University of Bath, 2006), available at http://www.researchgate.net/profile/Ramon_Ortiz/publication/
267220759_Review_of_Revealed_Preferences_Studies_on_Children's_
Environmental_Health/links/544fca980cf201441e934e6f.pdf.

40. Holly A. Hill, Laurie D. Elams-Evans, David Yankey, James A. Singleton, and Yoojae Kang, "Vaccination Coverage Among Children Aged 19–35 Months – United States, 2017," *Morbidity and Mortality Weekly Report* 67, no. 40 (October 12, 2018): 1123–1128.

41. These numbers are somewhat smaller than what I previously reported in Murphy, "The Willingness-to-Pay," 71–73. This is a result of an improvement in my methodology for performing this calculation, which can be found at Ryan H. Murphy, "Putting a Price on the Large Personal Cost of Failing to Vaccinate," *InsideSources*, April 25, 2019, https://www.insidesources.com/putting-a-price-on-the-large-person al-cost-of-failing-to-vaccinate/.

42. The inchoate theory backing "keep money in the economy" could be construed as an extraordinarily crude version of Keynesianism, but the myopia of "keeping money in the economy" has very little to do with modern New Keynesian economics or similar theories.

43. See Michael Pacione, "Local Exchange Trading Systems as a Response to the Globalisation of Capitalism," *Urban Studies* 34, no. 8 (October 1997): 1179–1199.

44. James Feyer, "Trade and Income – Exploiting Time Series in Geography" (*NBER Working Paper* no. 14910, Cambridge: National Bureau for Economic Research, 2009).

45. Valentina Bisinella, Paola Federica Albizzati, Thomas Freuergaard, and Anders Damgaard, "Life Cycle Assessment of Grocery Carrier Bags" *Environmental Project* no. 1985 (Copenhagen: Danish Environmental Protection Agency, 2018),

17–18. I have chosen to report the number for conventional cotton bags; their figure for organic cotton bags is actually far *worse*.

46. Barry K. Goodwin, Michele C. Marra, and Nicholas E. Piggott, "The Cost of a GMO-Free Market Basket of Food in the United States," *AgBioForum* 19, no. 1 (2016): 25–33.

47. Julia Belluz, "Americans Spend Billions on Homeopathy. The Best Evidence Say They are Wasting Their Money," *Vox*, March 11, 2015, https://www.vox.com/2015/3/11/8190427/homeopathy.

48. United States Department of Agriculture, "Organic Market Overview," last updated April 4, 2017, https://www.ers.usda.gov/topics/natural-resources-environment/organic-agriculture/organic-market-overview.aspx.

49. Ilya Somin, "Over 80 Percent of Americans Support 'Mandatory Labels on Food Containing DNA," *The Washington Post*, January 17, 2015, https://www.washingtonpost.com/news/volokh-conspiracy/wp/2015/01/17/over-80-percent-of-americans-support-mandatory-labels-on-foods-containing-dna/?utm_term=.aa4c8126ee4e.

50. For example, see Consumer Reports, "Which Car Brands Make the Best Vehicles," last updated February 21, 2019, https://www.consumerreports.org/cars-driving/which-car-brands-make-the-best-vehicles/.

51. Caplan, "Market Failure."

Chapter 5

Bohemian Status-archy

Compared to Europe, academic economics in nineteenth-century United States was an intellectual backwater.[1] The Marginal Revolution—the foundational moment of modern economics—originated with three different individuals working independently, none of whom was an American. Instead, the most historically important American economist in the nineteenth century was the iconoclast and general purpose weirdo, Thorstein Veblen. Professionally, he had trouble finding employment, and his personal life was occasionally scandalous. But his *The Theory of the Leisure Class* would have a lasting mark on sociology and economics. Through this work he introduced the concept of conspicuous consumption.

Conspicuous consumption is one of the few social scientific concepts that has truly pervaded the lay consciousness. "Keeping up with the Joneses"—making sure you have a car, house, and entertainment center as nice as everyone else on your street—is a problem people are keenly aware of, and is seen as one of the deficits of capitalism. For if you extract little actual pleasure or usefulness from the goods you buy, and the long hours you spend working are to merely avoid falling behind the consumption patterns of your peers, conspicuous consumption could potentially be ruinous for your well-being. Robert Frank, an economist and modern expounder of the ideas of Veblen, sees conspicuous consumption as not only entrapping particular periods of time (e.g., midcentury America) or particular places (e.g., Miami Beach), but as a continual source of hardship in the modern world.[2] (For a breezier take on how crass consumerism signals status, I would point to the work of Paul Fussell.[3])

There are rock-solid theoretical foundations for the argument that conspicuous consumption is a deeply embedded aspect of the human experience. The "reductionist" explanation—which is true in broad strokes—is that,

61

especially for men, the cues for status are the currency for finding a mate.[4] If you observe that you are low status, your psychology perceives a low likelihood of reproductive success and you start taking actions in response to that. As a result, for example, we are jealous in our day-to-day lives of those who are slightly higher than us in the status hierarchy, and much less so of the super-rich and famous.[5] We don't actually try to keep up with the Kardashians; the person one step up from you at work is far more likely to elicit your ire. From the standpoint of evolution, a Porsche performs a similar function to the elaborate tail of a peacock attempting to attract a peahen. A recent paper in social psychology is called, in fact, "Peacocks, Porsches, and Thorstein Veblen."[6] Both the peacock's tail and the Porsche are credible signals of status, although they are otherwise purposeless, costly ornaments. Humans today experience this as conspicuous consumption.

The technical reason why conspicuous consumption is socially harmful is that status is a "positional good." Status really is a zero sum game; if I have more of it, by nature it means others have less. So if I invest time or money or energy into seeking status, I may transfer status to myself, but the transfers of status for society all net to zero, overall. From the perspective of the public, the time, money, and energy I spent on conspicuous consumption amount to wasted resources. The economics going on in the background here are actually identical to those of rent-seeking, the concept described in chapter 2.

The aforementioned Robert Frank has written about conspicuous consumption for both scholarly and educated lay audiences. If you are reading this, I am willing to wager that you either have a bachelor's degree or will eventually have one. Among my audience or that of Robert Frank, how many believe that a Range Rover or a fist full of diamonds actually confers high status? I would wager that contrary to most contemporary presentations of conspicuous consumption, you would associate them with low status people who happen to have money for whatever reason. In other words, *goods that are conventionally thought of as conspicuous consumption actually denote low status*. And that is in the minds of the educated elite: you.

Any behavior can be thought of in terms of signaling of some sort. If we want to have some amount of confidence that what we observe is status signaling and conspicuous consumption, the best means of observing it is to find instances of one-upmanship, where the only apparent purpose of what we are observing is one-upmanship. I can provide three concrete examples of one-upmanship which uncannily parallel the ecological irrational behavior described in the previous chapter. Because of my own interests, all three will in some way relate to food. Additionally, each is a zanier act of one-upmanship on the previous one. What I will choose will be, necessarily, extreme examples, as one-upmanship is otherwise difficult to see. These examples I wish to use as motivation for the idea that a lot of modern conspicuous consumption looks like the opposite of what most of its expositors think of it as. Among the educated, cultural elite, it is not about revelry in the excesses of capitalism. It is now about costly private actions against the institutions of modernity, and here, especially markets and globalization.

Consider first the relentless one-upmanship in the area of food fads. Start with "natural," a scientifically meaningless term used by marketers to distinguish their authentic foodstuffs from the big bad machines of global capitalism. After the big bad machines of global capitalism started using the term, too—and why not, the word doesn't actually mean anything—we moved on to organic. "Organic" had the benefit of actually having a definition, but amounted to a set of boxes you had to check in order to claim you are organic. The big bad machines of global capitalism can check boxes as well as anyone else, so it wasn't that long before you saw organic being sold at Walmart. From there we got buy local, followed by the farm-to-table movement. Somewhat transparent one-upmanship appears to be the fundamental motive of Michael Pollan's *The Omnivore's Dilemma*, one of the primary statements for the foodie movement.[7] There are still various frontiers of stupid one-upmanship, such as the fact that urbane progressives are now going hunting for the sake of authenticity.[8] Others are even trying out DIY animal slaughter.[9]

Second, for many, buying local is not enough. They have gone much further, with conspicuous consumption behaving like a fractal. Instead of using "buy local" as a rule of thumb, others demand that, regardless of the cost and the presence of relevant alternatives, the origins of all consumption must be limited to their local geography. This practice, whose stated purpose is to limit environmental impact, began with the "100-mile diet." Following a few iterations, the practice culminated with an effort by a small family to eliminate all environmental impact of their actions for an entire year.[10] This was only true in a very superficial sense. Most of the limitations reflected little critical assessment of their actual effects on the environment; in the words of journalist Andrew Potter, they were "totally disconnected from any actual environmentally sound agenda."[11]

Since Potter's book was published, the pattern has continued, with another personal memoir published on only eating foods produced within ten miles of your home.[12] A similar recent fad has been "zero waste babies," whose parents try to make their own difficult lives even crazier by not throwing anything out while caring for their newborn children. While the buy local movement, in general, can perhaps be thought of in terms of other motivations, there is no other reading of the *X*-mile diets except that they are purely symbolic and performative, meant to outdo the previous "innovators." Potter calls these acts of conspicuous (anti-) consumption "conspicuous authenticity."

Another similar practice is freeganism, which is the next step up on vegan-
ism and involves literal dumpster diving to save the environment. I have no
intention to attack vegetarianism in its various forms, generally speaking—I
am not objecting to any particular set of values. But freeganism, which has
actually been taken seriously in academia,[13] takes on precisely the same con-
tours as the one-upmanship of the *X*-mile diets. Freegans seek not only to
avoid all animal products, but to reclaim as much wasted food from society
as possible, instead of purchasing it. On certain margins, I am sure there are
specific examples of types of food that are regularly disposed of and should
be somehow consumed. But beyond examining the barriers preventing the
consumption of such food, there is almost nothing recommending the morality of the freegan ideology. One estimate of the environmental impact of a
vegan diet for is that it will cause the release 1.5 tons of carbon per year.[14]
Even incorrectly assuming that freegans eliminate the carbon impact of their
food consumption *entirely*, all of this effort only roughly results in the same
impact on the climate as the elimination of a single roundtrip ticket from New
York to Los Angeles, in comparison to the baseline of the standard vegan
diet.[15] Carefully considered environmental and economic analyses these are
not; freeganism is symbolic and performative, poorly attuned to pursuing its
stated goal, and in practice calibrated for one-upping the behaviors of others.

When I first became aware of the ubiquity and systematic nature of these
consumption patterns, it was not from commentary within academia, but
from the writings of a few journalists and satirists. Robert Frank had made
conspicuous consumption, in the conventional sense, the central topic of his
2011 popular nonfiction book, *The Darwin Economy*, with no reference to
this shift, for example. But since then, Elizabeth Currid-Halkett, a professor
of public policy at University of Southern California, has outdone anything
I could ever hope to do in describing this phenomenon in terms of exhaustive descriptiveness.[16] Currid-Halkett provides three groupings of such goods
or behaviors: in her terminology, inconspicuous consumption, conspicuous
leisure, and conspicuous production. These sets of goods allow the elite to
signal their differences away from others in an age where flashy consumer
goods are as accessible as they have been never before.

The category of "conspicuous production" includes goods whose origins
story, like "organic," "fair trade" or "authentic," is valued, instead of characteristics of the physical good itself. "Conspicuous leisure" pertains to the
obsession the elite have with doing something useful or productive in their
leisure time. Currid-Halkett's primary example of conspicuous leisure is
motherhood, where the elite are able to spend far more time doing things for
children (e.g., breastfeeding[17]), even if it is often apparently not that beneficial.
The last category, "inconspicuous consumption," includes various goods like
paying for gardeners or nannies. On the surface, examples of inconspicuous

consumption have less overlap with my own conceptualization of conspicuous consumption. But Currid-Halkett concludes in describing inconspicuous consumption as "often invisible and reveal[ing] status but often only to one's peer group, [and] perhaps the most pernicious divide between the elites and the rest."[18] The canonical example of inconspicuous consumption is a very subtle kind of nail polish colors that are hard to observe and which function to distinguish the elites from non-elites.[19]

In addition to the three categories put forth by Currid-Halkett, there's also Andrew Potter's "conspicuous authenticity." I follow Potter in seeing three periods of conspicuous consumption, as reproduced in table 5.1. The most recent, "new conspicuous consumption," is synonymous with Currid-Halkett's three groupings and "conspicuous authenticity." "Old conspicuous consumption" is what most people think of as conspicuous consumption—oversized SUVs and fistfuls of diamonds. Conspicuous consumption prior to old conspicuous consumption, which Potter describes in passing, is the conspicuous consumption of the ancients and the old aristocracy, and I label that "classical conspicuous consumption."

It is worth elaborating on classical conspicuous consumption briefly. As described by economic historian Deirdre McCloskey, the ancients looked down upon the idea of engaging in commerce and trade.[20] Often, in ancient and medieval times, the children of successful incipient bourgeoisie were ushered off to seek the education and habits of the aristocratic class so as to enter the aristocracy, as opposed to continuing the family business. (Today, this attitude persists in the condescending attitude the humanities has toward business schools and STEM.[21]) To demonstrate that you belong among the aristocracy, you needed to pursue areas of study that hold little or no instrumental value, such as learning dead languages, pastimes like fencing, or pointless exercises in etiquette. It was only when people began seeing innovation and commerce as serving praiseworthy social goals—and the bourgeoisie

Table 5.1 Periods of Conspicuous Consumption

	Period		
Attribute			
	Classical	Old	New
Class	Aristocracy	Bourgeoisie	Bohemian-Bourgeoisie
Epithet	Old Money	Nouveau-Riche	Hipster
In Fiction	*Great Expectations*	*The Great Gatsby*	*Portlandia*
Cliché	Chivalry; Etiquette	"Keeping up with the Joneses"	Authenticity; Local; Non-Profit
Home	Estates; Townhouses	Suburbs	Gentrifying Cities
Education	Liberal; Dead Languages	Master of Business Administration	Master of Fine Arts

as seeing their social role as having its own dignity—did economic growth begin taking off. McCloskey argues that the ancient and medieval condescension toward commerce is the reason why it took so long in human history to achieve persistent economic growth. I believe that is an exaggeration, but it is possible that stubbornly prioritizing learning Latin and praising skills in fencing, over prioritizing learning accounting and praising innovation, single-handedly delayed the end of grinding, near-universal poverty for a couple of millennia.

New status signaling is a return to aligning what we deem to be praiseworthy with what is *against* trade, innovation, and globalization, just as it was earlier under classical status signaling. This is in contrast to aligning the praiseworthy with the *fruit* of trade, innovation, and globalization. To concretize this shift, consider one narrative history of the origins of European cuisine. For a time, spices, acquired internationally, were the focus of European cuisine. That is to say, early European cuisine was once much more similar to cuisine elsewhere in the world. But eventually, trade expanded, causing the price of spices to drop considerably, so spices lost their function as a status symbol. European cooking became centered on food with purer tastes, because foods of purer taste, unlike spices, the peasantry would be unable to afford.[22] Keeping "good" food one step ahead of what the mere plebs can afford (or understand) has followed the one-upmanship described earlier—think, for example, of the common insistence that one must actually visit a foreign country to get an authentic, praiseworthy experience. Heaven forbid that high quality food be available via a convenient supermarket or restaurant.

As I said, prior to the work of Currid-Halkett, there was some basic awareness that the sands of status signaling had shifted, but it was not in the halls of academia. Besides her work and the work of Andrew Potter, the shift had been noted earliest[23] and most emphatically by David Brooks, who painted the picture of a world where money has ceased to be a very effective correlate of status. An artist, musician, or college professor, making livable but unexceptional salaries, are higher in the pecking order than businesspeople making several hundred thousand dollars a year.[24] Others who have had a more positive spin on the transformation of the new values of the upper social class include Brink Lindsey,[25] Richard Florida,[26] and the controversial public intellectual, Charles Murray.[27] Where I first encountered it was through satirist Christian Lander.[28]

Lander's shtick, if you are unfamiliar, is to be found in his pair of books (following a blog) listing and describing "stuff white people like," with "white people" referencing high social class Westerners.[29] "Stuff white people like" is about new status signaling. For example, this is very explicit in his entries on not owning a television, watching TV shows by Anthony Bourdain, and buying peacoats at army surplus stores. Lander spoke at Google and makes this still more explicit, stating,

> [W]hat the book . . . talks about white people as . . . more of a class than a race thing. And I think a lot of people would agree with it as you read through it. But the other thing it's fundamentally about is a different generation of people who still have the same desire for status and competition among neighbors, but unlike in the past when that competition and status was determined by material wealth like the size of your house, or how much your car cost, or the size of your diamond ring, it's been replaced by authenticity [and] environmental awareness . . . I don't know about you . . . I'm not impressed when I see a Bentley, because I know it gets eight miles to the gallon. That's awful. I am impressed when I see plug-in cars. . . . Or . . . someone was telling me about the guy who's driving this GM fuel vehicle? Unbelievable. Water is exhaust! That stuff impresses me. And so it's about this sort of shift that we're still as competitive as ever, in saying [points at shirt] this t-shirt is more vintage than that one . . . or things along those lines. I think that comes through in the book. It's about competition.[30]

The TV shows *Portlandia* and *The Goode Family* use new status signaling as their entire premise, and whispers of it can be heard in the 1980s sitcom, *Family Ties*. An entire 2006 episode of *South Park*, "Smug Alert," featured one of the families becoming so smug that they move to San Francisco and smell their own farts. New status signaling has been referenced in two of the top webcomics, *Cyanide and Happiness*[31] and *Saturday Morning Breakfast Cereal*.[32] The website, *tvtropes*, catalogues still other examples of this appearing in other media.[33]

The academic literature was previously small, but it is now growing, while tending to focus on conspicuous environmentalism and what social psychologists have called "Blatant Benevolence,"[34] providing firmer empirical support for the arguments offered here.[35] For instance, one study found that "green" products appear to signal status in wealthy neighborhoods, but not poor neighborhoods.[36] Besides examples relating to environmentalism, another recent study has found a large increase in the willingness-to-pay for organic goods when in the presence of an acquaintance.[37] Additionally, two separate articles[38] have produced models of hipsters as converging to similar appearances despite preferences for appearing unique, echoing the sarcastic subtitle of Lander's first book, "the Unique Taste of Millions."

The concept of status signaling is well-known in the social sciences and allows for a certain continuity in approach from biology to psychology to economics. Beyond the work of Robert Frank, I would point to Geoffrey Miller's *Spent* as presenting preferences and evolution in the context of a unified framework of consumer behavior and personality psychology.[39] His book also describes new status signaling in passing,[40] and Miller is one of the contributors to the academic literature on blatant benevolence. Despite this, I cannot endorse most of his prescriptions, for reasons that I will delve into in chapter 8.

With all that said, let me connect the argument more explicitly with ecological irrationality. The way I described new status signaling is as a signpost for ecological irrationality. The reasons why I think it signifies it I hope are now obvious; if you are familiar with the various cultural references, they cluster tightly around ecological irrationality and to some extent, they embody it. But this presents a conceptual difficulty. "Status" is a perfectly rational thing to desire. So in what sense is seeking status by conspicuously rejecting the modern institutional environment *irrational*?

There are two ways of thinking about this contradiction. One is that the stated goal of most of these behaviors is pro-social, while what is occurring in practice (private rent-seeking) is anti-social. At the same time, I do not doubt that the vast majority of people partaking in these actions believe that buying local (or what have you) is to act pro-socially. But all status-seeking behavior, historically, took on the appearance of being pro-social. "Status-seeking never disappears," writes Andrew Potter,[41] "when it is exposed to the light, it simply scurries away and hides until it can transform itself into a subtler and less obvious form." As anyone who has ever been a teenager can attest, getting a good spot in the pecking order is a deeply embedded aspect of the human psyche, and it does not require conscious, rational thought to pursue. Some of our mental modules direct us against modernity, while others give us an instinctual desire for status. Together, these modules work in concert to push us toward making consumer choices that we believe are altruistic, even while the choices fulfill selfish purposes. In that sense, our psychology is causing the means we choose not to match the ends we desire, and new status signaling is still best thought of as an irrational behavior.

But I may be still somewhat open to calling this behavior "rational"; recall in the last chapter that I defined "rationality" in a particular way for a particular purpose; in other contexts, I am open to ostensibly outrageous behaviors being thought of as rational because of the ways in which they are rationalizable.[42] That buying either Porsches (per old status signaling) or hybrids (per new status signaling) could be individually rational because it buys status is an argument of psychologist Douglas T. Kenrick and marketing scholar Vladas Griskevicius.[43] In this alternative framework, new status signaling is individually rational but hypocritical. Our psychology may in this way be smarter than us, knowing that what we need for selfish purposes in the social context is status, while allowing us to blithely believe we are pursuing moral, altruistic ends. Currid-Halkett puts it thusly,

As I write, I continue to ask myself the extent to which my choices are conscious, and if conscious, what are my motivations? They are not status-driven in any intentional way . . . this is just how we do things; it is in the air. It feels unconscious and intuitive, like one's personal sense of morality or the desire to eat when hungry.[44]

A similar means of "rationalizing" ecological irrationality would be the concept of social desirability bias, a phenomenon often favored as an explanation by Bryan Caplan himself.[45] In this case, people fall in line with what is socially approved or sanctioned, as opposed to promoting what actually is true or effective, in order to be thought of as a good person. In my view, this is essentially the same idea as status signaling, but conceived of from a different angle. In the terminology of game theory, from which all this originates, social desirability bias is status signaling in a pooling equilibrium, in which everyone feels obligated to follow the crowd. Pinker, following legal scholar Dan Kahan, has argued on similar grounds.[46]

I do not believe that, for the purposes of this book, which interpretation of new status signaling you prefer really matters. Whether new status seeking is irrational because the means do not match the ends, or it is rational because it serves a background rational purpose, is not particularly important. The fact remains that we are systematically biased toward incorrect models of social interaction (e.g., Trade Is Bad), and the fact that an aspect of our psychology and social interactions has glommed onto that is circumstantial. Regardless, new status signaling retains its function as a signpost for the phenomenon of ecological irrationality.

We can also show that new status signaling and old status signaling lead to tangibly different policy implications. Robert Frank's policy proposal is a consumption tax, meaning in layman's terms (approximately[47]), a sales tax or a value-added tax. I would support a consumption tax, in comparison to many other forms of taxation, but I do not support this justification. Geoffrey Miller, with a few fanciful extensions, is in agreement with Frank.[48] A consumption tax may function to dissuade those who are still taken in by crass consumerism from conspicuous consumption. But regarding those who are presently operating at the top *social* class, which is not necessarily the same thing as the top *economic* class, new status signaling is ubiquitous, not old status signaling. And we would have reason to believe that new status signaling will continue to percolate downward to lower social classes since, well, they are trying to signal they belong in higher social classes.

What does that mean? The goods that denote status are a moving target. Goods associated with old status signaling are reasonably approximated by a general tax on goods (when paired with conventional excise taxes), but there is little expectation that goods associated with new status signaling are similarly associated. While the artisanal baked goods may cost six times more than a pack of cookies at a grocery store, new status signaling at many of its extremes operates in the underground, informal economy, or grey markets that do not always collect taxes (think the *X*-mile diets or DIY). Elsewhere, our public policies may favor or even subsidize goods that function to convey status, such as degrees in the humanities or more lenient regulatory requirements (e.g., zoning, city council favoritism) for local retail ventures.

And why would anything else be expected? The political elite largely has the same values of the top social class, so *whatever* it is at the moment that confers status for that class will be viewed as praiseworthy—and deserving of subsidy, not public disincentives. As said by the online cartoonist Zach Weinersmith of *Saturday Morning Breakfast Cereal*, "A lot of generational looking-down-one's nose can be condensed to 'You're doing the wrong kind of perpetual status seeking.'"[49] Michael Munger, a political scientist, has frequently argued that many kinds of public policy effectively "assume a unicorn." Instead of describing how a possible policy proposal would be desirable given what we know about how a government operates, a proponent will assume an idealized government will enact the proposal.[50] This is a particularly egregious example of that. If we were to actually tax the status-seeking behaviors of people in the elite (i.e., the status-seeking that most matters), it would require the elite to agree that we should tax goods or behaviors that the elite believe are *pro*-social behaviors. The idea that this can ever be enacted is virtually nonsensical.

And now that we are into the politics, I want to clarify a particular point. Many of the behaviors or habits I've described are commonly associated with the left, but this association is overblown. Conservatives—not necessarily its intellectuals but the overall population of self-identified conservatives—are more likely than leftists to be skeptical of genetically modified organisms[51] and the benefits of trade.[52] Even among libertarian idols (if fictional), the character Ron Swanson of the sitcom *Parks and Recreation* once proclaimed, "People who buy things are suckers." Years before the right swerved in a populist direction in America, journalist Rod Dreher noted the block of voters on the right who are opposed to our modern institutional environment, affectionately anointing them "crunchy cons."[53] Enemies of modernity have no political party. They are populists, and populists are embedded on both sides of the political spectrum.

Lastly, what I am calling "new status signaling" is analytically distinct from "virtue signaling," an epithet used by the deranged populists to attack those who call them deranged. Following the horseshoe theory of politics, the economic views of deranged populists, crunchy cons, conventional bohemians, and the broader new status signaling class are actually quite similar, even if the populist right at the moment appears inordinately preoccupied with showing up the cultural left for the sake of it. Perhaps acting deranged will be the new countersignal. My preferences do not at all lie in an outcome where signaling vice or identity politics succeeds new status signaling, if this is the direction society is actually moving in. If I were to dictate to society as to what "should" denote status, it would be to somehow align status with pro-social behaviors that are actually effective,[54] or to align status with cost-benefit analysis.

Let me recap the argument of the book so far. Political systems often yield uninspiring outcomes, and when economists were confronted with this fact, they reached into their standard methodological toolkit (rationality, equilibrium, and efficiency) and concluded it was the result of bad incentives. But upon closer examination, if the methodology is applied sufficiently rigorously and consistently, the analytics show that democratic political systems should operate just fine.

One way of overturning this result is to assume that voters are systematically biased. Empirical evidence exists that voters are biased in such ways, relative to the opinions of experts. This can also be placed in a somewhat conventional economic framework by asserting that it is painful to be rational, so we only do so when it is cheap, hence "rational irrationality."

As presented, this argument, taken literally, requires peculiar psychological assumptions. It would involve an otherwise rational economic actor, while voting, to realize that the benefits of being irrational exceed the costs, and therefore, to rationally choose to be irrational. This is implausible or, at best, discomforting. The problem is resolved by making more explicit ties between rational irrationality and "Folk Economics"—the theory that our brains are built to interpret social (especially economic) relations in society in ways that do not reflect the modern institutional environment. Differences of opinion between those who have studied the issues and the layperson are readily understandable in these terms, especially as they pertain to policies relating to attitudes toward foreigners and the prospects for mutually beneficial exchange.

These differences create tensions felt toward our modern institutional environment on which our relative prosperity is built—namely, capitalism, globalization, science, pluralistic democracy, and the rule of law. Recognizing these tensions does not require an implausible psychological mechanism, and in fact, fits well with mainstream psychology. To emphasize these mechanisms and their nature, I call this phenomenon "ecological irrationality" instead of "rational irrationality."

But this analysis suggests that these mechanisms may easily come into play in private actions, not just voting behavior. To identify such instances, I have identified four "signposts" to use in searching for it—Folk Economics, authenticity, Folk Biology (especially the naturalistic fallacy), and, presented in this chapter, new status signaling. In order to identify unambiguous instances of private irrationality, I need to focus on instances where private choices are systematically ill-suited means to attain a given end. The instances I identify the most rigorously are buying local to help the environment, buying fair trade to help the global poor, and the failure to vaccinate children. There are additional examples I provide of private irrationality as well, but I do not show these as rigorously.

The second half of this book will describe the implications of the similarity of ecological irrationality in markets and politics. Others have attempted to provide solutions for ecological irrationality changes to our democratic political systems. I will first assess how well these solutions should be expected to work given the importance of private sector ecological irrationality. Second, I will link ecological irrationality to the social scientific concept known as social capital, showing how too much social capital may exacerbate ecological irrationality. Third, I will discuss the DIY movement as an example of ecological irrationality and use that as a launching point for "what to do about" ecological irrationality in your personal life, the present chapter operating as an important prelude for it. The discussion of DIY leads into a discussion of "Social Luddism," a phenomenon I describe through which experts and those who possess specific skills attempt to use social suasion for their own selfish benefits at the expense of others. The final main chapter wraps these ideas together in a reflection on the role of experts in society.

NOTES

1. For an earlier version of this argument, see Ryan H. Murphy, "The New Aristocrats: A Cultural and Economic Analysis of the New Status Signaling," *Briefing Paper* (London: Adam Smith Institute, 2016).

2. Robert Frank, *The Darwin Economy: Liberty, Competition, and the Common Good* (Princeton: Princeton University Press, 2011).

3. Paul Fussell, *Class: A Guide through the American System* (New York: Simon and Schuster, 1983).

4. For a popularized exposition, see Matt Ridley, *The Red Queen: Sex and the Evolution of Human Nature* (New York: MacMillan, 1994).

5. Vilayanur S. Ramachandran and Baland Jalal, "The Evolutionary Theory of Psychology and Jealousy," *Frontiers in Psychology* 8 (2017): 1619.

6. Jill M. Sundie, Douglas T. Kenrick, Vladas Griskevicius, Joshua M. Tybur, Kathleen D. Vohs, and Daniel J. Bear, "Peacocks, Porsches, and Thorstein Veblen: Conspicuous Consumption as a Sexual Signaling Mechanism," *Journal of Personality and Social Psychology* 100, no. 4 (April 2011): 664–680.

7. Michael Pollan, *The Omnivore's Dilemma: A Natural History of Four Meals* (New York: Penguin, 2006). Specifically, this is Elizabeth Currid-Halkett's

interpretation of a criticism of Pollan by Mark Grief. See Elizabeth Currid-Halkett, *The Sum of Small Things: A Theory of the Aspirational Class* (Princeton: Princeton University Press, 2017), 125.

8. Emma Marris, "Hipsters Who Hunt," *Slate*, December 5, 2012, http://www.slate.com/articles/health_and_science/science/2012/12/hunting_by_liberal_urban_locavores_is_a_trend_good_for_the_environment.html.

9. James E. McWilliams, "The Butcher Next Door," *Slate*, June 6, 2012, http://www.slate.com/articles/life/food/2012/06/diy_animal_slaughter_urban_hipsters_think_it_s_a_good_idea_it_isn_t_.html.

10. Colin Beaven, *No Impact Man: The Adventures of a Guilty Liberal Who Attempts to Save Our Planet, and the Discoveries He Makes About Himself and Our Way of Life in the Process* (New York: Farrar, Strauss and Giroux, 2009).

11. Potter, *The Authenticity Hoax*, 131–132.

12. Vicki Robin, *Blessing the Hands that Feed Us: What Eating Closer to Home Can Teach Us about Food, Community, and Our Place on Earth* (New York: Viking, 2014).

13. Christopher Schlottmann and Jeff Sobo, *Foods, Animals, and the Environment: An Ethical Approach* (New York: Routledge, 2018).

14. Lindsay Wilson, "The Carbon Foodprint of 4 Diets Compared," *Shrink That Footprint*, accessed June 28, 2019, http://shrinkthatfootprint.com/food-carbon-footprint-diet.

15. Joseph Nevins, "Kicking the Habit: Air Travel in the Time of Climate Change," *YES!*, December 13, 2010, https://www.yesmagazine.org/planet/kicking-the-habit-air-travel-in-a-time-of-climate-change.

16. Currid-Halkett, *The Sum of Small Things*.

17. Currid-Halkett, *The Sum of Small Things*, 79–92.

18. Currid-Halkett, *The Sum of Small Things*, 45.

19. Currid-Halkett, *The Sum of Small Things*, 46–48.

20. Deirdre McCloskey, *Bourgeois Dignity: Why Economics Cannot Explain the Modern World.* (Chicago: University of Chicago Press, 2010), 22–30.

21. For example, see Steven Conn, "Business Schools Have No Business in the University," *The Chronical of Higher Education*, February 20, 2018, https://www.chronicle.com/article/Business-Schools-Have-No/242563.

22. Maanvi Singh, "How Snobbery Helped Take the Spice Out of European Cooking" *NPR*, March 26, 2015, https://www.npr.org/sections/thesalt/2015/03/26/394339284/how-snobbery-helped-take-the-spice-out-of-european-cooking.

23. Aspects of the observation were anticipated by Daniel Bell, *The Cultural Contradictions of Capitalism* (New York: Basic Books, 1976). Also applicable and preceding Brooks by many years is the framework developed in Pierre Bourdieu, *Distinction: A Social Critique of the Judgement of Taste* (Cambridge: Harvard University Press, 1984). Elizabeth Currid-Halkett and David Brooks both make use of Bourdieu's framework in discussing the phenomenon.

24. David Brooks, *Bobos in Paradise: The New Upper Class and How They Got There* (New York: Simon & Schuster, 2000), 178–185.

25. Brink Lindsey, *The Age of Abundance*.

26. Richard Florida, *The Rise of the Creative Class* (New York: Basic Books, 2002).

27. Charles Murray, *Coming Apart: The State of White America, 1960–2010* (New York: Crown Forum, 2012).

28. Christian Lander, *Stuff White People Like* (New York: Random House, 2008); Lander, *Whiter Shades of Pale*.

29. Christian Lander, *Whiter Shades of Pale*, 142.

30. See 18:01 of Christian Lander, "Christian Lander: 'Stuff White People Like' | Talks at Google," *Talks at Google*, July 17, 2008, https://www.youtube.com/watch?v=KfRgjW4hFcU.

31. Rob DenBleyker, [no title] *Cyanide and Happiness* no. 2932, September 22, 2012, http://explosm.net/comics/2932.

32. Zach Weinersmith, "The Greatest Generation," *Saturday Morning Breakfast Cereal*, August 7, 2018, https://www.smbc-comics.com/comic/the-greatest-generation.

33. tvtropes, "Bourgeois Bohemian," accessed Juned 28, 2019, https://tvtropes.org/pmwiki/pmwiki.php/Main/BourgeoisBohemian.

34. Gilbert Roberts, "Competitive Altruism: From Reciprocity to the Handicap Principle," *Proceedings of the Royal Society of London B* 265 (March 1998): 427–431; Vladas Griskevicius, Joshua M. Tybur, Jill Sundie, Robert B. Cialdini, Geoffrey F. Miller, and Douglas T. Kenrick, "Blatant Benevolence and Conspicuous Consumption: When Romantic Moves Elicit Strategic Costly Signals," *Journal of Personality and Social Psychology* 93, no. 1 (July 2007): 85–102; Vladas Griskevicius, Joshua M. Tybur, and Bran Van Bergh, "Going Green to Be Seen: Status, Reputation, and Conspicuous Conservation," *Journal of Personality and Social Psychology* 98, no. 3 (March 2010): 392–404. However, the literature using mating priming in the laboratory setting has come under fire. See David R. Shanks, Miguel A. Vadillo, Benjamin Riedel, Ashley Clymo, Sinita Govind, Nisha Hickin, Amanda J. F. Tamman, and Lawa M. C. Puhlmann, "Romance, Risk, and Replication: Can Consumer Choices and Risk-Taking Be Primed by Mating Motives?" *Journal of Experimental Psychology: General* 144, no. 6 (December 2015): e142–e158.

35. See also competitive altruism, for example, Charlie L. Hardy and Mark Van Vugt, "Nice Guys Finish Last: the Competitive Altruism Hypothesis," *Personality and Social Psychological Bulletin* 32, no. 10 (October 2006): 1402–1413.

36. Joel Berger, "Are Luxury Brand Labels and 'Green' Labels Costly Signals of Social Status? An Extended Replication," *PLOS ONE* 12, no. 2 (February 7, 2017): e0170216. See also Steven Sexton and Alison Sexton, "Conspicuous Conservation: The Prius Halo and Willingness to Pay for Environmental Bona Fides," *Journal of Environmental Economics and Management* 67, no. 3 (May 2014): 303–317; c.f. Shanks et al., "Romance."

37. Seon-Woong Kim, Jayson L. Lusk, and B. Wade Brorsen, "'Look at Me, I'm Buying Organic': The Effect of Social Pressure on Organic Food Purchases," *Journal of Agricultural and Resource Economics* 43, no. 3 (2018): 364–387.

38. Jonathan Touboul, "The Hipster Effect: When Anti-Conformists All Look the Same," arXiv:1410.8001 (February 2019); Paul E. Smaldino and Joshua M. Epstein, "Social Conformity despite Preferences for Distinctiveness," *Royal Society Open Science* 2 (March 2015), 140437.

39. Geoffrey Miller, *Spent: Sex, Evolution, and Consumer Behavior* (New York: Viking, 2009). See also Geoffrey Miller, *The Mating Mind: How Sexual Choice Shaped the Evolution of Human Nature* (New York: Doubleday, 2000).

40. Miller, *Spent*, 120, 256.

41. Potter, *The Authenticity Hoax*, 125.

42. Ryan H. Murphy, "The Rationality of Literal Tide Pod Consumption," *Journal of Bioeconomics* 21, no. 2 (July 2019): 111–122.

43. Kenrick and Griskevicius, *The Rational Animal*, 143–160.

44. Currid-Halkett, *The Sum of Small Things*, 95.

45. Bryan Caplan, *The Case against Education: Why the Education System is a Waste of Time and Money* (Princeton: Princeton University Press, 2018), 222–224.

46. Pinker, *Enlightenment Now*, 356–359.

47. Frank's proposal differs from consumption taxes you may be more familiar with. He wishes to structure its calculation more along the lines of the present-day U.S. income tax than at point of sale, and to make it steeply progressive. In addition to Frank's book, see Robert Frank, "The Progressive Consumption Tax: A Win-Win Solution for Reducing American Income Inequality," *Slate*, December 7, 2011, https://slate.com/business/2011/12/the-progressive-consumption-tax-a-win-win-solution-for-reducing-american-economic-inequality.html.

48. Miller, *Spent*, 308–329, c.f. 287–288.

49. Weinersmith, "Greatest Generation" (see rollover text).

50. Michael C. Munger, *The Thing Itself: Essays on Academics and the State* (Mungerella Publishing, 2015), 9–20.

51. Razib Khan, "Do Liberals Oppose Genetically Modified Organisms More Than Conservatives?" *Gene Expression*, June 11, 2013, http://blogs.discovermaga zine.com/gnxp/2013/06/do-liberals-oppose-genetically-modified-organisms-mor e-than-conservatives/#.WUBZVty1uM9.

52. Bradley Jones, "Support for Free Trade Agreements Rebounds Modestly, but Wide Partisan Differences Remain," *Factank*, April 25, 2017, http://www.pewresear ch.org/fact-tank/2017/04/25/support-for-free-trade-agreements-rebounds-modestly-but-wide-partisan-differences-remain/.

53. Rod Dreher, *Crunchy Cons: How Birkenstocked Burkeans, Gun-Loving Organic Gardeners, Evangelical Free-Range Farmers, Hip Homeschooling Mamas, Right-Wing Nature Lovers, and Their Diverse Tribe of Countercultural Conservatives Plan to Save America (or at least the Republican Party)* (New York: Crown, 2006).

54. For example, in terms of the "effective altruism" movement.

Chapter 6

Anarchy, State, and Dystopia

I will discuss four alternative approaches to reforming our political institutions, all of which could arguably mitigate the effects of ecological irrationality.[1] Most prominently, political philosopher Jason Brennan has argued in favor of *epistocracy*, which would place certain restrictions on democracy that would shift more political power in the hands of the more informed. (Caplan hinted at this approach himself.[2]) The second approach is to eliminate the state altogether and give *all* decision-making power to the free market. But there is a willingness-to-pay for irrationality in markets, meaning it does not simply disappear when people bear the cost, even if eliminating the state is otherwise feasible. Third, some scholars elsewhere have argued that, under the correct conditions, autocratic political institutions would rationalize governmental policy. Finally, *futarchy*, an idiosyncratic approach originating with economist Robin Hanson, proposes that societies vote democratically on which values to pursue, but betting markets could be a better way of choosing the means to achieve those values.

Methods of reducing the role of democratic (or more precisely, majoritarian) institutions, I conclude, are solutions we should consider only with caution. But they are also serious ideas that should not be dismissed out of hand. Some of the far left has muddied the waters considerably in discussing political institutions, insisting that only stringently majoritarian political institutions that allow 50.001 percent of the population to make any decision it wishes may "count" as a democracy. (In more staid analysis of political institutions, the "50.001% does whatever it wants" is known as "mob democracy" or Ochlocracy.) The fact that mob democracy, which has never really existed meaningfully in a historically sense, has also never coincided with socialism, is the wordplay that allows modern-day socialists to claim that "true socialism has never been tried," and that the Soviet Union didn't "count" as socialism. Recent criticism of the Electoral College has arisen because it allowed the loser of the popular vote in the 2016 U.S. presidential election to win, and these criticisms have been couched in terms of the Electoral College being anti-democratic.[3] Similarly, the left has argued that recent court decisions such as *District of Columbia v. Heller*[4] and *Citizens United v. FEC*[5] have circumvented the popular will.

But this goes both ways. *Roe v. Wade* circumvented the popular will with respect to abortion. *Brown v. Board of Education* circumvented the popular will (the case was in Topeka, Kansas, the population of which was mostly white) with respect to segregation of public education. *Reitman v. Mulkey* circumvented a 1964 California ballot initiative which achieved over 65 percent of the vote to amend the state's constitution to guarantee landlords the right to discriminate. One can argue that some of these decisions only overturned U.S. state actions that were not democratic because Jim Crow Laws were in place. But this point does not apply to all Supreme Court decisions still championed by the political left.

Much has been made about whether the United States "counts" as either a democracy or a republic from commentators on both sides of the political spectrum. The answer to this question, according to legal scholar Eugene Volokh, is it's both.[6] While the discussion above has limited itself to the United States, similar issues arise in all democracies. Limiting the power of what a 50.001 percent majority is allowed to do is a pedestrian question in political science, and many such limits (including judicial review) are part of our package of modern institutions. Some of the possible changes to our political institutions which follow are simply incremental changes to our package of modern institutions. Others, however, are indeed quite radical.

Given that democracy may be itself understandably interpreted as one of our modern institutions, I wanted to preface the discussion of political institutions by noting incremental changes to political institutions are wholly consistent with seeing democracy as an important part of our institutional bundle. "Democracy" as necessarily uniformly majoritarian is, at best, misleading. It is ahistorical. It is a means of bullying anyone who will not accede to a radical change from our liberal democratic political order as an enemy of democracy. At the same time, I recognize that some of the proposals found here are hardly incremental changes. I am considering two of them (epistocracy and futarchy) because they are meant explicitly as responses to Caplan. I am considering two others (anarcho-capitalism and one brand of autocracy) because they are a natural outgrowth of the theoretical discussion of the others.

One final alternative solution to ecological irrationality that I will not explore in-depth is the creation of a constitutional amendment which would prohibit interference with trade and other expressions of ecological irrationality. When we consider economically beneficial constitutional amendments, the intention is usually to prevent a special interest from sneaking through a bit of antisocial legislation, or forcing ourselves to follow rules that will be beneficial in the long run.[7] The problem of ecological irrationality is of another nature. In effect, there would need to be a constitutional supermajority in favor of passing a meta-rule which contradicts the mental model of how people think about the world. To say the least, that does not seem like a likely series of events.

On the other hand, there is also no widespread support for any of the other changes to political institutions found in this chapter, so I am not being entirely fair when raising that point. Suppose we set my objection aside and assume a constitutional amendment against ecological irrationality were to be passed. Whether such an amendment would "work" would raise issues like how the text is worded or how judges would interpret it. And history has taught us that if there isn't some deep societal support for what is found in a written constitution, the formal wording will not have teeth.[8] Those kinds of questions would determine whether the constitutional amendment would "work." They are important questions, but have little bearing on how we theoretically conceptualize ecological irrationality, unlike the other sets of political institutions I will analyze. As such, I will not consider constitutional amendments any further.

EPISTOCRACY

The first of the four proposals, which is far more incremental than it first appears, is Brennan's *Against Democracy*,[9] which received respectful coverage in progressive outlets including *The New Yorker* and *Vox*.[10] His work surveys the literature on the extreme ignorance of the American public, and classifies members of the franchise as either "hobbits" (those who do not care about politics and are politically unengaged), "hooligans" (those who are engaged in politics but are hopelessly partisan), or "vulcans" (those who evaluate evidence on policy dispassionately). An overwhelming percentage of the population is either a hobbit or a hooligan. One of Brennan's most forceful points is that, contrary to the arguments (or hopes) of political scientists, attempting to make our democracy more "deliberative" turns unengaged hobbits into partisan hooligans, while conditioning hooligan voters to gain even greater goonish tendencies.[11]

Brennan's solution is to put more power in the hands of the informed (the vulcans). He suggests a handful of competing proposals that would introduce epistocracy while maintaining democratic procedures side-by-side.[12] For example, a representative group of the population could be enfranchised by lottery, and after being selected, the group must participate in small group discussions to gain competence on issues.[13] Or, tests could be required to vote, or tests or credentials could confer extra ("plural") votes (e.g., a college graduate's vote counts more than once). Brennan also suggests an "epistocratic council" could be formed with difficult exams as a membership requirement. This council would have no power to make law, but it would have veto power over legislation passed by the democratic branches. Finally, a system could be devised that would allow you to statistically simulate what each voter's political opinions would be if they were informed, and use the results of the statistical simulation in place of the vote. Despite the title of Brennan's book, it is not actually clear that all of these political institutions are actually any more anti-majoritarian than judicial review. Brennan suggests as much. The larger, more important concern is that some of these procedures may systematically discriminate against certain demographic groups.

Similar arguments are advanced by economist Garett Jones in a forthcoming book, *10% Less Democracy*, who also uses Caplan's work as a starting point.[14] Some of Jones's recommendations are more modest or more surgically tailored to preserving democracy than are Brennan's proposals. For example, politicians are more informed than voters and have better incentives to be informed. This suggests that the reduction of political pressure on politicians to ensure that their votes won't harm their reelection campaign is a good thing. To accomplish this, Jones suggests, among other things, an incremental change: *extending* the length of terms served by legislators. Longer term lengths would allow politicians to pay closer attention to their staff and other policy experts, in place of the voters. This institutional proposal is elitist, but it is only anti-democratic in the sense that it isn't strictly majoritarian. It remains substantively democratic.

In my own research, I approached the same question as Jones and Brennan, but with a different emphasis. What I looked at was the demand curve for irrationality. As established in chapter 4, it should be expected to look like any other demand curve. But even under current democratic institutional arrangements, public policy is biased toward elite (meaning, for the most part, informed) opinion.[15] Our political institutions already have certain epistocratic elements in place. It is only under pure majoritarian democracy you actually get the "will of the people." In all systems of elected legislators, you get "the will of the legislators" (so long as that they are still popular enough to be reelected). Both Brennan and Caplan note that democracies work better than they should work given how uninformed and biased "the will of the people" actually is.[16]

Elected officials are themselves systematically more educated and intelligent than the franchise; they have a lower "demand for irrationality." Furthermore, the higher up in government you go, the more you have incentive to be informed. Unlike voting in general, a legislator or executive official is bearing a cost when they indulge their irrationalities, because their votes and decisions tangibly matter. Under mob democracy, voters have the incentive to continue engaging in irrationality until the marginal benefit of doing so reaches zero (jargon: economic satiation). Meanwhile, politicians face an upward-sloping cost curve—the more they are irrational in voting, the more they actually make the world worse, which is something presumably at least some of them care about. All this is to say that politicians have a lower demand for irrationality while facing more of the cost of irrationality than do voters.

But there is something counterintuitive going on in the background of this analysis. If you can curb *some* irrationality by shifting power from the mob to the politicians, how far can you keep going in that direction to curb irrationality? If you sit down with a (conventionally drawn) demand curve for irrationality and draw a cost or supply curve for an autocrat, you would immediately conclude that the autocrat would be far more rational than any democratically elected politician. A near-neoclassical demand curve would actually imply a perfectly rational autocrat. As long as the autocrat cares somewhat about those whom the autocrat is governing, the autocrat would set aside his or her economic biases and figure out what actually works. The only alternative is to assume that the autocrat (or politician) is a psychopath who really only cares about looting the country.[17] This may be a likely explanation for why the model does not seem to "fit" the real world.[18] Throughout their works, both Caplan and Brennan fervently reject that voters are self-interested, instead arguing that voters are approximately altruistic but irrational. But perhaps self-interest should re-enter the picture if we are considering radically different institutional contexts.

The issue, it seems, is that autocracy creates *risk*. The mob in a mob democracy gets whatever it wants; 50.001 percent says they want *x*, *x* happens. An autocrat is selected by a figurative lottery, and with some probability you end up with a Robert Mugabe, and some probability you end up with a Lee Kwan Yew. Society gets disastrous results with Mugabe or gets rapid growth under Yew. There are also other senses of "risk" that are posed by mob democracies, but that is not what I am trying to describe here. The "risk" I am referring to is narrowly about deviations in outcomes from what would be attained under mob democracy. I am simplifying and zeroing in on that the band of possibilities, both good and bad, are widened with less majoritarian political institutions.

Where most countries are, however, is somewhere in between autocracy and mob democracy. Legislators must operate within certain bounds such that they can still expect to get reelected, but within those bounds, they have capacity for both good and evil. Longer congressional terms, for example, are longer leashes for good or evil. This suggests a spectrum, which appears as figure 6.1 below, from mob democracy on one end to complete political discretion (autocracy) at the other. As modeled here, the average draw that we get for introducing more constraints on democracy is positive, but it increases the risk of a really bad outcome as well. Very nearly all developed countries (including Singapore, which is not as autocratic as is commonly portrayed[19]) are somewhere in the middle of this spectrum.

"Epistocracy" in this graph can be interpreted as an attempt both to move in the direction of autocracy (more power in the hands of fewer individuals) and *inside* the curve to a point that was previously impossible to get to, if Brennan is correct. However, this formalization clashes, again, with Brennan's rejection of the self-interested model of political behavior. There is little to fear from an autocrat or epistocracy if self-interest can be ruled out. But bad apples exist, and the bad apples become bigger problems the more you concentrate power.[20]

And maybe even this is too optimistic. While many development economists believe that autocrats can play an important role in achieving growth miracles, William Easterly argues that this is an illusion, and that on average, there is no positive effect on growth.[21] Upon working out the logic of my own argument and later reflecting on those of Brennan and Jones, I decided to dive into the data myself.[22] The logic of my model, and my reading of Caplan, suggested that more constraints on democracy could be beneficial. Brennan and Jones may see their arguments as more narrowly tailored, but the goodness of small generic movements away from democracy is entailed by the titles of their works, if nothing else.

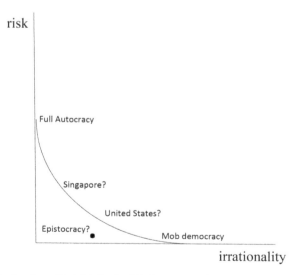

Figure 6.1 The Irrationality-Risk Tradeoff? *Source:* Author.

There is readily available data on democracy, the most notable being the *Polity IV* dataset. It gives you an integer for each country and year from −10 to +10, with −10 being a complete autocracy and +10 being a complete democracy. A score of +10 does not require a mob democracy, with "democracy" conceptualized here more along the lines of our bundle of modern institutions. I could look at the relationship between this variable and different measures of policymaking. Here, I chose market institutions and the aforementioned *Economic Freedom of the World* index.[23]

An empirical exercise like this (i.e., measuring the effects of democracy on economic freedom) has been done numerous times with numerous methodologies, with most studies finding positive effects of democracy on economic freedom.[24] But those studies consider the linear relationship, meaning what happens, more or less, when you graph the variables against one another and draw a line of best fit through them. My question was instead, whether a country with a *Polity IV* score of +8 or +7 or +6 or +5 could outperform a country with a +10 rating. In doing so, we are raising the question: *in recent history, where there is modestly less democracy than is normally observed in Western Countries, will there be better or worse policy in the future than there would be otherwise?*

I dove into this general framework in dozens of different ways, starting with a method that would allow each individual *Polity IV* score to have its own independent effect on policy (e.g., a score of "10" would have its own effect, as would a score of "9" or "−2")). I looked at different measures of democracy. I broke the economic freedom index into its constitutive parts. I replaced the variable for each individual *Polity IV* score with a simple U-shape that would allow the effect of democracy to "peak" (this being much less statistically challenging for the data to show). I did other things. I found very, very little evidence that I would say supports the perspective that slightly less democracy will improve policy. I still found, nonetheless, the standard (linear) patterns in the data that support a general positive relationship between democracy and market-oriented policy.

What this underscores to me is that, just as ecological irrationality is not just about public versus private decision-making (i.e., chapter 4), the challenges Caplan poses have little to do with "democracy," if we are considering how political institutions across the world in practice vary. If, among the various approaches outlined in this chapter, Brennan and Jones are the most correct, then the institutional reforms they propose are better framed as conventional means of improving democratic decision-making. What incremental epistocratic reforms would introduce would scarcely differ from "restrictions on democracy," like due process rights or the First Amendment. Framing solutions to the challenge of ecological irrationality as rejecting democracy only makes discourse in exploring these issues unnecessarily contentious. Opportunities for institutional reform here are possible, but they should be approached with caution.

ANARCHO-CAPITALISM

But instead of trying to fix the system, what if we figuratively burn it all down? An alternative set of institutions to liberal democracy that is discussed frequently in certain corners of academia is anarcho-capitalism. In contrast to other theories of anarchy, anarcho-capitalism holds that in the absence of state intervention altogether, societies would develop private institutions that perform conventionally governmental legal and regulatory functions using competitive market forces. Scholars favoring this set of institutions find empirical examples existing historically in, for example, Medieval Iceland,[25] periods in the recent history of Somalia,[26] and the American Wild West.[27] Recent analytical presentations of the system of institutions can be found in the works of economists Peter Leeson,[28] Ed Stringham,[29] and Avinash Dixit.[30] A moral case is made by philosopher Michael Huemer.[31] While models differ, most presentations of anarcho-capitalism center on competitive private courts, security, and insurance companies taking the roles of the provision of law and justice currently held by modern-day states.

Possible criticisms of anarcho-capitalism are numerous,[32] but my purpose in bringing it up is not to debate the merits of anarcho-capitalism in general. Rather, I wish to argue that, even if it functions as presently imagined by its advocates, it is *not* a solution to ecological irrationality, except in some very narrow senses. Under the assumptions of anarcho-capitalism, we should expect less irrationality in the absence of the state than a society would get under a mob democracy, but it is ambiguous whether the modern liberal democratic order would yield more or less irrationality than under anarcho-capitalism.

In anarcho-capitalism, consumer sovereignty holds, and there is some cost to "supplying" irrationality. Let us jump headfirst into what this implies. Consider racist housing covenants (private contractual agreements attached to properties) that would prevent non-whites from entering a community. In our modern institutional environment, these are legally unenforceable. But they would be enforceable under anarcho-capitalism, provided that individuals are willing to bear the cost of enforcing them. For similar reasons, other rules can arise to enforce autarky (no trade) or to ban vaccines, or any number of other irrational private rules or governance. While some of these ideas are possible in some sense today (e.g., setting up a commune where no one gets vaccinated), it is much easier to sort a like-minded community in anarcho-capitalism. That community would then be capable of "seceding" from the more rational global community, exactly *because* anarchy is functioning as effectively as its proponents argue it will. Communities where people are able to associate with others and live as they wish are the utopias of Robert Nozick's *Anarchy, State and Utopia*. But, per my interpretation of ecological irrationality, some of Robert Nozick's[33] "utopias" become dystopic because *people get what they want*.[34] Anarcho-capitalism would yield a massive reduction in transaction costs to form whatever "utopia" a group of individuals wishes, including autarkic "utopias" or predatory cults, relative to what is possible in the present day.[35]

This is speculative, but that is the point. *We don't know what the supply of irrationality looks like in the absence of all state institutions*. Some positive amount of irrationality will be provided under anarcho-capitalism. It will be less than the amount of irrationality under mob democracy (because market actors feel the cost of their actions), and it will be greater than zero. In the present day, decision-makers (i.e., politicians and bureaucrats) who have systematically lower demand for irrationality and some amount of incentive to get the right answer (because their decisions matter) are empowered to make decisions. In this second case, there will be less irrationality than there is under mob democracy, but more than zero. Whether or not one amount of irrationality is greater than the other is contingent on the exact shape of the demand and supply curves under the various sets of institutions, regarding which we have little or no knowledge. This result differs from what would be found if the near-neoclassical demand curve for irrationality were to hold. If it held, societies under anarcho-capitalism would feel some cost of their actions and immediately eliminate all irrationality from their lives.

There is a theoretical—or really, terminological—objection to my argument: what if people are merely expressing their preferences? A famous finding by Nobel Laureate Thomas Schelling, for example, is that only a mild taste for living near people who look like you would quickly result in a highly segregated society.[36] In the earlier example of racist housing covenants, are racist housing covenants to merely follow the logic of how a taste for discrimination would function in markets, as was worked out decades ago?[37] But my analysis is premised on the idea that racism is not something people prefer for its own sake, and rather that people exhibiting racist tendencies do so because they falsely believe it will make them better off—that is, they are acting instrumentally irrational. Racism "for its own sake" is reprehensible, but not ecologically irrational.

Rather, I assume that discrimination arises for the ecologically irrational reason of the fear of outsiders, because it is essentially the textbook form of the mental module of fear of outsiders. In reality, "racism for its own sake" may look an awful lot like ecological irrationality, because the reasons underlying the intuitions against outsiders are not fully conscious. It is not as if people declare, "I perceive you to be part of the outgroup due to the cultural norms I grew up with, therefore I think you are less than me" prior to doing something racist. Doing X for its own sake is always a weak explanation, and I would hold to the position that apparent "racism for its own sake" really just amounts to the mental module of fear of perceived outsiders.

This point is more important than it may appear. Ecological irrationality expressed privately, resulting in racism, or other expressions of ecological irrationality should be viewed as a social loss, not simply "revealed preferences" for racism. Otherwise, one cannot consistently compare ecological irrationality, as expressed within a modern set of institutions, to ecological irrationality, as expressed under anarcho-capitalism, without evaluating both as social losses. They are the same phenomenon; to argue that ecological irrationality expressed privately is just "revealed preferences" is to confuse comparative analysis with terminological word games.

If we are willing to say that revealed preferences in anarcho-capitalism would somehow sanctify ecological irrationality because people expressed a willingness-to-pay for autarky, then to be consistent, we should be advocating the types of trade restrictions that would arise under anarcho-capitalism, not free trade. I belabor this point somewhat because I anticipate it will be the primary response by anarcho-capitalists. But if the level of ecological irrationality supplied under anarcho-capitalism is considered a good because it is now "revealed preference," then ecological irrationality and rational irrationality are neither good nor bad—they are just preferences. In that case, the sin of government policy is being imprecise in how it supplies ecological irrationality. If ecological irrationality is the bad, then we should choose the set of institutions that will minimize it, not redefine ecological irrationality to only be a social loss when expressed through public policy.[38]

I wish now to callback to Caplan's brief statement on the unimportance of private irrationality. Caplan's position is that in markets, the informed are able to be rational, while with government, irrational decision-making is forced on all. The perspective promulgated here is that if ecological irrationality is the objective bad and if we can stop people from figuratively smacking themselves in the head with a frying pan, it's good. Second, there are actually ambiguities about whether a perfectly rational person in an anarcho-capitalist society would be better off than in a modern-day democracy, at least for issues pertaining to ecological irrationality. For instance, one recent estimate found that a surprising proportion of economic growth from 1960 to 2010 was simply due to allowing ethnic minorities and women to pursue their comparative advantage,[39] and such growth benefits society overall. Would that have also been achieved under Nozickian dystopias?

Or, if a significant population in the world decides not to engage in global markets, almost anyone's well-being will fall, because Trade Is Good. Those who no longer trade with you may have exited the stage of their own volition, but your income will fall regardless of whether that is because they are willing to pay or willing to vote to achieve less trade. Let me make it explicit, however, that I am not endorsing any form of imperialism in support of these goals. We should not be using paternalistic foreign intervention to open up markets. These issues are difficult enough to grapple with domestically, as we will see in chapter 10.

Lastly, I should mention that there are conventional externalities that could be exacerbated more under anarcho-capitalism via ecological irrationality than they presently are, for example, regarding health and sanitation. Suppose we compare our current set of institutional arrangements where regulations governing health and sanitation are already somewhat epistocratic. Suppose the less informed have a willingness-to-pay to choose regimes that are more congruent to folk biology than to hard science. If choices regarding health and sanitation have third party effects, and the anarcho-capitalist systems of addressing externalities are less than perfect, then the class of instances where anarcho-capitalism may perform worse than our present set of institutional arrangements is quite wide, indirectly because of ecological irrationality.

NEW AUTOCRACY

Next, I want to consider another radically different set of political institutions, which is the recent interest in reviving a form of complete autocracy. While the scholars I have in mind do not use ecological irrationality as a basis for autocracy, as I pointed out earlier, the first-approximation application of Caplan's model would imply that autocrats are fully rational. This deserves to be more fully addressed. To consider the point, we return to the work of Public Choice scholar Mancur Olson, whom we mentioned in chapter 2. Years after *The Logic of Collective Action* was published, Olson separately came up with another innovative analytical tool, this time to explain the origins of the state.[40]

Imagine we are in a pre-state society. Groups of people are spread across a geography, where they grow food and raise livestock. Some in the society live outside the groups and do not produce anything, instead traveling around and stealing from the productive groups. These people are called the Roving Bandits. Because the productive groups know these Roving Bandits are among them and at any moment could take what they produce, the productive groups do not invest and produce as much as they otherwise could, because it's not worth it if the fruits of their labor are simply taken by a Roving Bandit.

One day, a Roving Bandit decides that, instead of roving around, they take rule over one of the productive groups via force. The Roving Bandit then becomes the Stationary Bandit. The Stationary Bandit discovers that she should stop Roving Bandits from attacking the population she is currently victimizing, because those attacks take away from her ability to victimize them. She also realizes that if she only takes a percentage of what the productive group produces, she can take more from them over time. Then she realizes that she is in a special position in wanting to increase the total size of what the productive group produces, in such a way that no individual member of the productive group is interested. Logically, the Stationary Bandit begins making investments in infrastructure and the provision of law and order, so the productive group produces even more. We now have a government, which taxes while providing foreign defense, law, and infrastructure.

Let's pretend, for the sake of argument, that all states effectively behave this way, and are only interested in maximizing tax revenue. This is an analytical assumption with precedent.[41] What characteristics do we want from our political institutions, given that assumption? For one thing, we want a long term outlook. In the absence of a long term outlook, the government will tax and loot as much as it can immediately, while failing to invest to reap greater benefits down the line. This would also imply that we would want stability in rule, because again, we want the government to have incentive to look to the future. But under this model, the case for democracy is not strong. Political power under a democracy is fleeting. A stable autocracy, perhaps in competition with other stable autocracies, is what you would expect to provide the best governance, under the assumption that modern governments are best thought of as Stationary Bandits.[42]

It is not necessary to conceive of this narrowly in terms of autocracies. Other institutional arrangements make use of mechanisms with similar incentives. For example, "seasteading" is a movement promoting the possibility of competing new political or economic institutions into existence, by either creating a society on a boat or constructing a new platform or island.[43] If this is still too fanciful for your taste, seasteading can be understood in terms of other modern innovations in governance,[44] such as special economic zones and jurisdictions, and charter cities, these latter experiments being within the scholarly mainstream.[45]

Returning to the narrow question of hard autocracy, however, the issue simply is that the data in support of the hypothesis are too thin. The combination of good governance and an autocratic state is extremely rare. It arguably exists in the East Asian city states of Hong Kong and Singapore, the oil city states of United Arab Emirates and Qatar, the tiny European principality Liechtenstein, and historically, medieval Venice. (China is sometimes talked up as another example of this phenomenon, but quantitative measures of its governance tend to be middling at best.) The counterargument to this fact, however, is that our bundle of modern institutions, along with other variables like economic output per capita, education, and positive cultural characteristics, are highly correlated with one another. In terms of simple correlations, good governance, democracy, economic output, education, and culture are positively correlated.

So it is possible that the lack of empirical examples in the modern world of "good autocracies" is not because autocracy is bad, but because we haven't controlled for the other elements of the modern world. In another recent paper,[46] I searched for any autocracies out there whose governance is relatively good, after taking into account their economic output per capita, education, and culture. To do so, I used a combination of the data from *Worldwide Governance Indicators.*[47] To measure democracy, I used "Executive Constraint," a piece of the aforementioned *Polity IV* index, which I simplified into three possible values (from seven) to make the empirical tests less statistically demanding.

When I did this, Singapore immediately jumps off the page as a place with far better governance than would be expected. United Arab Emirates and Qatar did not have the cultural data I needed to fully assess them, and they appear borderline—their high levels of economic output per capita readily explain a fair amount of their governance. I couldn't assess Hong Kong or Liechtenstein at all because there is no Executive Constraint data for them, but even so, it is not actually clear that with data, either of these "countries" (Hong Kong is a Special Administrative Region of China, and Liechtenstein is the home of fewer than 50,000 people) would actually be considered autocracies. Both have legislative branches who hold at least some real power.

There was only one country in the world besides those we already mentioned that looks like a "new" example of a good autocracy, Rwanda. This fact isn't yet known in the public discourse—I say so in the year 2019—but Rwanda is light years ahead of where it was during its experience with genocide in 1994. Under Paul Kagame, Rwanda now scores very well in both *Worldwide Governance Indicators* and *Economic Freedom of the World.* According to World Bank data, Rwanda as of 2017 has seen its Real GDP per capita double since 2002, and more than triple compared to its nadir in 1994. Growth has been steady despite the turbulent world economy in the period. Rwanda also supports the hypothesis insofar as it is a small autocracy, a model similar to the various city states.

But there really aren't any other autocracies whose governance outperforms what you would expect given their economic output per capita, education, and culture. I used different tweaks to the definitions of culture, democracy, and governance to see if that would change anything, and it really didn't. The dearth of good autocracies is not the result of autocracies being entangled with other negative characteristics. They're just badly governed countries. Although my reading of Caplan's model implies that autocracy should eliminate ecological irrationality, autocracies are simply too good of a breeding ground for ruthless psychopaths to have much to recommend it.

The issue shouldn't be thought of as "the superiority of autocracy" as much as "what are the idiosyncrasies that allow autocracy to sometimes work out very well?" To a certain extent, this is what economist Alexander Salter (who articulated the argument reproduced here) has done, arguing that what the United Arab Emirates and Singapore have in common is that they operate in a way similar to a profit-seeking corporation.[48] But another factor the two countries have in common is their small size, and numerous small democracies also feature good governance, such as Estonia, Switzerland, and the African island of Mauritius. At least presently, if we try to isolate the common elements of the most effectively governed countries on the planet, autocracy is not one of them.

FUTARCHY

The final proposal in altering political institutions to address ecological irrationality is futarchy, proposed by economist Robin Hanson.[49] Under this model, we would keep our democracy insofar as we would vote on the values the government would pursue—increasing economic growth, improving health, protecting the environment, or whatever else—and how much weight to place on each of our desired ends.[50] But instead of using democratic institutions to tell us how to achieve those values, we would use a prediction market. You may be familiar with prediction markets from recent major elections. They are how you can effectively bet on who will be president in the next election. Prediction markets function almost identically to betting on sports, the accuracy of which is why it is so difficult to win bets on sports consistently.

The reason why prediction markets operate so well is the same reason that most credible economists advise you to invest in index funds,[51] instead of trying to pick individual assets. The rationale for this is known as efficient market hypothesis, and it is yet another application of the Chicago School's relentless focus on rationality, maximization, and equilibrium, discussed in chapter 2. The idea is that investors are focused on securing excess returns. This means that investors are intent on finding assets that are undervalued, given their risk. The notion that there is a figurative "twenty dollar bill on the sidewalk" is seemingly ludicrous—traders and analysts everywhere across the world are staring at the sidewalk (the market) looking for any stray nickels.

Meanwhile, you believe your random financial newsletter or that scream-ing man on television has found you a $20 bill on the sidewalk? Once you account for the costs of executing a trade, divergences between the efficient market hypothesis and reality, more or less, disappear. Scholars in finance and economics have scoured the world looking for anomalies to efficient market hypothesis. And while such anomalies are often published, they are typically difficult to replicate. When they do replicate, they are smaller than they previously appeared.[52] With all this in mind, we can mobilize the power of efficient financial markets to accurately predict the future value of any variable, or forecast the probability of an event occurring, using prediction markets. We can then use these predictions to determine which set of policies will do the best to achieve the goals democracy has chosen.

A prediction market would be similar to epistocracy's plural voting format. However, instead of demonstrating competence through a college degree or testing, your competency is demonstrated by your willingness to put money on the line. But it's not like we are handing rich people more votes. This would not be true here anymore than it is true in financial markets. What is rewarded in either is making correct predictions when the market is out of whack, not an ability to manipulate the market. In real life markets, as long as individual and institutional investors have access to capital (or have the capacity to borrow), a renegade wealthy person attempting to punch up the value of an asset is only creating an opportunity for arbitrage (profit) for the rest of the market. Hanson addresses many other such criticisms in his paper in *Journal of Political Philosophy*.

My concern is that, while I believe efficient market hypothesis is more likely than not to be true, it is too drastic of a departure from the status quo given the lack of broad agreement with efficient market hypothesis. On the one hand, public intellectuals associated with behavioral finance grossly overstate the frequency and obviousness of bubbles in financial markets. For instance, if you look at the prices of assets associated with the tech bubble, the housing bubble, and bitcoin *at the points in time they were first said to be a bubble*, shorting those assets would have actually lost you money in the long run. For each class of assets, post-crash prices of those assets later reverted to the path of the pre-crash prices, if you correctly assign the time to when they were first said to be "bubbles."[53]

But bubbles, carefully defined, still seem to exist in financial markets.[54] In general, the academic statements on behavioral finance are more nuanced than what you would pick up at an airport bookstore and are immune to most arguments presented by efficient market proponents. The point of disagree-ment isn't about how difficult it is to make more money than what an index fund will get you (it's incredibly difficult), but rather, how far prices can get out of whack before it becomes profitable to correct the price.[55] Can prediction markets get sufficiently out of whack for it to disrupt policymaking? I don't think we can be so confident in the answer to this question that we should actually want futarchy—at least yet. To summarize my position, efficient market hypothesis is my starting point, but we still understand financial markets imperfectly, and too imperfectly to enthusiastically recommend futarchy.

ASSESSMENT OF PROPOSALS

Futarchy has some advantages over epistocracy. If expert opinion is wrong and popular opinion is correct, futarchy should still end up with the right answer. However, futarchy must also be structured such that changes in values over time are not too capricious. Changes in values over time would be addressed by epistocracy, but at the cost of allowing the elite to partially dictate to the masses which values their political institutions ought to pursue. In their idealized forms, both futarchy and epistocracy would be real solutions for ecological irrationality, but I would urge caution if either proposal got off the ground. As stated above, I believe the epistocratic program should be reframed in terms of modest innovations in democratic political institutions. Regarding futarchy, it is reasonable to demand that additional demonstrations of proof-of-concept for prediction markets are first achieved. For instance, empirical demonstrations showing that prediction markets can actually be used to run monetary policy, as has been proposed by economist Scott Sumner,[56] would be an adequate intermediate step before further considering radically altering our political institutions.

Regarding the other, even more radical, proposals in their present form I do not see them as appropriate. We do not have a strong enough grasp of what makes "good autocracy" tick to make an appraisement of what it would even entail for us to safely "reform" a country from liberal democratic political institutions to Singaporean quasi-autocracy. And historical examples notwithstanding, any statement on how ecological irrationality will behave in anarcho-capitalism is purely speculative, and theory does not tell us whether ecological irrationality will be better or worse under this alternative set of institutions.

As stated at the outset of this chapter, we are exploring previously proposed solutions to ecological irrationality (and their natural extensions), even if the starting point for this book disfavors radical institutional changes. That does not mean it is not worthwhile to grapple with radical changes to institutions and fairly assess them. My conclusion has been that neither autocracy nor anarcho-capitalism offers good reason to believe they would improve on the status quo in addressing ecological irrationality, and each comes with great risk. However, there are relevant epistocratic reforms which would not be any more extreme than the recent suggestion to eliminate the Electoral College. Meaning, it probably should not be interpreted as that radical of a change. Meanwhile, futarchy can safely be shelved until more intermediate steps have been taken in the ambitious applications of prediction markets.

These conclusions are in part an outgrowth of the findings in chapter 4. If individuals were only ecologically irrational when it is of very low cost, then anarcho-capitalism would stand out as the best option, setting aside other objections to anarcho-capitalism. As is, we have two possible paths of reforming democracy, with some reason for caution regarding both. That is a lukewarm conclusion. In the following chapter, we will move on from comparing sets of political institutions to examining an important question at the nexus of political science and sociology, the implications of ecological irrationality for social capital, where my conclusion will be much less lukewarm.

NOTES

1. An earlier presentation of some of these arguments can be found in Ryan H. Murphy, "Rational Irrationality across Institutional Contexts," *Journal des Economistes et des Etudes Humaines* 21, no. 1–2 (December 2015): 321–335.

2. Caplan, *The Myth of the Rational Voter*, 197–199.

3. Andrew Prokop, "Why the Electoral College is the Absolute Worst, Explained," *Vox*, December 19, 2016, https://www.vox.com/policy-and-politics/2016/11/7/12315 574/electoral-college-explained-presidential-elections-2016.

4. Saul Cornell and Justin Florence, "The Right to Bear Arms in the Era of the Fourteenth Amendment: Gun Rights or Gun Regulation," *Santa Clara Law Review* 50, no. 4 (2010), 1050.

5. Timothy Egan, "The Disgust Election," *New York Times*, October 23, 2014, https://www.nytimes.com/2014/10/24/opinion/the-disgust-election.html.

6. Eugene Volokh, "The United States is Both a 'Republic' and a 'Democracy'—Because 'Democracy' is like 'Cash'," *The Washington Post*, November 14, 2016, https://www.washingtonpost.com/news/volokh-conspiracy/wp/2016/11/14/th e-united-states-is-both-a-republic-and-a-democracy-because-democracy-is-like-cas h/?utm_term=.9771330defdb.

7. Especially in the frame, for example, of James M. Buchanan and Roger Congleton, *Politics by Principle, Not Interest: Towards Nondiscriminatory Democracy* (Cambridge: Cambridge University Press, 1998).

8. Stefan Voigt, "Breaking with the Notion of Social Contract: Constitutions as Based on Spontaneously Arisen Institutions," *Constitutional Political Economy* 10 (October 1999): 283–300.

9. Jason Brennan, *Against Democracy* (Princeton: Princeton University Press, 2016).

10. Caleb Crain, "The Case Against Democracy," *The New Yorker*, October 31, 2016, https://www.newyorker.com/magazine/2016/11/07/the-case-against-democra

cy; Sean Illing, "Epistocracy: A Political Theorist's Case for Letting Only the Informed Vote," *Vox*, November 9, 2018, https://www.vox.com/2018/7/23/17581 394/against-democracy-book-epistocracy-jason-brennan.

11. Brennan, *Against Democracy*, 58–73.

12. Brennan, *Against Democracy*, 204–230.

13. This model follows Claudio Lopez-Guerra, *Democracy and Disenfranchisement: The Morality of Electoral Exclusions* (New York: Oxford University Press 2011).

14. As I am writing this, Jones's book has not yet gone to press, but he sketched his argument at a seminar at Southern Methodist University in September, 2016.

15. See Martin Gilens, *Affluence and Influence: Economic Inequality and Political Power* (Princeton: Princeton University Press, 2012) for more empirical support on the issue; c.f. Bryan Caplan, "The Logic of Gilensian Activism," *Econlog*, September 15, 2014, https://www.econlib.org/archives/2014/09/gilens_page_and.html.

16. Brennan, *Against Democracy*, 196–203; Caplan, *The Myth of the Rational Voter*, 166–181; c.f. Bryan Caplan, "Persuasion, Slack, and Traps: How Can Economists Change the World?" *Public Choice* 142, no. 1 (January 2010): 1–8.

17. C.f. Ryan H. Murphy, "Kissing Babies to Signal You Are Not A Psychopath," *Journal of Neuroscience, Psychology, and Economics* 9, no. 3–4 (2016): 217–225.

18. In unpublished material, Caplan addresses some of these concerns and reaches conclusions similar to mine. See Bryan Caplan, "Week 12: Dictatorship," accessed June 29, 2019, http://econfaculty.gmu.edu/bcaplan/e854/pc11.htm.

19. More serious exceptions would be small, developed autocracies like United Arab Emirates and Brunei Darussalam. We will return to countries like these later in the chapter.

20. My concern here perhaps fits in with what Brennan characterizes as the "Burkean" criticism of epistocracy. See Brennan, *Against Democracy*, 228–230.

21. William Easterly, *The Tyranny of Experts: Economists, Dictators, and the Forgotten Rights of the Poor* (New York: Basic Books, 2014), 307–338.

22. Ryan H. Murphy, "Imperfect Democracy and Economic Freedom," *Journal of Public Finance and Public Choice* 33, no. 2 (October 2018): 197–224.

23. James Gwartney, Robert Lawson, Joshua Hall, and Ryan H. Murphy, *Economic Freedom of the World*.

24. John W. Dawson, "Causality in the Freedom-Growth Relationship," *European Journal of Political Economy* 19, no. 3 (September 2003): 479–495; Jakob De Haan and Jan-Egbert Sturm, "Does More Democracy Lead to Greater Economic Freedom? New Evidence for Developing Countries," *European Journal of Political Economy* 19, no. 3 (September 2003): 547–563; Susanna Lundstrom, "The Effect of Democracy on Different Categories of Economic Freedom," *European Journal of Political Economy* 21, no. 4 (December 2005): 967–980; Martin Rode and James Gwartney, "Does Democratization Facilitate Economic Liberalization?" *European Journal of Political Economy* 28, no. 4 (December 2012): 607–619.

25. David D. Friedman, "Private Creation and Enforcement of Law – A Historical Case," *Journal of Legal Studies* 8, no. 2 (March 1979): 399–415; Carrie B. Kerekes and Claudia R. Williamson, "Discovering Law: Hayekian Competition in Medieval Iceland," *Griffith Law Review* 21, no. 2 (2012): 432–447.

26. Peter T. Leeson, "Better Off Stateless: Somalia Before and After Government Collapse," *Journal of Comparative Economics* 35, no. 4 (December 2007): 689–710; Benjamin Powell, Ryan Ford, and Alex Nowrasteh, "Somalia After State Collapse: Chaos or Improvement?" *Journal of Economic Behavior & Organization* 67, no. 3–4 (September 2008): 657–670.

27. Terry L. Anderson and Peter J. Hill, *The Not So Wild, Wild West: Property Rights on the Frontier* (Stanford: Stanford University Press, 2004).

28. Peter T. Leeson, *Anarchy Unbound: Why Self-Governance Works Better Than You Think* (Cambridge: Cambridge University Press, 2014).

29. Edward P. Stringham, *Private Governance: Creating Oder in Economic and Social Life* (Oxford: Oxford University Press, 2015).

30. Avinash Dixit, *Lawlessness and Economics: Alternative Modes of Governance* (Princeton: Princeton University Press, 2004).

31. Michael Huemer, *The Problem of Political Authority: An Examination of the Right to Coerce and Duty to Obey* (New York: Palgrave Macmillan, 2012).

32. Criticisms of anarcho-capitalism most similar to the themes explored here can be found in Brad Taylor and Eric Crampton, "Anarchy, Preferences, and Robust Political Economy," *Working Paper* (Toowoomba: University of Southern Queensland, 2009), https://papers.ssrn.com/sol3/papers.cfm?abstract_id=1340779 and Ryan H. Murphy, "Heterogeneous Moral Views in the Stateless Society," *Libertarian Papers* 7, no. 1 (2015): 39–54.

33. Nozick, I should say, was not an anarchist, but the models of governance in his utopias closely approached the anarcho-capitalist model.

34. Robert Nozick, *Anarchy, State, and Utopia* (New York: Basic Books, 1974).

35. Governments can overcome certain issues (especially with eminent domain) to force through societal changes even where there are holdouts. However, this benefit of government is often in dispute among anarcho-capitalists themselves. Moreover, the model I have in mind is a dystopic version of Nozick's utopias, which reflect other issues concerning transaction costs. C.f. Bruce Benson, "The Mythology of Holdout as a Justification for Eminent Domain and Public Provision of Roads," *The Independent Review* 10, no. 2 (Fall 2005): 165–194.

36. Thomas C. Schelling, "Dynamic Models of Segregation," *Journal of Mathematical Sociology* 1, no. 2 (1971): 143–186.

37. Gary S. Becker, *The Economics of Discrimination* (Chicago: University of Chicago Press, 1957).

38. This is analogous to the question of whether private communities in anarchy would keep out immigrants, with Hans-Hermann Hoppe affirming they would under anarcho-capitalism. The position here is that heavy immigration restrictions are incorrect regardless of whether done via legislation or an expression of willingness-to-pay. C.f. Hans-Hermann Hoppe, "The Case for Free Trade and Immigration Restrictions," *Journal of Libertarian Studies* 13, no. 2 (Summer 1998): 221–233.

39. Chang-Tai Hsieh, Erik Hurst, Charles I. Jones, and Peter Klenow, "The Allocation of Talent and U.S. Economic Growth," *NBER Working Paper*, no. 18693 (Cambridge: National Bureau of Economic Research, 2013).

40. Mancur Olson, *Power and Prosperity: Outgrowing Communist and Capitalist Dictatorships* (Oxford: Oxford University Press, 2000).

41. Geoffrey Brennan and James M. Buchanan, *The Power to Tax: Analytical Foundations of a Fiscal Constitution* (Cambridge: Cambridge University Press, 1980).

42. See Alexander W. Salter, "Sovereignty as Exchange of Political Property Rights," *Public Choice* 165, no. 1–2 (October 2015): 79–96; Alexander W. Salter, "Political Property Rights and Governance Outcomes: A Theory of the Corporate Polity," *Journal of Private Enterprise* 31, no. 4 (Winter 2016): 1–20; Alexander W. Salter and Abigail Hall, "Calculating Bandits: Quasi-Corporate Governance and Institutional Selection in Autocracies," *Advances in Austrian Economics* 19 (2015): 193–213; c.f. Hans-Hermann Hoppe, *Democracy – The God That Failed: The Economics and Politics of Monarchy, Democracy, and Natural Order* (New York: Routledge, 2001); Paul Collier, *Wars, Guns, and Votes: Democracy in Dangerous Places* (New York: HarperCollins, 2010); Fareed Zakaria, *The Future of Freedom: Illiberal Democracy At Home and Abroad* (New York: W.W. Norton & Company, 2003).

43. Patri Friedman and Brad Taylor, "Seasteading: Competitive Governments on the Ocean," *Kyklos* 65, no. 2 (May 2012): 218–235.

44. Tom W. Bell, *Your Next Government? From the Nation State to Stateless Nations* (Cambridge: Cambridge University Press, 2017). For the broader point, see Paul Aligica and Vlad Tarko, "Polycentricity: From Polanyi to Ostrom, and Beyond," *Governance: An International Journal of Policy, Administration, and Institutions* 25, no. 2 (2012): 237–262.

45. For example, Paul Romer, "Technologies, Rules, and Progress: The Case for Charter Cities," *Center for Global Development Essay* (Washington, DC: Center for Global Development, 2010), https://www.cgdev.org/publication/technologies-rules-and-progress-case-charter-cities.

46. Ryan H. Murphy, "Governance and the Dimensions of Autocracy," *Constitutional Political Economy* 30, no. 2 (June 2019): 131–148.

47. I left out "Voice and Accountability" from my governance measure, since that component of *Worldwide Governance Indicators* is too close conceptually to democracy. *Worldwide Governance Indicators* has some conceptual overlap with *Economic Freedom of the World*, but I concluded *Worldwide Governance Indicators* served as a better test of the hypothesis.

48. Salter, "Political Property Rights."

49. Robin Hanson, "Shall We Vote on Values, But Bet on Beliefs?" *Journal of Political Philosophy* 21, no. 2 (June 2013): 151–178.

50. Another recent proposal, which is similar to futarchy, has been proposed by Eric Posner and E. Glen Weyl. However, my trepidation toward futarchy is far greater toward what Posner and Weyl propose, as the types of changes they discuss have not been vetted in the same way that prediction markets and efficient market hypothesis have. See Eric A. Posner and E. Glen Weyl, *Radical Markets: Uprooting Capitalism and Democracy for a Just Society* (Princeton: Princeton University Press, 2018).

51. Burton Malkiel, *A Random Walk Down Wall Street: The Time-Tested Strategy for Successful Investing*, 11th ed. (New York: W.W. Norton & Company, 2016).

52. Kewei Hou, Chen Xue, and Lu Zhang, "Replicating Anomalies," *The Review of Financial Studies* (forthcoming).

53. Scott Sumner, "Don't be Early in Bubble Predictions," *Econlog*, August 9, 2017, https://www.econlib.org/archives/2017/08/dont_be_early_i.html; Scott Sumner, "How Do We Evaluate Robert Shiller's Forecast?" *Econlog*, September 13, 2017, https://www.econlib.org/archives/2017/09/how_do_we_evalu.html.

54. Robin Greenwood, Andrei Shleifer, and Yang You, "Bubbles for Fama," *Journal of Financial Economics* 131, no. 1 (January 2019): 20–43.

55. Eugene Fama and Richard Thaler, "Are Markets Efficient?" *Chicago Booth Review*, June 30, 2016, http://review.chicagobooth.edu/economics/2016/video/are -markets-efficient.

56. Scott Sumner, "Nominal GDP Futures Targeting," *Journal of Financial Stability* 17 (April 2015): 65–75.

Chapter 7

Too Much Social Capital

When we last left off on the topic of the buy local movement, I discussed its supposed positive environmental impact and dismissed that rationale.[1] Yet another standard reason to buy local is that it "keeps money in the community," the same illiterate rationale for local currencies. There is one final justification for buying local that I have not yet discussed—that it helps *build* community. In the parlance of social science, this means it creates "social capital." In order to give a sense of what social capital means, I will first briefly discuss four major thinkers who contributed to its development—political scientists Alexis de Tocqueville, Francis Fukuyama, and Robert Putnam, and community activist Jane Jacobs—although there are of course numerous others who contributed to the development of the concept as well.[2]

In one of the founding documents in the field of political science, *Democracy in America*,[3] a major finding of Alexis de Tocqueville in studying early nineteenth-century United States was the peculiar ability of Americans to solve problems afflicting their communities on their own, without the swords of the state imposing a political solution from on high. While he did not use the term, de Tocqueville characterized Americans as possessing the social capital needed to allow you to stop your neighbor from parking in front of your mailbox by simply asking, at which point the neighbor would apologize. In places with less social capital, society needs to pay an enforcement officer to drive around and write tickets any time someone parks in front of a mailbox. In the absence of outside enforcement, societies without social capital are unable to resolve basic social conflicts. Whether societies appear to be capable of spontaneously cooperating and how desirable the society is to live in seem to be closely linked; in the words of a tweet from economist David

Andolfatto, "Forget GDP as a measure of living standards. Just give me two measurements: [1] How well do the toilets work? & [2] How well do people queue?" (@dandolfa, January 2, 2016).

Much later in history, in the postwar era, cities were slowly dying all across America. While New York City would eventually face its own urban decay and near-bankruptcy, for a time it had Robert Moses, the only person in the second half of the twentieth century in the United States who was able to ram through giant infrastructure projects successfully, seemingly at will, through realpolitik, brinkmanship, and Machiavellianism.[4] Playing antithesis to Moses's thesis was Jane Jacobs, as she organized against Moses's practice of gutting entire neighborhoods in Manhattan so he could replace them with highways and office buildings.[5] In the worldview of Jacobs, mixed-use zoning and the presence of urban neighborhood residents throughout cities serve as "eyes on the street," allowing locals to, effectively, police and govern themselves. Moses's highways cut through the heart of cities and destroyed the social capital that makes this possible.

Continuing in our less optimistic trajectory, we find Robert Putnam in *Making Democracy Work* and later *Bowling Alone* arguing that America rapidly lost its accumulated social capital over the course of the twentieth century.[6] Civil associations that today feel a bit dusty, like the Knights of Columbus, the Union Local, or the titular bowling leagues, were once central to people's lives. Today, they are not, and Putnam argued that the decline in social interconnectedness means that we as a society will be less able to make use of our public institutions effectively. To marshal evidence in favor of his hypothesis, Putnam showed that the density of these types of organizations in Italy hundreds of years ago predict which regions of Italy are wealthier today. Furthermore, the relationship between the historical civil associations and today's economic outcomes is closer than the relationship between historical economic outcomes and today's economic outcomes. To Putnam, something as banal as the decline in bowling leagues and the rise in "bowling alone" is predictive of a society's ability to make its political institutions function properly.

As a side note, the cover of some editions of *Bowling Alone* features an iconic drawing of a solitary man gravely looking down at a bowling ball in his hands. In 2016, *Pokémon Go* took the Western world by storm, causing American teens and Millennials to leave their houses and, contrary to their programming, to interact with strangers, as is frequently required for success in the game. In reaction to this, a meme circulated online of the *Bowling Alone* cover, with a prominent item from the game (a Pokéball) edited in place of the bowling ball. *Pokémon Go* created the rare opportunity for the West to accumulate social capital, but the fad died. The hypothesis that *Pokémon Go* had the potential to create social capital has actually been taken seriously within academia.[7]

Finally, in 1996, Francis Fukuyama published *Trust: The Social Virtues and the Creation of Prosperity*.[8] Fukuyama agreed in broad strokes that markets are what gets us to prosperity, but the standard economic story was missing a piece, social trust, which explains why Southern Europe is poorer than Northern Europe. In low trust societies that have markets, entrepreneurship is often confined to family businesses, because entrepreneurs can only truly trust their family members. High levels of social trust, as in, for instance Japan and Germany, allow for the creation of gigantic corporations. Gigantic corporations aren't necessary for everything, but they do help a lot in certain industries where tasks are highly complicated, like manufacturing automobiles.

Fukuyama's story builds on earlier work told by Edward Banfield in *The Moral Basis of a Backwards Society*.[9] For all the talk among social conservatives about the instrumental importance of family,[10] low trust societies place a very *high* importance on family. What makes these societies "backwards" is not that familial connections are weak, but that individuals in those societies are willing to rob, pillage, and maim others outside their family to help their relatives, if doing so passes a very rough cost-benefit analysis. This is "moral" in some narrow sense (you are helping your family), but societies that function well tend to be those where their members sometimes recognize that it is important to put the needs or desires of society ahead of a close relative.

The stories of these four authors have both complementary and contradictory elements, and you would struggle to put a group of social scientists in the same room and agree on a single definition of "social capital." Maybe social capital is best defined in terms of your willingness to leave your phone on the table at Starbucks without fear that someone will take it. Maybe it's best defined in terms of you knowing, off the top of your head, that your friend's cousin is a graphic designer who just lost her job, so maybe the place you work at could hire her. Or maybe social capital is instead better thought of as the informal rules by which we conduct our lives.[11]

But the precise definition is not especially important. We know social capital when we see it, if you keep in mind everything I just described. When the Japanese national soccer team departed the stadium in Russia upon losing the World Cup in 2018, they cleaned up their locker room, leaving it spotless and thanking the country with a card.[12] Then, fans of Japan stuck around at the end of the games to help the staff clean up. Unrelatedly, in November 2017, a Japanese train left twenty seconds early (9:44:20 instead of 9:44:40), and that minor snafu was so far out of accepted societal practice that the company felt the need to apologize.[13] Stories like these are what lots of social capital "looks" like, whatever the proper definition of social capital is.

The wide variety of definitions of social capital corresponds to similarly far-flung methods of approaching how to measure it. Putnam, as discussed, used the density of civil organizations. This was followed up with more elaborate U.S. subnational data in *The Social Capital Community Benchmark Survey*. In the realm of cross-country comparisons, where I am most familiar, most scholars use questions from the *World Values Survey*. Data used to measure social capital pertain to participation in civil organizations, volunteering, and politics, questions about general trust or trust in various institutions, and the importance of friends. Compared to many other kinds of variables, data for social capital are spotty and the different ways of quantifying and conceptualizing social capital will often yield differing results. For example, even though qualitative observation supports Fukuyama's choice of Japan to exemplify the high trust society, it is above average—but not an exemplar—in social trust using the *World Values Survey* data.[14]

But there is one distinction within the definition of social capital well worth making—between *bonding* social capital and *bridging* social capital. To understand the distinction, consider your own life and imagine there are three groups—your family, the group of people you consider your moral co-equal, and everyone else.[15] Bonding social capital increases how close you feel to other people you consider your moral co-equal. For instance, in a middling bonding social capital society, you're not going to steal someone's phone just because you know you could get away with it, but maybe you're not necessarily so altruistic that you will stop on the side of the road to help someone change their tire. In a high bonding social capital society, you probably go out of your way to help. In contrast, bridging social capital should be thought of in terms of bringing more people into the group that you consider your moral co-equal from the "everyone else" category.

Without waxing too poetic, building *bridging* social capital can be thought of "the entire developmental history of political institutions." The earliest human societies featured small groups each comprised of people who more or less trusted one another, with each group in constant quasi-warfare with any other group they came across (think "rob, pillage, and maim" above, in conjunction with no governance ruling these groups). The force that fostered larger groups was, generally, a religion. Bridging social capital eventually became extended to ethnicities, and then to entire nation-states. In the current state of affairs, we live in "imagined communities"[16] where we treat strangers as "honorary friends," and where our (general) willingness to cooperate with any of our fellow citizens mirrors earlier humans' willingness to cooperate within the community of their tribe, only at a much larger scale.[17] These developments were described already in chapter 3, but we now have the tools to better describe the process that unfolded historically.

So let us return to the original question—does "buy local" build social capital? The narrative here is that if a local community keeps out the soulless corporations, the local hardware store and café are more attuned to the needs of the local communities, get to know their customers, and form human relationships that allow for closer cooperation than does bloodless (or bloody) profit maximization. Is it true? The evidence is mixed,[18] but if it is true, the only reasonable reading of it is that it builds bonding social capital, not bridging social capital, in the senses I am using these terms.

The two conceptualizations of social capital by Putnam and Fukuyama also lead to an interesting paradox. Among recommended readings on social capital, Robert Putnam is probably ranked #1, but Fukuyama is arguably #1A. One of the primary motivating reasons for having social capital within Fukuyama's framework is to make the creation of giant, soulless corporations possible, as low social capital societies tend to be forced to rely on family run firms. If we take Fukuyama's rationale for granted, and we are buying local to build social capital, what we are saying is that we want to accumulate social capital by keeping out the corporations, then accumulate the social capital, and finally, gain the ability to cooperate easily and anonymously, all so we can... create giant soulless corporations? I am not claiming that anyone in particular takes this position, but the utter contradiction of one of the primary reasons for wanting to accumulate social capital is worth noting.

We can set aside that paradox and Fukuyama's argument. Let us instead assume what is intended by the buy local advocates is that we need social capital so we can make our local governments function properly, fix the metaphorical potholes, and enjoy taking part in the local community. Fine. But the problem is that, *generally* speaking, highlighting one kind of social capital tends to erode the other form of social capital.[19]

Consider two imaginary acquaintances of mine from New England, who are, we imagine, attending a Major League Baseball game between the Boston Red Sox and their rival, the New York Yankees. Bridging Social Capital Cosmopolitan Connor will go to a Red Sox game and take it in as a social event, a time to enjoy a couple incredibly overpriced beers. If he is interested in baseball, it is the more cerebral parts of the game, and he doesn't really care about the Red Sox any more than cheering on Liverpool soccer games, whom he adopted as his team while abroad because it was fashionable to do. He's the guy who, when everyone else is on their feet and cheering, will distantly murmur, "hurray, look how fun it is to cheer for laundry." In contrast, there is Bonding Social Capital Bro Brad, who watches the Red Sox religiously and oh no he just got arrested again for getting in a fight with a Yankees fan.

Massachusetts is a weird place—I have remarked to hometown friends, to their agreement, that in the city of Worcester, there are three types of people: those holding a master's degree in engineering, those who have been arrested for misdemeanor assault at a minor league hockey game, and those who have done both. But the height of the Red Sox-Yankees rivalry (circa 2000) was emblematic of what building bonding social capital in a secular society looks like, with all its beauty and ugliness side-by-side. The "Yankees Suck" chant, which peaked shortly after the turn of the millennium, could be heard when the Red Sox weren't even playing, including at Boston-area events like weddings and Bar Mitzvahs.[20]

You can imagine ways of encouraging Cosmopolitan Connor to feel the sublimity of solidarity in Red Sox Nation, or you can imagine ways of encouraging Bro Brad to get out of his element. But the former boils down to heightening the fellow-feeling among people within a set of boundaries, while the latter involves breaking down those very same boundaries. I am not saying that it is impossible to build both bonding and bridging social capital at the same time, but doing so is threading the needle. If what buying local does is to build bonding social capital, in doing so it is likely to impair bridging social capital. Maybe it starts with saying "we don't want a Walmart," but with enough bonding social capital, you start doing silly things like launching your own local currency to keep money in the community.

While too much bridging social capital at the expense of bonding social capital may bring about its own social issues (i.e., "atomism"[21]), that issue is not what I'm looking to focus on here. Bonding social capital, in potentially highlighting differences between local groups and outsiders, encourages ecological irrationality. Some level of bonding social capital is necessary such that individuals aren't constantly trying to cheat the system, but too many cooperative sentiments can impede the impersonal institutions in place that allow for social cooperation at an even larger scale to occur (e.g., international trade). What appears on the surface to be pro-social fellow-feeling within a community may actually throw sand in the gears of the rule of law or the division of labor. That sand will ultimately reduce our ability to cooperate at a global scale and produce the figurative and literal pencil. Modern institutions are built on the idea that all individuals have rights, and you must respect them. Enough bonding social capital so that individuals voluntarily respect one another's rights has paramount importance. More than that and, at the very least, you are entering the world of tradeoffs.

To circle this back a bit, note also that I am not necessarily rejecting the narrative that buying local encourages bonding social capital formation. I am arguing that the converse is likely to hold—that high levels of bonding social capital causes people to behave inappropriately within their institutional environment. This in turns leads to greater demand for buy local. More bonding social capital and more buying local could subsequently be mutually reinforcing, though that also is not what I am trying to argue.

Classical liberal readers may notice certain parallels between my argument and the position of F. A. Hayek on "atavism" and "social justice."[22] Hayek made a similar distinction among the issues as I am making, that it is a mistake to apply our instincts that developed regarding relationships in a small social group, to modern society. But Hayek's concerns were with the rhetoric surrounding the concepts of social justice and socialism, whereas my points are about how these issues pertain to our conduct in the ordinary business of our lives. Additionally, the relationship between the concerns of Hayek and how social capital can go awry has already been developed elsewhere by economist Shaun Hargreaves Heap.[23]

Discussions of social capital tend to veer toward bonding social capital, as do its empirical measures (e.g., trust, participation, and friendship), at least as I have used the terminology. And while the distinction is sometimes made in the data, most research treats social capital as homogenous (or if measured in different ways, as addressing the same fundamental hypothesis). Going forward, I will not always make the distinction between bonding and bridging social capital, but I want to stress that reasonable readings of most of what follows can only be interpreted meaningfully in terms of bonding social capital, not bridging social capital, again as how I have defined each term.

Now that my position is clear, I can speak to the existing literature on social capital. First, I will lead in with the uncomfortable open secret among urban economists that the much-beloved Jane Jacobs was, more or less, a NIMBY ("Not in my backyard").[24] While many of her arguments, such as that elevated highways wreck neighborhoods and destroy social capital, are correct, she substantively fought private development, not simply centrally planned infrastructure projects, while favoring the kinds of density restrictions that are now disastrous for modern day economic growth. This is true despite her insights into spontaneous order that many free market intellectuals today deeply appreciate.[25] In the recent fights over exclusionary zoning and gentrification, she would be standing with parochial complaints, not for economic development. Regardless of the optics and rhetoric, she stood for regulation and against markets.

TEXTBOX 7.1 SOCIAL CAPITAL, LOCAL GOVERNANCE, AND ZONING

The informed position across the political spectrum is that zoning restrictions are incredibly onerous for the economy.[26] Rises in housing costs are an underlying cause of slowing real wage growth and higher returns to capital.[27] Simply stated, how poorly – and anti-socially – local governments in the United Stated have been run over the last fifty years will hopefully discredit the American veneration of federalism and local governance, as the empirics supporting these ideas have always been thin.[28] If social capital is facilitating communities' ability and desire to "self-govern" this way, that would imply a very high cost of social capital. My conclusion here actually squarely contradicts the conclusion of Ilya Somin, who in considering rational *ignorance*, argues local governance is superior in combatting the problem.

Jacobs, though, was likely correct that postwar Manhattan neighborhoods really were close communities that created human benefits beyond what can be measured using GDP statistics. The point, however, isn't that bonding social capital serves no purpose, but that too much can eventually be a bad thing. Jacobs celebrated her "eyes on the street" and community governance, but as economists Samuel Bowles and Herbert Gintis have argued,[29] community governance functions through the mechanism of making the "us" versus "them" distinction. You want enough of community governance to facilitate cooperation and friendships, but beyond that point, community governance means raising metaphorical fences to keep outsiders out. The example of this that is most salient as of 2019 is bonding social capital mashed up with the soft-fascist policy of "if you see something, say something." The primary social outcome of the policy has been a spike in calling the cops on minority children for selling candy bars and similar innocuous activities, a phenomenon branded as "The Summer of Snitches."[30]

Or, consider the Amish in America, the North American Protestant group who originated historically from the Anabaptists, and are most famous today for living without technology. The Amish exemplify a combination of high bonding social capital with low bridging social capital. According to one observer, "On the one hand, the Amish had a pronounced pro-social attitude... On the other hand, these neighborly behaviors were confined to in-group members. There was a conspicuous degree of prejudice towards out-group members, especially ethnic and religious minorities."[31]

Presenting difficulties for the social capital literature is that social scientists have been unable to create a clear distinction between types of civil associations which create trust, and those which create distrust. Recalling a colleague from Bosnia claiming that her country's problem was "too much social capital," political scientist Bo Rothstein laments, "Many of the people of Bosnia have been involved in social networks that create the hate and mistrust that laid foundation for discrimination, ethnic cleansing, concentration camps, and murder of civilians. The same can probably be said about Northern Ireland and Israel/Palestine, to take two more examples from the depressing pile."[32]

Ecological irrationality causes societies to go off the rails, falling into populism. More ecological irrationality piled on populism gets you to authoritarianism in its various shapes and forms. Putnam argued at length that social capital supports our institutions. If that were to be the case, we certainly want more of it. But while the positive relationship between social capital and institutional quality may be evident in the low trust society of Italy, as Putnam found, this may not hold in all times and places. Elsewhere, political scientist Sheri Berman has argued that civil associations, the telltale sign of social capital, were instrumental in the demise of Weimar Republic.[33] A group of scholars recently has studied this historical question rigorously and found that the density of civil associations in interwar Germany was predictive of the vote share for the Nazi Party, pricking Putnam in the eye by titling their paper, "Bowling for Fascism."[34] Besides facilitating populism and authoritarianism, there is empirical evidence that social capital may at times actually *promote* corruption[35] and can facilitate lobbying and rent-seeking,[36] which do not sound very much like "making democracy work."

As a final illustration of this mechanism of "too much social capital," I conjecture that it is the reason there are so many cultural differences between baseball played in the United States and baseball played in Japan.[37] Baseball in Japan puts significant emphasis on strategies and fundamentals in such a way that is purely performative (e.g., the sacrifice bunt). Teams in the United States have realized over recent decades that these strategies are useless or counterproductive,[38] while they remain ingrained in Japanese baseball. The positive behaviors described above which follow from the culture of Japan may also lead to excessively "cooperative" or "selfless" brands of play which do not actually serve any instrumental purpose. More serious illustrations of social capital inhibiting Japan include excessive barriers to performing layoffs[39] and a fear of outsiders. "For centuries, Japan's insularity protected it from conflict" write political scientist Keiko Hirata and educational researcher Mark Warschauer. "Today, though, in an era of globalization, that same insularity shuts Japan off from the immigrants, ideas and markets it needs to thrive. While other countries in Asia, such as Korea, China, and Singapore are embracing globalization, Japan has stagnated."[40]

In addition to heightening the salience of the outgroup, I would also conjecture that bonding social capital may give rise to more ecological irrationality through its interaction with the elementary forms of sociality, as modeled by anthropologist Alan Fiske.[41] According to Fiske, people in groups will default into thinking in terms of one of four kinds of social relationships: communal sharing, authority ranking, equality matching, and market pricing. These relational norms inform which behaviors are permitted or required in the course of social interaction. Simply respecting property rights and contractual obligations corresponds to the market pricing social relation, and such norms are the sociological undercurrent necessary for markets.

If someone perceives that a relationship should be governed by one set of relations and observes it being governed by another, the person will feel moral disgust.[42] Examples of this disgust include anger at "price gougers" in the course of disaster relief,[43] and the unease people feel toward markets for organs, regardless of the benefits that using market pricing may confer.[44] There is a small literature[45] showing similar situations where monetary incentives *reduce* individuals' willingness to say, supply their labor. The explanation for this is that by offering the incentive, you have moved across perceived sets of relations. Yet over time, social relationships have increasingly shifted from others to frameworks of market pricing, with little practical ill effect – think of the changes in social attitudes toward charging interest, for example.[46]

Suppose then, that social capital shifts these bounds such that individuals in a society are more likely to believe that a relationship should be governed by communal sharing instead of market pricing. This, I believe, is one of the deeper psychological foundations in play here, where high levels of social capital lead to more ecological irrationality. Very high levels of bonding social capital may shift the perceived social relation to communal sharing instead of market pricing, the continued use of market pricing causes moral disgust, and people get mad at the market. I am, to some extent, mixing positive and normative statements here; maybe we do want more relations to be governed by communal sharing. But if they are, it is at the cost of people failing to behave appropriately within the strictures of their institutional environment.

What does the data look like? In the course of investigating the relationships between social capital and social outcomes in the past, I applied the basic statistical methods I am competent enough to perform and found some evidence that there can be too much social capital. If you test the relationship using quadratic term (i.e., "X^2"), meaning you allow the relationship between economic output per capita and social capital to take a U-shape instead of a straight line, you find that models tend to fit an inverted-U to the data, meaning there is a "peak" optimal level of social capital.

In one such case, more social capital means more economic output, but only to a point, after which it means less. It is possible to find results suggesting that even the United States is on the "wrong" side of the curve, implying we have too much social capital relative to what would be economically beneficial—and the United States has far less social capital than does Japan or Northern Europe. Elsewhere, theory[47] and empirics[48] have suggested that social capital has the inverted-U-shape in explaining innovation and economic growth. Such a relationship also holds with other cultural variables that have become more recently fashionable within academia (the "deep roots" literature[49]). I should say that other scholars have argued that the data support a linear relationship, but many others have found the inverted-U.

What are the effects of social capital on the institutions of capitalism and globalization? Some economists have suggested that social trust promotes them,[50] but after poking around the data a lot, I had problems seeing a robust relationship. Part of the problem is that we have pretty spotty data for social capital, no matter how you quantify it. But there is one area of public policy that unambiguously relates to social capital. The more social capital, the larger government spending is relative to GDP. "Less social capital" in this context is interrelated with diversity (social science jargon: fractionalization) because people are racist.[51] Putnam himself has stated that immigration reduces social capital for this reason, and is somewhat at a loss about what to do about it.[52] There is direct evidence that immigration reduces support for the welfare state.[53] The intention of this book is not to take any position on whether social spending or transfer payments should be higher or lower in the United States or in Northwest Europe, but one clear fact is that immigration and diversity reduce the desire of present-day democracies to engage in many forms of government spending.

If it hasn't been clear enough, let me state outright that my claim that social capital is something we can have too much of isn't an outlier within scholarly research, especially given the social disincentives to making this argument. The first instance I have identified of substantively similar claims is a 1996 essay in *American Prospect* magazine by sociologists Alejandro Portes and Patricia Landolt[54] (while Putnam himself acknowledges the "dark side of social capital" in *Bowling Alone*[55]). But the idea that maybe it's a *good* thing that a culture of communitarianism in the United States is weaker than that of Northern Europe is not a popular proposition for either side of the political spectrum. On this point in the immigration debate, social democrats have fretted about immigration reducing social capital and support for the welfare state,[56] while the populist right is simply ignorant, in the United States insisting that immigration will increase the government spending,[57] despite this point being unsupported by complete analyses.[58] But regardless of its narrow effects on the welfare state, perhaps less social capital is simply one additional tally in favor of raising legal immigration rates in the West.[59]

From the perspective of tradeoffs, we may not even actually want to be at the ecological irrationality-minimizing level of social capital, because community begets happiness. If you want to argue that you like the local restaurant because of the sense of community it engenders, I will not argue with you. The optimal level of social capital should account for such facts. On the other hand, tightly knit communities are not for everyone, and they may be seen as stifling, as can be observed in the movie *Footloose*, the collected works of Stephen King, or the twenty-first-century equivalent of small town gossip: the cesspools of petty tyranny found in town-based Facebook groups or at Nextdoor.com.[60] Whatever the optimal level of bonding and bridging social capital is, social capital at high levels and ecological irrationality can make people behave wildly inappropriately and do very stupid things. Like thinking the key to financial success is doing-it-yourself.

NOTES

1. For an earlier take of this point, see Ryan H. Murphy, "The Perils of Buying Social Capital Locally," *Journal of Private Enterprise* 33, no. 2 (Summer 2018): 67–81.

2. Most notably, see James Coleman, "Social Capital and the Creation of Human Capital," *American Journal of Sociology* 94 (1988, Supplement): S95–S120; Glenn C. Loury, "A Dynamic Theory of Racial Income Differences," in *Women, Minorities, and Employment*, ed. Phyllis A. Wallace and Annette M. LaMond (Lexington: Lexington Books, 1977), 153–188, and Mark S. Granovetter, "The Strength of Weak Ties," *American Journal of Sociology* 78, no. 6 (1973): 1360–1380.

3. Alexis de Tocqueville, *Democracy in America*, ed. Eduardo Nolla, trans. James T. Schneider (Indianapolis: Liberty Fund, 2012).

4. While opinions differ on Moses, one starting point on Moses is Robert Caro, *The Power Broker: Robert Moses and the Fall of New York* (New York: Knopf, 1974).

5. Jane Jacobs, *The Death and Life of Great American Cities* (New York: Vintage, 1961).

6. Robert Putnam, *Making Democracy Work: Civic Traditions in Modern Italy* (Princeton: Princeton University Press, 1993); Robert Putnam, *Bowling Alone* (New York: Simon & Schuster, 2000).

7. Oriol Marquet, Claudia Alberico, Deepti Adlakha, and J. Aaron Hipp, "Examining Motivations to Play Pokémon Go and Their Influence on Perceived Outcomes and Physical Activity," *JMIR Serious Games* 5, no. 4 (October–December 2017): e21; Alexander M. Clark and Matthew T. G. Clark, "Pokémon Go and Research: Qualitative, Mixed Methods Research, and the Supercomplexity of Interventions," *International Journal of Qualitative Methods* 15, no. 1 (December 2016): 1–3. See also Mark Lutter, "Pokémon Coming Together: The Revival of American Civic Culture," *The Daily Caller*, July 11, 2016, https://dailycaller.com/2016/07/11/pokem on-coming-together-the-revival-of-american-civic-culture/.

8. Fukuyama, *Trust*.

9. Edward Banfield, *The Moral Basis of a Backwards Society* (New York: The Free Press, 1958).

10. For example, W. Bradford Wilcox, Paul Taylor, and Chuck Donovan, "When Marriage Disappears: The Retreat from Marriage in Middle America," *Heritage Lectures* no. 1179 (2011); Murray, *Coming Apart*, 153–171.

11. C.f. Claudia R. Williamson, "Informal Institutions Rule: Institutional Arrangements and Economic Performance," *Public Choice* 139, no. 3–4 (June 2009): 371–387.

12. Lindsey Ellefson, "After Defeat, Japan's World Cup Team Leaves behind Spotlessly Clean Locker Room and a 'Thank You' Note," *CNN*, July 3, 2018, https://www.cnn.com/2018/07/03/football/japan-belgium-russia-thank-you-locker-room-trnd/index.html.

13. *BBC*, "Apology after Japanese Train Departs 20 Seconds Early," November 16, 2017, https://www.bbc.com/news/world-asia-42009839.

14. If you rank all countries that have been surveyed in the two most recent waves of the *World Values Survey*, Wave 5 and Wave 6 using question V24, "Most People Can Be Trusted," and subtract those saying "no" ("need to be careful") from "yes" ("most people can be trusted"), Japan ranks sixteenth out of seventy countries.

15. Although I just defined social capital in terms of "I know it when I see it," the phrase has such wide ranging usage that there are additional uses, including within academia, that do not mesh well with what I have described. "Social capital" is sometimes used as a synonym for "social skills" or "social IQ," which in my view is a skill that should be seen as a form of human capital. It is also sometimes meant as a capital accrued over time within a social group, in the sense of "favors owed" or "social standing," which in my view is better thought of as "political capital." Additionally, other presentations of bridging social capital can be more literal or microcosmic than my presentation, describing bridging social capital as the literal number of acquaintances someone has, not who one is willing to freely cooperate with. See Tristan Claridge, "Explanations of Different Levels of Social Capital," *Social Capital Research & Training*, January 28, 2018, https://www.socialcapitalresearch.com/levels-of-social-capital/ for a reasonable summary of the many clashing definitions.

16. Benedict Anderson, *Imagined Communities: Reflections on the Origin and Spread of Nationalism* (New York: Verso, 1983).

17. This description of the history of political institutions echoes Fukuyama, *The Origins of Political Order* and Paul Seabright, *The Company of Strangers: A Natural History of Economic Life*, 2nd ed. (Princeton: Princeton University Press, 2010).

18. Daniel Shoag and Stan Veuger, "Shops and the City: Evidence on Local Externalities and Local Government Policies from Big-Box Bankruptcies," *Review of Economics and Statistics* 100, no. 3 (July 2018): 440–453; Jeremy Jackson, Art Carden, and Ryan A. Compton, "Economic Freedom and Social Capital," *Applied Economics* 54 (2015): 5853–5867; Art Carden, Charles Courtemanche, and Jeremy Meiners, "Does Wal-Mart Reduce Social Capital?" *Public Choice* 138, no. 1–2 (January 2009): 109–136; Stephen J. Goetz and Anil Rupasingha, "Wal-Mart and Social Capital," *American Journal of Agricultural Economics* 88, no. 5 (December 2006): 1296–1303; Troy C. Blanchard and Todd L. Matthews, "The Configuration of Local Economic Power and Civic Participation in the Global Economy," *Social Forces* 84, no. 4 (June 2006): 2241–2257; Troy C. Blanchard, Charles Tolbert, and Carson Mencken, "The Health and Wealth of U.S. Counties: How the Small Business Environment Impacts Alternative Measures of Development," *Cambridge Journal of Regions, Economy, and Society* 5, no. 1 (March 2012): 149–162.

19. See Marilynn B. Brewer, "The Psychology of Prejudice: Ingroup Love or Outgroup Hate?" *Journal of Social Issues* 55, no. 3 (1999): 429–444; Shaun P. Hargreaves Heap and Daniel John Zizzo, "The Value of Groups," *American Economic Review* 99, no. 1 (March 2009): 295–323.

20. Amos Barshad, "'Yankees Suck! Yankees Suck! The Twisted, True Story of the Drug-Addled, Beer-Guzzling Hardcore Punks Who Made the Most Popular T-Shirts in Boston History," *Grantland*, September 1, 2015, http://grantland.com/feat ures/yankees-suck-t-shirts-boston-red-sox/.

21. One such issue that could arise is an atomistic individualism, which has long been a criticism of the many stripes of liberalism. See, for instance, Geoffrey Hodgson, *Economics and Utopia* (London: Routledge, 1998); c.f. Tibor Machan, "Liberalism and Atomistic Individualism," *Journal of Value Inquiry* 34, no. 2–3 (September 2000): 227–247; Douglas J. Den Uyl and Douglas B. Rasmussen, "The Myth of Atomism," *The Review of Metaphysics* 59, no. 4 (June 2006): 841–868.

22. F. A. Hayek, "The Atavism of Social Justice," in *New Studies in Politics, Philosophy, and Economics* (New York: Routledge, 1978), 57–68.

23. Shaun P. Hargreaves Heap, "Social Capital and Snake Oil," *Review of Austrian Economics* 21, no. 2–3 (September 2008): 199–207. For a much different take on markets and social capital, but with a similar worldview, see Mark Pennington, *Robust Political Economy: Classical Liberalism and the Future of Public Policy* (Northampton: Edward Elgar, 2011), 81–110 and Art Carden, "Inputs and Institutions as Conservative Elements," *Review of Austrian Economics* 22, no. 1 (September 2009): 1–19.

24. Edward Glaeser, *The Triumph of the City: How Our Greatest Invention Makes Us Richer, Smarter, Greener, Healthier, and Happier* (New York: Penguin, 2011), 144–147; Angus Deaton, "On Tyrannical Experts and Expert Tyrants," *Review of Austrian Economics* 28, no. 4 (December 2015), 410–411. See also M. Nolan Gray, "How Should We Interpret Jane Jacobs?" *Market Urbanism*, June 30, 2018, https:// marketurbanism.com/2018/07/30/how-should-we-interpret-jane-jacobs/.

25. See the *Cosmos + Taxis* 4, no. 2–3 issue for several examples.

26. For a wide cross-section of topics and authors on this point, see Chang-Tai Hseih and Enrico Moretti, "Housing Constraints and Spatial Misallocation," *American Economic Journal: Macroeconomics* 11, no. 2 (April 2019): 1–39; Glaeser, *The Triumph of the City;* Lisa Prevost, *Snob Zones: Fear, Prejudice, and Real Estate* (Boston: Beacon Press, 2013); Edward Glaeser and Joseph Gyourko, "The Economic Implications of Housing Supply," *Journal of Economic Perspectives* 32, no. 1 (Winter 2018): 3–30; Matthew Yglesias, *The Rent is Too Damn High: What to do about It, And Why It Matters More than You Think* (New York: Simon & Schuster, 2012).

27. Matt Rognlie, "Deciphering the Fall and Rise in Net Capital Share: Accumulation or Scarcity?" *Brookings Papers in Economic Activity* (Spring 2015): 1–54; Kevin Erdmann, *Shut Out: How a Housing Shortage Caused the Great Recessions and Crippled Our Economy* (Lanham: Rowman & Littlefield, 2019).

28. Robert A. Lawson and Walter Block, "Government Decentralization and Economic Freedom," *Asian Economic Review* 38, no. 3 (1996): 421–434; Aurelie Cassette and Sonia Paty, "Fiscal Decentralization and the Size of Government: a European Country Empirical Analysis," *Public Choice* 143, no. 1–2 (2010): 173–189; Dean Stansel, "Interjurisdictional Competition and Local Government Spending in

U.S. Metropolitan Areas," *Public Finance Review* 34, no. 2 (March 2006): 173–194; c.f. Clint Bolick, *Grassroots Tyranny: The Limits of Federalism* (Washington, DC: Cato Institute, 1993).

29. Samuel Bowles and Herbert Gintis, "Social Capital and Community Governance," *The Economic Journal* 112 (November 2002): F419–F436.

30. Zuri Davis, "Is This the Summer of Snitches?" *Reason*, June 30, 2018, https://reason.com/blog/2018/06/30/burrito-bob-police-bart-san-francisco; Brandon Griggs, "Living While Black," *CNN*, December 28, 2018, https://www.cnn.com/2018/12/20/us/living-while-black-police-calls-trnd/index.html.

31. Robert Biswas-Diener, "The Subjective Well-Being of Small Societies," in *Handbook of Well-Being*, ed. Ed Deiner, Shigehiro Oishi, and Luis Tray (Salt Lake City: DEF Publishers, 2018), 4–5.

32. Bo Rothstein, *Social Traps and the Problem of Trust* (Cambridge: Cambridge University Press, 2005), 101.

33. Sheri Berman, "Civil Society and the Collapse of the Weimar Republic," *World Politics* 49, no. 3 (April 1997): 401–429.

34. Shanker Satyanath, Nico Voigtlander, and Hans-Joachim Voth, "Bowling for Fascism: Social Capital and the Rise of the Nazi Party," *Journal of Political Economy* 125, no. 2 (April 2017): 478–526.

35. Daron Acemoglu, Tristan Reed, and James A. Robinson, "Chiefs: Economic Development and Elite Control of Civil Society in Sierra Leone," *Journal of Political Economy* 122, no. 2 (April 2014): 319–368.

36. Emily Chamlee-Wright and Virgil H. Storr, "Social Capital, Lobbying, and Community-Based Interest Groups," *Public Choice* 149, no. 1–2 (October 2011): 167–185.

37. Robert Whiting, *You Gotta Have Wa*, 2nd ed. (New York: Vintage, 2009).

38. Tom M. Tango, Mitchel G. Lichtman, and Andrew E. Dolphin, *The Book: Playing the Percentages in Baseball* (Dulles, VA: Potomac Books, 2007); Ben Lindbergh, "Sabermetrics is Killing Bad Dugout Decisions," *Fivethirtyeight*, January 14, 2016, https://fivethirtyeight.com/features/sabermetrics-is-killing-bad-dugout-decisions/.

39. Hiroko Tabuchi, "Layoffs Taboo, Japan Workers Are Sent to the Boredom Room," *New York Times*, August 16, 2013, https://www.nytimes.com/2013/08/17/business/global/layoffs-illegal-japan-workers-are-sent-to-the-boredom-room.html.

40. Keiko Hirata and Mark Warschauer, *Japan: The Paradox of Harmony* (New Haven: Yale University Press, 2014), 6.

41. Fiske, "The Four Elementary Forms of Sociality."

42. Fiske and Tetlock, "Taboo Trade-offs."

43. See Michael C. Munger, "They Clapped: Can Price-Gouging Laws Prohibit Scarcity?" *Library of Economics and Liberty*, January 8, 2007, https://www.econlib.org/library/Columns/y2007/Mungergouging.html.

44. Jason Brennan and Peter Jaworski, *Markets without Limits* (New York: Routledge 2015).

45. Bruno S. Frey and Felix Oberholzer-Gee, "The Cost of Price Incentives: An Empirical Analysis of Motivation Crowding-Out," *American Economic Review* 87,

no. 4 (September 1997): 746–755; Dan Ariely, Anat Bracha, and Stephen Meier, "Doing Good or Doing Well? Image Motivation and Monetary Incentives in Behaving Prosocially," *American Economic Review* 99, no. 1 (March 2009): 544–555; Antoine Beretti, Charles Figuieres, and Cilles Grolleau, "Using Money to Motivate Both 'Saints' and 'Sinners': A Field Experiment on Motivational Crowding-Out," *Kyklos* 66, no. 1 (February 2013): 64–77. However, at least one meta-study has claimed these effects have been strongly overstated. See Judy Cameron and W. David Pierce, "Reinforcement, Reward, and Intrinsic Motivation: A Meta-Analysis," *Review of Educational Research* 64, no. 3 (September 1994): 363–423.

46. Pinker, *The Better Angles of Our Nature*, 635–637; c.f. Brennan and Jaworski, *Markets without Limits*.

47. Angelo Antoci, Fabio Sabatini, and Mauro Sodini, "Economic Growth, Technological Progress, and Social Capital: The Inverted U Hypothesis," *Metroeconomica* 64, no. 3 (July 2013): 401–431.

48. Carmen Echebarria and Jose M. Barrutia, "Limits of Social Capital as a Driver of Innovation: An Empirical Analysis in the Context of European Regions," *Regional Studies* 47, no. 7 (2013): 1001–1017; F. Xavier Molina-Morales and M. Teresa Martinez-Fernandez, "Too Much Love in the Neighborhood Can Hurt: How an Excess of Intensity and Trust in Relationships May Produce Negative Effects on Firms," *Strategic Management Journal* 30, no. 9 (September 2009): 1013–1023; M. Ann Fadyen and Albert A. Canella Jr., "Social Capital and Knowledge Creation: Diminishing Returns of the Number and Strength of Exchange," *The Academy of Management Journal* 47, no. 5 (October 2004): 735–746.

49. Oana Borcan, Ola Olsson, and Louis Putterman, "State History and Economic Development: Evidence from Six Millennia," *Journal of Economic Growth* 23, no. 1 (March 2018): 1–40.

50. Results from economists Niclas Beggren and Christian Bjornskov find positive effects of trust on the legal system and possibly positive effects on lighter regulatory policy, the latter taking the form of *preventing* reforms in the "wrong" direction. For many dimensions, I would also expect trust to improve the quality of the legal system, although I would speculate that more social trust would eventually lead to more stringent labor regulation. See Niclas Beggren and Christian Bjornskov, "The Market-Promoting and Market-Preserving Role of Social Trust in Reforms of Policies and Institutions," *Southern Economic Journal* 84, no. 1 (July 2017): 3–25. Other research supports the idea that trust leads to deregulation. See Phillippe Aghion, Yann Algan, Pierre Cahuc, and Andrei Shleifer, "Regulation and Distrust," *Quarterly Journal of Economics* 125, no. 3 (August 2010): 1015–1049; Markus Leibrecht and Hans Pitlik, "Social Trust, Institutional and Political Constraints on the Executive and Deregulation of Markets," *European Journal of Political Economy* 39 (September 2015): 249–268.

51. Alberto Alesina, Edward Glaeser, and Bruce Sacerdote, "Why Doesn't the United States Have a European-Style Welfare State?" *Brookings Papers on Economic Activity* 2 (2001): 187–277.

52. Robert Putnam, "*E Pluribus Unum*: Diversity and Community in the Twenty-first Century," *Scandinavian Journal of Political Studies* 30, no. 2 (June 2007): 137–174.

53. Alberto Alesina, Armando Miano, and Stefanie Stantcheva, "Immigration and Redistribution," *NBER Working Paper* no. 24733 (Cambridge: National Bureau of Economic Research, 2018). Theoretically, see Urs Steiner Brandt and Gert Tinggaard Svendsen, "How Robust is the Welfare State When Facing Open Borders? An Evolutionary Game-Theoretic Model," *Public Choice* 178, no. 1–2 (January 2019): 179–195.

54. Alejandro Portes and Patricia Landolt, "Downsides of Social Capital," *American Prospect* 26 (May–June 1996): 18–26. A more developed statement from Portes can be found in Alejandro Portes, "Social Capital: Its Origins and Applications in Modern Sociology," *Annual Review of Sociology* 24 (August 1998): 1–24. Portes points to four costs of social capital, one of which is fear of outsiders. The one aspect of social capital outlined here not on Portes's list is excessive solidarity can lead to inappropriate behavior given our institutional environment.

55. Putnam, *Bowling Alone*, 350–363. To be precise, Putnam outlines a tradeoff between social capital and "tolerance," and finds reasons to be skeptical, while I emphasize the tradeoff being between bridging and bonding social capital (table 8, 355), with bridging social capital here having a certain amount of conceptual overlap with "tolerance." Putnam notes that bonding social capital is a far greater danger than bridging social capital (358, 362). While Putnam downplays the dangers of social capital, there is likely less disagreement between my position and his than it appears at first glance.

56. Jonas Hinnfors, Andrea Spehar, and Gregg Bucken-Knapp, "The Missing Factor: Why Social Democracy Can Lead to Restrictive Immigration Policy," *Journal of European Public Policy* 19, no. 4 (2012): 585–603.

57. For example, Mark Krikorian, "Immigration + Welfare = Bad News," *National Review*, August 8, 2012, https://www.nationalreview.com/corner/immigration-welfa re-bad-news-mark-krikorian/.

58. Alex Nowrasteh, "The Fiscal Impact of Immigration," in *The Economics of Immigration: Market-Based Approaches, Social Science, and Public Policy*, ed. Benjamin Powell (New York: Oxford University Press, 2015), 38–69.

59. For the broader immigration issue, see Benjamin Powell, ed. *The Economics of Immigration: Market-Based Approaches, Social Science, and Public Policy* (Oxford: Oxford University Press, 2015).

60. Paul Thornton, "Nextdoor, Where Every Neighborhood is Under Siege," *Los Angeles Times*, May 5, 2018, http://www.latimes.com/la-ol-opinion-newsletter-ne xtdoor-20180505-htmlstory.html#.

Chapter 8

The Poverty of DIYism

The DIY movement celebrates and encourages the performance of various tasks and activities yourself, instead of using markets and paying someone to do it for you.[1] Generally speaking—although not universally—this movement is another instance of ecological irrationality. First, I will be addressing the DIY presumption that doing it yourself is more financially prudent than buying a good through the market. There are obviously instances where doing it yourself does makes sense. The issue is that the mental model most people have for figuring out when to do it yourself is incorrect. After making the case that doing it yourself isn't more financially prudent, I will explore other kinds of explanations of DIY and tie them back to the discussion from chapter 5 on status signaling.

Recall that Trade Is Good, Thomas Thwaites' toaster, and Andy George's $1,500 chicken sandwich. The reasoning underlying Trade Is Good, as in chapter 1, is really the concept of comparative advantage from the field of international trade, with trade essentially functioning as a form of technology. What comparative advantage means is that, if we all do what we are best at and trade with one another, society overall will have more goods and services in the end. A highly productive person is made more productive by specializing in their comparative advantage and "outsourcing" other work, even if the highly productive person is more effective at doing the outsourced tasks. For instance, suppose a statistician is extremely efficient at data entry, but the statistician is the only one really capable of doing data analysis with a high degree of competence. The statistician can be more productive by hiring someone else to perform data entry, even if the new person performs data entry more imperfectly and slowly. While there are provisos and exceptions, the logic of comparative advantage is the same logic which dictates what gets produced and where it gets produced in the global supply chain.

If we apply this logic to DIY, something doesn't fit, exactly. We are not in the position to costlessly hire the perfect person who can perform household tasks for us, pay them for the individual task, and bid them farewell. But what about businesses? If comparative advantage were the only variable in play, businesses would want to divvy up every task in front of them each day and contract with an individual whose comparative advantage most closely corresponds to each task. Instead of doing that, businesses typically hire with the expectation of employing the employee for an extended period of time, even though that particular individual will not have a clear comparative advantage in every task assigned to them. What gives?

This was what perplexed Nobel Laureate Ronald Coase in his 1937 article, "The Nature of the Firm."[2] The logic of comparative advantage, applied relentlessly, would suggest there should be daily or hourly re-contracting as workers continuously seek the highest paying use of their labor, and employers seek the cheapest and best labor for the tasks they need done. But this isn't what we see when we look into the world. Instead of constant re-contracting in an ocean of chaos, firms appear, as economist D. H. Robertson describes and Coase quotes, as "islands of conscious power in this ocean of unconscious co-operation like lumps of butter coagulating in a pail of buttermilk."[3] Some other force is pushing workers into the long-run relationships found in those islands of conscious power known as firms.

Coase solved the puzzle by noting the significance of how costly it is to contract with a new worker each time you need a new task to get done. This kind of cost is known as a *transaction cost* and has spawned an entire subfield of economics research.[4] Recent technological trends have been in the direction of drastically reducing these costs. The world with companies and apps like Uber, Postmates, TaskRabbit, and Fiverr look much more like the chaos that Coase imagined than what conventional long-run employment looks like.[5] These innovations make it possible to efficiently contract for individual tasks, whereas relatively recently it was far too inconvenient and uncertain to identify a stranger who would be willing to drive you to the airport for $25 with ten minute's notice. Still, most people in the labor market remain in conventional forms of employment. Adam Smith famously said, "The division of labor is limited by the extent of the market." Similarly, how far we can take comparative advantage is limited by the extent of transaction costs.

This is how you should think about DIY, if your goal in doing it yourself is to be financially responsible. Whatever hours you are willing to "work," work them in exchange for compensation in your area of comparative advantage. Contract out for tasks that are relatively straightforward to contract out for. DIY for tasks where it is too costly or annoying to go through the process of contracting out. "But," you may be thinking, "It's more expensive for me to buy a complete table than it costs for the lumber and hardware I would need to buy to construct one." This may be true, but only in a trivial sense.

Your own time is valuable, and you can observe its value in the wage rate that you demand. "Cost" means more than the number of dollars you must remove from your wallet to do something. If you include any reasonable value of what wage your labor commands when you are working an hour at the job that is your comparative advantage, you will find, predominantly, that building the table is more expensive. The other major consideration that is neglected is an honest appraisement of the cost of "capital" when you purchase the tools to build the table (with a reasonable expectation as to how many more times they will be used before they need to be replaced). Another is the risks implicit in your lack of expertise—for example, how confident are you that you cleaned out your mason jars correctly when making your DIY homemade pickles? If you *do* run the analysis correctly and you find that it saves money, good for you. DIY. I am not advocating dogmatism and I do not think the world is so neat and tidy that there are no exceptions to the rule, even forgetting transaction costs.

The DIY evangelist may accept that time is valuable, while insisting on two important caveats. First, most labor markets aren't so flexible that you can will yourself another hour of work into existence and have the money for it tacked onto your paycheck. Second, you may enjoy DIY tasks, and you should not assign the same value you demand in exchange for working as you do when enjoying the experience of DIY. Regarding the first, I would agree, we do not operate in a world of zero transaction costs. But workers are not utterly incapable of taking steps that would increase their time working at their comparative advantage. Suppose you want to be "financially responsible," that is your real motivation, and your present leisure/labor mix involves too much leisure. What you then should be doing is keeping an eye out for a new job or a new (or expanded) role in your current firm that would achieve something closer to your ideal mix. You shouldn't be spending several hours a week on yard work to avoid paying someone to do that for you.

Moreover, "taking on another hour of work in your comparative advantage" is something that can be quite broad. For academics like myself, performing a few extra hours of research per week would certainly perform this function. For others, this could mean a small part-time job, or just turning that DIY activity you truly enjoy and are good at into something you do for compensation on the side. If you honestly believe that working toward learning a new skill or set of ideas will increase your pay over time, such an investment could be consistent with working another hour in your comparative advantage as well.

Regarding the second caveat raised by the DIY evangelist, I agree that DIY activities are sometimes more fun than "working," but we need to be careful about what we mean by that. In virtually every job, there are tasks each week that you actively enjoy, tasks that are annoying but only modestly so, and tasks that are awful. The reason you are being paid at the wage rate you command is to perform the parts of your job that you do not like, not the parts you enjoy or don't mind. There are many people who have careers where parts of their job are more enjoyable than the less entertaining hours spent on leisure each week.[6] Compare in your head, if nothing else, how much you enjoy joking or gossiping with coworkers versus the more aggravating hours of television you catch yourself watching.

Here is a concrete example. I think I enjoy cooking—not so much that I am fascinated or exhilarated, but I am rarely annoyed by it. I can recall parts of my more purely leisurely leisure time that I find less enjoyable than some of my time cooking. But I rapidly lose interest in performing the task of cooking. If I were to do it all day, it would become physically demanding. For it to be worth the transaction cost for a restaurant to hiring me, I would need to do repetitive tasks all night and promise to show up for work at particular periods of time. But if I *really* like cooking, that is less an argument that DIY is generally a good use of my time than it is an argument that I should get a second job as a line cook. Many cooks enjoy aspects of their job, and the "work" involved applies to certain parts of the job that are exhausting or otherwise a pain. I get to skip the bad parts when I DIY, for the most part. To adequately take these facts into consideration, the cost of the DIY "work" that you enjoy should merely reflect the cost of holding your attention over a period of time. DIY that you do not enjoy falls into a different category.

Let's go into more detail regarding your attention. You may "enjoy" building a table, but you enjoy lots of other things. Because I am a strange person, I "enjoy" working with spreadsheets on a computer, but the appropriate value of my labor (specifically, my attention) is not zero if someone asks me to work on a spreadsheet for them. *You should value your labor in performing enjoyable DIY at the hypothetical wage rate you would demand in exchange for working more hours while only doing the parts of your job you enjoy doing.* Recall again—I am not arguing that everyone is able to inform their boss that they will take on more work this way, but that if your leisure/labor mix is off, you are able to move yourself in the desirable direction over time. For me, the wage rate is how much I would need to be paid to work on a spreadsheet puzzle. For a more normal person, it is how much you would need to be paid to take on more hours doing the fun parts of your job. My best guess for how much to charge for your attention in the United States in 2019, very roughly speaking, is $20/hour for an educated, midcareer worker, $50–$100/hour for a high income worker, and around the minimum wage for a college student.

The second labor rate is what you would need to be paid if you were to take on additional work doing stuff you dislike—such as dealing with coworkers you don't like, doing HR paperwork, or cleaning a bathroom. This is the appropriate labor rate for shoveling snow or other DIY tasks that give you no pleasure. For the educated, midcareer worker, this is $75–$100/hour, for the high income worker this could be something like $250–$1000/hour, and something like $15/hour for a college student. These wage rates should roughly correspond to what additional income you would be able to get on the market if all you cared about was money, to the point that your work life is miserable.

While this shouldn't be taken too literally, you can think of the wage rate you need to be willing to take a job formulaically. For instance:

wage = value of attention + work boredom + work stress + feeling tired + etc.

If a work activity is the equivalent of leisure, everything else equals zero and you are only left with the value of your attention. As an activity becomes more like shoveling snow or something you personally find very unpleasant, you should demand a higher and higher wage for doing them. This holds whether you are willing to perform a task for pay or in your individual calculus for deciding whether to do something yourself.

Considering the issues this way conforms your thinking to conventional cost-benefit analysis. Doing so doesn't make your thinking soulless or your life meaningless—if the numbers don't provide more informed decisions, you are using the wrong numbers. If you think this way, the question of whether you should perform a task isn't about whether you are "getting things done" or "not being wasteful," but being effective at allocating your time.[7] The answer to the question of how you can be financially responsible, shockingly, is that you can just work more. If you are convinced that you really enjoy a DIY task that much, then you should seriously consider doing it for money.[8] The determinants of DIY should be the transaction cost of hiring someone to do the task for you. How much DIY to do has nothing to do with the conscientiousness of DIYers or the laziness of those who contract out to a specialist.

Of course, if you *do* perform the task as your job already, sure, do it yourself on the side to save a little money. It's your comparative advantage!

One other rationale for DIY besides financial prudence is the desire to customize the final product. While many firms are willing to customize a product for you, I will not deny that in various circumstances the only way to get just what you want is to DIY.[9] Just recall the value of your own time when deciding to DIY—if a high-powered lawyer thought the price that contractor quoted her was high, she ought not to forget calculating the actual cost of three of her weekends.

But I do not think that DIY is really all that motivated—in a deeper sense—by wanting to save money. The rhetoric surrounding DIY proponents as to why DIY is cheaper is that, because the person you are buying the good from is making money, you are somehow being taken advantage of by not doing it yourself ("that's how they make their money" or "the profits come out of your wallet"). Surprise, surprise, our modern institutional environment is only intended to screw over you, the little guy: the rhetoric of ecological irrationality. If DIY really was a reliable rule of thumb for saving money, it would actually be quite damning of our institutions. But fortunately, it is only in the imaginary world of the enemies of our institutional environment that accurate cost-benefit analyses would reliably show that DIY is the key for financial prudence.

But as before, the argument is not confined just to the left—and it's not even confined to Rod Dreher's "crunchy cons" on the right, whom I alluded to in chapter 5. Romanticizing "living off the land" and doing *everything* yourself enjoys a certain cachet among many libertarians, even though libertarians are ostensibly the greatest champions of markets. This attitude is the libertarianism of *Parks and Recreation* character Ron Swanson. Historically, it may have roots in "rugged individualism," and, less obviously, American Transcendentalism, the latter of which was intertwined with incipient nineteenth-century libertarianism.[10] Modern rugged individualists living off the land purportedly with nothing but their guile and grit actually live in the shadow of the rule of law, the social safety net, and civil society, all the while without contributing to them. Instead of achieving self-sufficiency, they effectively mooch off modern institutions.[11] Self-proclaimed "libertarianism," when refracted through the lens of the DIY mythology and ethos, itself evinces ecological irrationality.

A similar attitude was famously expressed in a novel by libertarian science fiction author Robert Heinlein.

> A human being should be able to change a diaper, plan an invasion, butcher a hog, conn a ship, design a building, write a sonnet, balance accounts, build a wall, set a bone, comfort the dying, take orders, give orders, cooperate, act alone, solve equations, analyse a new problem, pitch manure, program a computer, cook a tasty meal, fight efficiently, die gallantly. Specialization is for insects.[12]

This attitude is not quite the same as fooling yourself into believing you have achieved complete self-sufficiency, but it is a clear continuation of the libertarianism of rugged individualism.

DIY is not a path to fiscal prudence and it exists across the political spectrum, but why? Ecological irrationality is one explanation for why

Westerners proselytize DIY. Other explanations are certainly possible. A weak explanation, though, is that you do it yourself because you enjoy doing it for the sake of it. It is a weak explanation because it is almost tautological; the original question is no different than asking *why* do you enjoy doing it? If you enjoy admiring what you yourself create, *why* do you admire what you created yourself more than what you purchased using the fruit of your comparative advantage? Or, if you want to create something for a loved one, *why* does creating something for a loved one do more for them than using your strengths and abilities to their greatest (i.e., working at you comparative advantage) in order to acquire that for them?

These questions are somewhat similar to the impish question asked by economists—why give gifts instead of giving money?[13] If you care about the well-being of the person you are giving the gift to, they are a better judge of what to buy typically, right? But as economist Tyler Cowen has pointed out, allowing cost-benefit analysis to encroach on the realm of the family (as in the case of gift-giving) may itself signal something negative about how you feel about your family, whether that is your intention or not.[14] On the narrow point, this is a reason to tread carefully and not to troll your family members too aggressively with economics. On the broader point, we should keep in mind that there may be something deeper going on in the background with respect to DIY.

Of the deeper explanations out there, the one that has been best explored is what behavioral economist Michael I. Norton and his colleagues call the "IKEA Effect"—that people are willing to pay more for something when they played some role in building it.[15] In a later paper, after examining a few alternative hypotheses (e.g., the IKEA Effect arises because people enjoy the process of making things) they argue that the IKEA Effect arises for two reasons—that people wish to signal to themselves that they are capable of performing a certain task, and that they wish to show to others that they are capable of doing so.[16]

The authors of the IKEA Effect call it signaling competence. We can then ask why it is of special importance to signal you are competent in that which is not your comparative advantage. But, more importantly, signaling competence is a hair's breadth away from "showing off," which in turn is almost synonymous with signaling status. Don't think of "status" here literally in terms of who is elected Prom Queen, but rather in terms of relative quality of genes expressed through capabilities, which in the evolutionary context, amounts to the same thing as signaling status. Does this mean we've effectively circled back to DIY as yet another outlet for signaling status?

To address that indirectly, let us return to the previously mentioned Geoffrey Miller, who elaborated on status signaling in his 2009 book, *Spent*, and at various points he acknowledged the existence of new status signaling.

Beyond status signaling, his book devotes quite a bit of time to how, more specifically, humans have the desire to express their type of personality and their intelligence. His thesis, ultimately, shows how marketing functions to convince people that products allow them to express their personality or intelligence, while Miller thinks the products in question are mostly a waste of money.

Toward the conclusion of the book, in a chapter titled "The Centrifugal Soul," Miller describes what he thinks people should do about the collection of facts he has assembled. Contrary to my expectation, Miller actually attempts to *teach* the reader how to better signal status (and type of personality and intelligence; he never draws a fine line between them in the chapter in question). This is because it is impossible to escape status hierarchies—they will always reemerge.

> Of course, human nature always leads such renouncers [of conspicuous consumption] to construct new status hierarchies of their own, based on costly behavioral displays of conscientiousness, introversion, and emotional stability...
>
> Modern renouncers are more likely to join the voluntary-simplicity movement by subscribing to *Real Simple* magazine and carrying a *Slow Food USA* tote bag. In either case, the renouncers remain awesomely self-deceived in believing that they have left behind the whole castle of self-display just by escaping the dungeon of runaway consumption. Since this type of self-deception looks naïve and witless to those who understand the evolutionary origins and functions of self-display—including my dear readers, by now—the renunciation strategy itself ends up looking stupid and childish. It speaks highly of the renouncer's conscientiousness and agreeableness, but poorly of their intelligence, experience and insight.
>
> It seems far more self-aware and creative to take a hard, conscious look at one's self-display strategies—to assess their true social and sexual goals, their reliability and efficiency of trait displays, and the many alternatives that are available.[17]

But most of his recommendations then fall entirely in line with what would soon be popular in the *Real Simple* and *Slow Food USA* (i.e., new status signaling) crowd—including buying goods at thrift shops or artisans, or doing-it-yourself. DIY thereby fits neatly with the constellation of goods described in chapter 5. But it's puzzling to *advocate* for status signaling, even if it is signaling more effectively; status signaling remains an anti-social behavior.

Yet even there, Miller grossly overstated his case. By the time Miller's book was published in 2009, society was already gaining awareness that buying a $13 croissant from an artisan is silly. While Miller wrote, "Fortunately, there are alternatives to buying new, branded, mass-produced products at full retail price from anonymous sales staff in unmemorable stores. They are not easier, but they carry much higher signaling value about one's personal traits"[18] recall that in 2009, Christian Lander's *Stuff White People Like*, in referencing exactly these types of signaling strategies in 2008, sarcastically subtitled his book, "the Unique Taste of Millions." Just as the formal mathematical models mentioned in chapter 5 show that a preference for uniqueness can lead to identical behavior, the desire to outsmart conventional signaling mechanisms leads to herding behavior. By the time Miller advocated anti-mass consumerism to better express our individuality, it was already ubiquitous across several million identical hipsters from Portland to Williamsburg. In the parlance of game theory, Miller's separating equilibrium had long already been a pooling equilibrium.

Miller does recognize that conspicuous consumption is harmful and advocates a consumption tax, but paradoxically, what he argues for in "The Centrifugal Soul" would simply be better at avoiding the tax without losing the signals of status. Moreover, earlier in the book, he criticizes a whole other class of consumer spending, not for being expressive but for being "self-stimulating," and, therefore, "narcissistic." Included in his list of "narcissistic" goods are simple sources of amusement, like hot chocolate and escapist fiction.[19] While Miller justifies this in terms of the literature in psychology on narcissism, it is difficult to conclude anything besides that he is framing it rhetorically as a persuasive definition to impugn these conventional consumer behaviors as exercises in narcissism.

What I would advocate, if we were to focus on using social science to help people live fuller, happier lives, would be to take a literature review on what practices or behaviors relate to greater subjective well-being, combine it with cost-benefit analysis, and hand it off to let people decide on their own what to do. Regarding the broader topic of this chapter, that may create some room for DIY, because people like experiencing novel things. But whatever it is in our brains that is falsely telling us that doing it ourselves is an effective practice of fiscal prudence is wrong. Furthermore, while status-seeking behavior is something we will never actually escape, it is a negative externality that people should be discouraged from doing when they have the presence of mind to avoid it. In any case, it is actively counterproductive to teach people how to do it better.

Finally, I can see two interrelated sources of disagreement that people of good faith could have with the preceding discussion. One is that "signaling competence" conceptually differs from "signaling status," and that signaling competence does not impose the same kinds of negative externalities that signaling status imposes. The other is that a more generous reading of Miller—in my mind, an excessively generous reading—is that the social signaling he is talking about facilitates the sorting of people into different subcultures or cliques just as much as it is about jockeying for status within a group. The question in my mind then, is, why is this best expressed through the mechanism of doing it yourself? I suspect that most responses to that would have to be worded carefully in order not to have a lot of overlap with ecological irrationality.

Even so, supposing a rationale could be proposed, we would be left in the conceptual conundrum of whether situations in which our psychology is lying to us ("doing it yourself is cheaper") in pursuit of unconscious ends should be thought of as rational—see chapter 5. Such a rationale would also be cold comfort to any true DIY evangelist who has spent a lifetime scoffing at those consumerist lemmings for wasting their money buying chairs at the furniture store. People get quite upset when you tell them that skills they have sunk time and energy into acquiring are not useful. The DIY evangelist is a special case of individuals who spend an exhausting amount of time trying to convince you for whatever ineffable reason that their skills are actually useful, when either the back-of-the-envelope calculation or a careful laboratory experiment would tell you they are not. These actions are a form of rent-seeking in the private sphere, and should be thought of with the same contempt we hold a lobbyist looking for a handout. They are the Social Luddites, and the topic of the next chapter.

NOTES

1. An earlier version of this argument can be found in Ryan H. Murphy, "The Diseconomies of Do-It-Yourself," *The Independent Review* 22, no. 2 (Fall 2017): 245–255.

2. Ronald H. Coase, "The Nature of the Firm," *Economica* 4, no. 16 (November 1937): 386–405.

3. Coase, "The Nature of the Firm," 388; D.H. Robertson, *Control of Industry* (London: Nisbet & Co. Ltd., 1923), 85.

4. Oliver E. Williamson, *The Transaction Cost Economics Project: The Theory and Practice of the Governance of Contractual Relations* (Northampton: Edward Elgar, 2013); Steven N. S. Cheung, "The Transaction Cost Paradigm," *Economic Inquiry* 36 (October 1998): 514–521.

5. Michael C. Munger, *Tomorrow 3.0: Transaction Costs and the Sharing Economy* (Cambridge: Cambridge University Press, 2018).

6. For a related point explored much more formally, see Martin J. Biskup, Seth Kaplan, Jill C. Bradley-Geist, and Ashley A. Membere, "Just How Miserable is Work? A Meta-Analysis Comparing Work and Non-Work Affect," *PLOS One* 14, no. 3 (March 2019): e0212594.

7. This chapter can be viewed in terms of Gary S. Becker, "A Theory of the Allocation of Time," *The Economic Journal* 75, no. 299 (September 1965): 493–517.

8. A common attitude that can arise is that the act of exchanging money is corrupting or makes something less enjoyable. Regarding the "but now it's your job" effect, I would remind the reader that as stated before, when you take a job, you are accepting to take the good parts with the bad. The bad parts are what people dread. Regarding the deeper, philosophical objection regarding the corrupting nature of exchange, see Jason Brennan and Peter M. Jaworski, *Markets without Limits*.

9. The issue here is conceptually closer to transaction costs than it may appear. Specifically, it is about what economists call the thinness of markets.

10. Allen Mendenhall, *Literature and Liberty: Essays in Libertarian Literary Criticism* (Lanham, MD: Lexington Books, 2014), 25–30; Thomas Peyser, "Capitalist Vistas: Walt Whitman and Spontaneous Order," in *Literature and the Economics of Liberty: Spontaneous Order in Culture*, ed. Paul A. Cantor and Stephen Cox (Auburn, AL: Ludwig von Mises Institute, 2009), 263–292; Brian Doherty, *Radicals for Capitalism: A Freewheeling History of the Modern American Libertarian Movement* (New York: Public Affairs, 2007), 36–38.

11. Adam Ozimek, "Dear Homesteaders, Self-Reliance is a Delusion," *Forbes*, July 29, 2017, https://www.forbes.com/sites/modeledbehavior/2017/07/29/the-delus ion-of-self-reliant-off-the-grid-living/#c126e4c343d2.

12. Robert Heinlein, *Time Enough for Love*, reissue ed. (New York: Ace, 1988): 248.

13. Joel Waldfogel, "The Deadweight Loss of Christmas," *American Economic Review* 83, no. 5 (December 1993): 1328–1336.

14. Tyler Cowen, *Discover Your Inner Economist: Use Incentives to Fall in Love, Survive Your Next Meeting, and Motivate Your Dentist* (New York: Plume, 2008), 89–92.

15. Michael I. Norton, Daneil Mochon, and Dan Ariely, "The IKEA Effect: When Labor Leads to Love," *Journal of Consumer Psychology* 22, no. 3 (July 2012): 453–460.

16. Daniel Mochon, Michael I. Norton, and Dan Ariely, "Bolstering and Restoring Feelings of Competence via the IKEA Effect," *International Journal of Research in Marketing* 29, no. 4 (December 2012): 363–369.

17. Miller, *Spent*, 256.

18. Miller, *Spent*, 258.

19. Miller, *Spent*, 58–59.

Chapter 9

Social Luddism

"Luddism" refers to the historical rebellion by industrial workers in response to the installation of labor-saving machines in factories. Luddites correctly perceived that these machines could put them out of their jobs—at least in the short-run, they would be made worse off by the introduction of new technology. As a result of this perception, they destroyed the machines. This is a fuller illustration of the tight relationship between trade and technology, as in chapter 1. There are temporary "losers" with the introduction of trade or technology, but these disruptions are the only way we get economic growth.[1] Per the early twentieth-century economist Joseph Schumpeter,

> Capitalism is essentially a process of (endogenous) economic change. Without that change or, more precisely, that kind of change which we have called evolution, capitalist society cannot exist, because the economic functions and, with the functions, the economic bases of its leading strata—of the strata which work the capitalist engine would crumble if it ceased: without innovation, no entrepreneurs; without entrepreneurial achievement, no capitalist returns and no capitalist propulsion . . . *stabilized capitalism is a contradiction in terms.*[2] [Emphasis added.]

We can empathize with someone who has lost his or her job, but growth cannot proceed if Luddism is allowed to win.

Neo-Luddism, on the other hand, embraces the destruction of technology and an end to growth, or even a return to the state of nature, today.[3] It is antithetical to the assumed starting place of this book—that our counterintuitive set of modern institutions is tremendously beneficial. But Neo-Luddism also contrasts with the original Luddism insofar as it is ideological, as Neo-Luddites do not make their arguments out of personal self-interest. Frequently, Neo-Luddism is intertwined with radical environmentalism. At the "reasonable" end of Neo-Luddism you'll find innocuous people who just seem to like camping a lot. At the other end you'll find the Unabomber; Neo-Luddism was the professed ideology of the terrorist Ted Kaczynski.[4] Neo-Luddism can thereby be as non-coercive as your choice of hobbies or as coercive as a mail bomb.

What concerns me is a modern form of Luddism that *is* self-interested, but *is not* coercive—what I am calling Social Luddism.[5] You can find a taxonomy of the varieties of anti-growth social action in figure 9.1. Social Luddism differs from conventional Luddism as it promotes itself peacefully (speech and persuasion in place of destroying property), while it differs from Neo-Luddism insofar as it is rent-seeking and self-interested, not ideological. Readers familiar with political economy may see parallels between what I am called "ideological" and "self-interested" and the "Baptists and Bootleggers" theory of legislation. According to this theory, you can find ideological parties ("Baptists") and self-interested parties ("Bootleggers") coming together to support any piece of legislation, just as the unlikely duo of Baptists and bootleggers came together to support alcohol prohibition, as the story goes. This characterization is correct and I have labeled figure 9.1 to reflect it.[6]

Social Luddites, then, are metaphorical self-interested bootleggers who use social suasion to seek rent. In many or most cases, Social Luddites may also *believe* their own stories about why what they know is useful even though it isn't. In this case, there is also a Baptist element to their behavior.

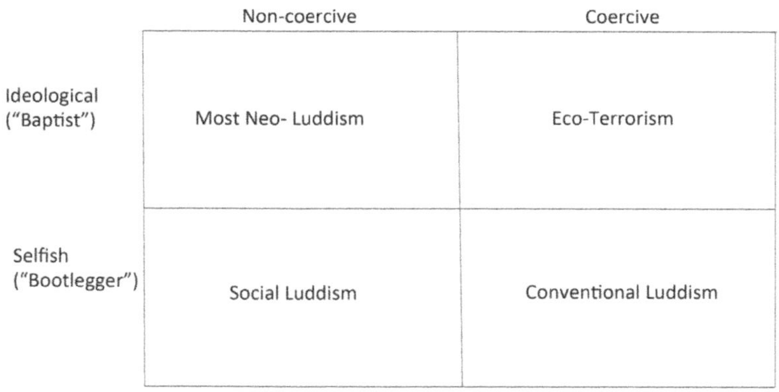

	Non-coercive	Coercive
Ideological ("Baptist")	Most Neo- Luddism	Eco-Terrorism
Selfish ("Bootlegger")	Social Luddism	Conventional Luddism

Figure 9.1   Taxonomy of Private Anti-Growth Social Action. *Source*: Author.

But just as people rationalize arguing for policies they stand to benefit from as being beneficial for the public ("what is good for General Motors is good for America"), Social Luddites may believe stories which are, ultimately, rationalizations.

What is listed in figure 9.1 is not exhaustive; other forms of nonviolent rent-seeking exist in markets besides Social Luddism. For instance, firms may invest in barriers to entry so as to maintain market (monopoly) power.[7] Some of these investments are legal and some of them are illegal. While conventional examples of barriers to entry pertain to hard economic incentives, the Social Luddite barriers to entry pertain to the imposition of *social* barriers or sanctions to maintain demand for the Social Luddite's labor services. However, Social Luddism is not limited to the enforcement of barriers to entry and includes other social rent-seeking behaviors meant to increase their income or status.

How do you convince others to believe in something that is in your own narrow self-interest, but is actually contrary to theirs? You need to fool people in ways they want to be fooled. The most effective way for the Social Luddite to seek rent or status is by playing to the tension between how people wish the world worked and how our institutional arrangements actually work. In other words, by and large, Social Luddites take advantage of the ecological irrationality of those around them. As such, this chapter can be viewed as a continuation of chapter 5, with those who have attained status through their hostility toward modern institutions now willing to spend resources on keeping their status. With that in mind, let's take a look at some concrete examples.

The example of Social Luddism that has most permeated culture is expertise in tasting wine, which is something that doesn't actually exist. While we cannot directly test wine expertise meaningfully, we can ask closely related questions that should change the mind of whoever is willing to change their mind on the topic. The first is, if wine expertise exists, shouldn't wine experts rate the same wines similarly in quality, without first observing which wines are which? Or, if a wine expert is given three of the same glasses of wine, shouldn't the expert give the wine the same (or even a similar) rating? Or, shouldn't there be a reasonably strong correlation among experts in which adjectives they use to describe a wine?

Wine experts are unable to do these things, or are far less able to do them than one would expect.[8] Moreover, getting these things right is not setting an especially *high* bar for defining the existence of expertise in wine tasting; rather, it is a remarkably *low* bar. These tests are akin to requiring someone claiming to be a literary critic to be literate. And this also isn't just about wine—similar issues arise in the expert evaluation of Stradivarius violins.[9] More fancifully, another similar paper published in 2010 found that diners are unable to reliably distinguish dog food from pâté, although I would not put as much faith in that particular result.[10]

This does not mean you can buy boxed wine or a random $2 bottle of wine and expect the same level of quality as a $20 bottle of wine. But it does raise a few issues. One is that, if experts can't consistently distinguish between the quality of most wines, the point at which "diminishing marginal returns to wine quality" may set in is at lower prices than many wine drinkers think. Second, the nature of the human capital accumulated by wine experts is the ability to speak a specifically refined gibberish that sounds convincing or profound to the general public, while sounding close enough to the refined gibberish of other wine experts. Some wine experts' livelihood depends on playing this game. For an amateur wine expert, it is a means of gaining status associated with wine expertise. But either way, the time and energy sunk into "learning" wine expertise are waste from a social standpoint. That time and energy could be used in creating skills that are actually socially useful. Meanwhile, wine could remain a product with various gradations of quality, but without the exaggerations or fabrications from wine experts.

While there are not the same kind of hard empirics on the matter, similar arguments could obviously be extended to craft beer. "Craft" seems to imply "skill," but light, cheap beer is actually often more difficult to make than craft beer.[11] In another timeline where light beers are considered artisanal and hoppy India Pale Ales (IPAs) are associated with big business, the beers we now call craft would be called crass or unsubtle, in comparison to the skill and craftsmanship needed to brew a light beer. To put this point somewhat impishly, neither craft beer nor sparkling water are thought of as being in bad taste, as light beer is. Economists often speak of bundling—putting two consumer goods together and selling them as one—as being useful and valuable for consumers. So, why not think of light beer as a bundle of craft beer and sparkling water, served in one glass? The standard reasons given for drinking light beer, like lower alcohol content, less heaviness, and easier flavor, make sense in the context of this interpretation. Light beer is a prepackaged, low alcohol, beer cocktail of beer and sparkling water. The only reason why this *sounds* bad is that it is putting a high status good (craft beer) in the same terms as a low status good (light beer), which is uncomfortable for those who have invested a lot of time and energy into appreciating craft beer.

TEXTBOX 9.1 SOME FURTHER THOUGHTS ON CRAFT BEER

While it has become a hip pastime among the upper-middle class to travel around visiting local microbreweries, it is remarkable how *similar* microbreweries are to one another. As of 2019, most microbreweries will feature an IPA, a wheat beer, a dark beer like a milk stout or a porter, a beer similar to mass American domestics that has been begrudgingly brewed for the annoying person in the party who doesn't want to try a *real* beer, and a fad zany beer made with an ingredient like gingersnap cookies or Szechuan peppercorns. I would argue that there is greater variation across the hamburgers of large fast food chains than there is variation between the selections found at two randomly chosen microbreweries.

Do not forget either that, prior to more effective refrigeration later in the post-war era, early beer aficionados would *travel* in order to try Coors beer at its source. If you recall the plot of *Smokey and the Bandit*, it was about smuggling Coors into eastern half of the United States, where it was otherwise unavailable. Multiple U.S. Presidents made special arrangements for Coors to be made available at the White House during this era.[12] Coors, in effect, was the original craft beer, in terms of how people thought of it.

Many craft beer experts will try to craft their own beer, meaning, DIY beer. Unless you live in an area where the government has made it especially difficult to buy beer (in which case I would suggest moving), learning to brew your own beer does not pass a cost-benefit analysis for the novice. It may make sense for someone who has already sunk effort into gaining the expertise and buying the equipment, but simply listing the costs of water, yeast, grain, and hops is a very incomplete assessme for most people, for the same reasons given in the previous chapter regarding DIY. And as hinted at before, more broadly speaking, the DIY advocate, in insisting that DIY is smart and that people who buy goods are being duped by businesses, are Social Luddites fighting to maintain the status associated with the human capital for DIY that they sunk time and energy into accumulating. If you see the direct parallels between the wine connoisseur and the DIY advocate, and how they seek status (or rent), you have the intuition of what Social Luddism is.

Unsurprisingly, the wine expert or beer snob values "authenticity" and buy local, which in turn means the currency they deal in is ecological irrationality, creating how-to guides for attaining status by doing something socially counterproductive.[13] Much of that and what was said above goes for foodieism more generally. I have no doubt that certain difficult-to-reach restaurants, whether in an inconvenient suburb or village of a distant country, have amazing, inexpensive food. But apply the value of your time from the previous chapter to what food you could get for the same true economic cost at a less distant restaurant before getting convinced to sink effort into traveling somewhere.

Besides hipsters, some of these practices have been championed by economist Tyler Cowen. While I agree with much of Cowen's writing on food[14] and culture,[15] I am highly skeptical of some of his more audacious claims about the quality of goods that seem defined in terms of having high non-financial barriers to accessing them, such as that the best restaurant in the world is located in the Faroe Islands.[16] I am hardly someone who claims that the world must always allocate its scarce resources efficiently, but the circumstances that would allow something like this to hold are next to impossible.

Let's move on from food. Many American high school students will read Ray Bradbury's *Fahrenheit 451*, learning the dangers of censorship in the process. The central theme of censorship is the plain reading of anyone who has read and understood the book. "Anyone" that is, except Ray Bradbury himself, who wrote *Fahrenheit 451* not to decry censorship, but to whine that people were watching television instead of reading his stories.[17] To Bradbury, feeling competition from a new technology amounted to book burning. The entire exercise of writing the book was Social Luddism; fortunately, his efforts went for naught and the book was salvaged as a paean for civil liberties instead of egotistical rent-seeking.

In chapter 2, I recounted the history of Public Choice theory. The early response by many conventional political scientists to Public Choice was, unsurprisingly, Social Luddism. Per James Buchanan himself, "Successful invasion of an established discipline by 'outsiders' generates strong emotions," with political scientists seeing "their own intellectual capital threatened with rapid depreciation, and they are led to resist."[18] Political scientists responded to their new competitor analogously to how Ray Bradbury responded to television.

Some journalists have engaged in Social Luddism as a response to the rise of the internet. While the internet spreads its share of misinformation, it also drastically removed barriers to entry for those who wish to write on current events without a degree or credential. This is unfortunate for those who do have such degrees or credentials, even as most have adapted gracefully. An example of responding *without* grace is Murray Chass, a baseball writer who was bought out[19] of his contract as a journalist and started a blog (murraychass.com), prefacing its "About" section with, "This is a site for baseball columns, not for baseball blogs. The proprietor of the site is not a fan of blogs." Or, David Warsh, an economics journalist who left *Forbes* and *The*

Boston Globe for his own site, a blog. Warsh on the blog insists "Economic Principals.com is an experiment in online economics journalism—a Web-based independent weekly commentary on the production and distribution of economic ideas. It is not a blog." It sure *sounds* like a blog, plus brazen elbowing of the blogosphere competition. The claims by Chass and Warsh ultimately do not really matter materially, but they illustrate Social Luddism perfectly.

Another insignificant example, though one that would still doubtlessly upset certain people, is the use of the font, Comic Sans. I will not fully commit to this as an example, but the YouTube popular science channel, *Vsauce*, describes the opposition to Comic Sans, in almost precisely the terms of Social Luddism. Argues the host, "Discerning type aficionados may recognize Comic Sans so quickly because it is a threat. Type design is a specialized discipline, but now anybody with a computer can take a stab at it, without your approval. They don't need you."[20] Comic Sans is annoying and "ugly" precisely because of how it is perceived to have encroached on those who have invested in gaining skills in design.

The book and movie[21] *Moneyball* tell the story of how the Major League Baseball franchise, the Oakland Athletics, were able to successfully compete for a number of years on a shoestring budget, using insights that outsiders gleaned from baseball statistics.[22] Most people think of *Moneyball* as being about applying data analytics to sports, or if you want to be a little more edgy, it is about behavioral economics,[23] or it is about entrepreneurship.[24] It's actually about Social Luddism, applied specifically to baseball. (The *Moneyball* mindset was likely the genesis of my thoughts presented in this chapter, going back to when I was a high school student.) Those wielding baseball statistics are the innovators, playing the role of the innovative manufacturing firms with new machines, while baseball scouts with expertise play the role of the factory workers smashing the machines, only using words instead of weapons. In the theatrical version of *Moneyball*, the dramatized Social Luddite scout proclaims, "Baseball isn't just numbers. It's not science, if it was, anybody can do what we're doing, but they can't because they don't know what we know. They don't have our experience and they don't have our intuition." People who tell you to trust either their experience or intuition tend to be Social Luddites.[25]

At earlier points in time, baseball players were more resistant to statistics, jealously guarding their expertise in playing and later commentating on the game with assertions of "you can't know better than me unless you played the game." One recent example is Jayson Werth, a rare holdout who stated in 2018, as he was about to retire, that "[Teams] have these super nerds, as I call them, in front offices who know nothing about baseball but they like to project numbers and project players . . . I think it's killing the game. . . . When they come down, these kids from MIT or Stanford or Harvard, wherever they're from, they've never played baseball in their life."[26] A trend running in parallel with this has been noted by film critic and journalist Sonny Bunch on the negative attitude of filmmakers and other artists have expressed toward those who criticize them but do not themselves make art.[27]

Sentiments similar to "you can't know better than me unless you played the game" can be traced in baseball history far back into the nineteenth century. Bill James, in his masterful analytic history of baseball, compiled sets of facts from every decade of baseball from the 1870s to the 1990s. He was able to identify in each decade a veteran or retired player claiming that baseball is actually now bad, far worse than baseball of his day.[28] Either baseball has become continually worse over time, even as nutrition has improved, the sport racially integrated, the baseball glove was invented, and pitchers started pitching overhand, or these players each were wrong and were instead expending resources to guard the value of their expertise against those with less experience. While James's book is now more than a decade old, evidence of old players still complaining about how the game is now bad has been documented as recently as 2018.[29]

While players are incentivized to champion the period of time they played, fans tend to valorize a golden age of baseball, the period of which, if it isn't coincidentally when they were twelve years old, tends to be the 1950s. Elsewhere in his book, James demonstrates how distorted this perspective is.[30] Attendance in baseball declined throughout the 1950s. Journalists and teams at the time blamed the rise of television which, in terms of Luddism, is a little bit on the nose. The supposedly beloved New York Giants and Brooklyn Dodgers left for new cities for the simple reason that fans weren't showing up to the games. The Giants, "in the biggest city in the nation, a team with an unparalleled wealth of tradition, boasting uncounted millions of loyal fans who would wail and lament thirty years for their lost team, a team featuring one of the greatest and most exciting players who has ever played this game—was drawing 9,000 people a game." *Baseball in New York in the 1950s was dying.* The idea that *this* is the era of baseball to romanticize is ahistorical and a little bit silly.

As in baseball, myths of classic periods of time, romanticized and promulgated by experts, are fully ensconced in the humanities and pop culture, from action films to orchestral music. According to the "learned" view, whatever is new is bad or incomparable to the classic period. But as documented by online filmmaker Kirby Ferguson, "Everything is a Remix," or stated less politely, *everything* is a rip-off of something else (see https://www.everythingisaremix. info/). For example, per Ferguson, there is very, very little that is innovative in the work of Led Zeppelin, with many of their most iconic sounds simply lifted from other artists, including the opening of "Stairway to Heaven." And while many know that there are predecessors to *Star Wars*, Ferguson shows that many of the most iconic shots from the film were directly lifted from earlier movies by George Lucas. Classic rock and the creation of the modern blockbuster were not flashes of genius, but small bits of evolution of an ongoing process combining already existing pieces of material into new-ish cultural artifacts.

And that process is still ongoing today. Setting aside genres that are actually dead (e.g., in films, romantic comedies, and westerns), as a first—but not final—approximation, the "best" of whatever subgenre in existence is something that appeared relatively recently. By "best" I mean most enjoyable in whatever way it is meant to be enjoyed (many experts will conflate "best" with "historically important" because experts are better equipped to argue about what is historically important). Today, we have more skills and technology to create better cultural products. But just as importantly, the world is now far more capable of plucking people from society to specialize in a subgenre and to create new entries in that subgenre, in a way that it never did before. This holds even if you are cynically convinced that the majority of artists or academics are wasting their time with fads, politicized drivel, and pompous nonsense. The number of people working in almost *any* area after heavily investing in the development of their skills simply dwarfs that of earlier eras. Ninety percent of everyone who ever held a PhD at any point in human history were still alive as of 2015, according to one estimate, for example.[31]

Perhaps there is an area of human achievement (I am not sure which) where there was an old master in the art from an earlier epoch who truly was so ahead of everyone else that the master's output is still better today than the best of all the modern practitioners, despite all the technological advantages any form of art or expression now has. But the fact that the storied superiority of an old master is present in literally *every* genre (whether Beethoven, Alfred Hitchcock, or Jimi Hendrix) invites skepticism. Why is it that, for all the cases we can objectively assess it, like the physics of Newton versus the physics of Hawking, that you would be laughed out of the room for suggesting the work of the old master is still better? Newton's science isn't better than what you would find in a remaindered physics textbook, after all.

For a very specific example, consider that film buffs will sometimes explain the greatness of Orson Welles as a filmmaker in *Citizen Kane* by recalling his then-innovation of cutting a hole on the movie set so he could get a low enough shot to evoke the intended mood.[32] That Welles did this may make him important historically, but it has nothing to do with how enjoyable the film is today, when contemporary films produced will use these tactics whenever it is appropriate. These types of arguments and anecdotes are a common form of "gotchas" used by Social Luddites when arguing for one thing or another. That Welles did it first is unrelated to its quality today—these kinds arguments are little more than trivia.

Exceptions to this presumption of progress across types of human achieve-ment (e.g., professional boxing is probably worse today) are demonstrative of how much society must change for the old masters to be superior to the new. Such a claim isn't "scientism" or "whiggism" as much as it is reflecting on the fact that such a large number of smart people is dedicated to every pursuit of interest, even tiny subgenres or heterodoxies,[33] that it is ridiculous to argue, as the experts will, that the classic work of the old master is better. And regarding whiggism, nothing I am saying here is about inevitable human progress; if our institutional environment collapses, then the twenty-first cen-tury will in fact be the classic period for any subgenre, not the future-present. "Things are getting better, on average," is roughly synonymous with per capita GDP growth. Constant claims that everything around us isn't what it once was while GDP increases is GDP trutherism. But if GDP begins to trend downwards, the presumption disappears.

People whine endlessly and perpetually about the decline of culture. Either this is always wrong or we need to go all the way back in time when literacy rates were much lower to find a time when culture was good. Steven John-son has investigated the popularity of middle-highbrow work like Charles Dickens, which is often cited as what was popular when culture was good and people were willing to pick up a book, versus the popularity of middle-highbrow cultural products of today. He found that the sales of a typical Charles Dickens novel relative to the size of the population of Great Britain at the time are dwarfed by the penetration of middle-highbrow cultural products like *The Sopranos* in recent history.[34] Quite the opposite of "dumbing down" has happened in mass media over time.

We still read the philosophy of Classical Athens. At its peak, it had far fewer than 100,000 people with rights, all of them men.[35] We have two pos-sibilities. One is that there isn't a better statement on philosophy from *some-one* in the modern world than the statements of the few dozen or so people who decided to start a philosophy club in Classical Athens. The second is that many philosophers and their lay audience are so heavily invested in hav-ing learned the work of the Classical Athens philosophy club that they work hard to convince everyone that the Classical Athens philosophy club is still relevant. Which is more likely?

Let me also emphasize the distinction between philosophy itself (original-ity of ideas does not matter; the origins of concepts are trivia) and the study of the *history* of philosophy (where the origins of ideas are a key point). With that in mind, I would argue that the notion that the "Great Books" curriculum is somehow the secret sauce for critical thinking and wisdom is itself Social Luddism. The amount of time one must spend reading the "Great Books" per unit of knowledge is utterly preposterous. While there is something to be said for the Hirschian idea that an important purpose of education is to bring students up to speed on the cultural ideas used in public discourse,[36] one hardly needs to read a 300-year-old book to accomplish the small task of learning what it is and why it is important. Assertions and pseudo-arguments in favor of actually going and reading the "Great Books" amount to a colossal make-work scheme for those who have gone through the trouble of studying the "Great Books" closely. With luck, these curricula will continue to fizzle out along with other forms of education that amount to classical status signaling, like finishing schools or fencing.

One could *ad hoc* another social function served by any of the "classics." I wouldn't be opposed to certain, limited framings. For instance, because the human mind is so good at following narratives, learning philosophy through a historically unfolding story may make different perspectives sink in more deeply. Or reading an original text may inspire more conversation than simply reading and understanding a secondary source that tells you, far more comprehensibly, what the text says. But these are distant from claims that the classics are actually preferable to read on their own merits or worthy of your time compared to the relevant alternatives. They aren't.

Romanticizing earlier periods reflects the pessimism of ecological irrationality. If you believe in GDP statistics showing how rapidly things have changed for the better, the idea that almost every form of human art, expression, or study actually had its golden period somewhere between 20 years ago and 4,000 years ago makes little sense. As a first approximation, the golden period of whatever it is we are talking about is today. In exchange for high status or a paycheck, the Social Luddite expert preys on irrational pessimism by lecturing on the greatness of the mythical past, instead of recognizing the excellence of the present. While one may question the practical importance of all this, Social Luddism has permeated much of our culture, including that which is thought of as highbrow.

A final and substantive example of Social Luddism is the modern war against the development and implementation of metrics, big data, algorithms, and artificial intelligence (AI). There is a significant possibility that algorithms and the use of artificial intelligence will be an important source of economic growth in the future,[37] and cultural pushback preventing the implementation of algorithms is dangerous for future technological progress. Obviously, if algorithms outcompete experts, that is bad for the job prospects for experts, although the rest of the world would be better off with the expert employed elsewhere in the economy.

As documented by behavioral economist Daniel Kahneman, algorithms already win in many cases, even with complex tasks like medical diagnoses, though the human mind is disinclined toward using algorithms in place of human judgment.[38] A formal meta-analysis published in the year 2000 found algorithms to already be superior in medicine.[39] While Social Luddites blather on about how AI cannot grasp the subtleties of human creation, AI has already gone as far as making novel scientific discoveries.[40] The resistance documented by Kahneman can be thought of as the naturalistic fallacy and ecological irrationality, as in chapter 4. People are just very resistant to exactly these kinds of technologies. From *2001: A Space Odyssey* on, whenever artificial intelligence appears in fiction, it will almost inevitably malfunction or try to kill everyone.[41] Giving dire warnings about algorithms or AI is very much fooling people in the way they want to be fooled.

Two recent books opposing these technologies can be found in *Weapons of Math Destruction* by Cathy O'Neil[42] and *The Tyranny of Metrics* by Jerry Muller.[43] While I would agree with these works that the technologies may challenge our moral intuitions and, improperly specified, lead to bad consequences, they should be free to compete with expertise. Expertise, after all, can also fail on either of these margins. We should give algorithms a chance, as we would give a more "natural" human competitor a chance. To do otherwise is to carry water for the Social Luddite experts who are really just worried about keeping their jobs, economic progress be damned. It would be a gross error to allow modern Social Luddites to take a metaphorical hammer to our most promising new machines of today because these new machines make us feel squeamish.

A provocative example of AI is the application of artificial intelligence to criminal justice proceedings. One way it can be used is to better anticipate recidivism rates (i.e., who is at risk of reoffending). In response to this technology, many reference *Minority Report*, as if citing a science fiction story makes you informed about the costs and benefits of an application of artificial intelligence. Instead, one can recognize that the current criminal justice system already has demonstrable inequities and failings, and investigate how AI can be used to mitigate them. In response to Cathy O'Neil, public policy analyst Caleb Watney writes,

> But places where human bias is most prevalent offer some of the most exciting opportunities for the application of algorithms. Humans appear to be really, really bad at administering justice by ourselves. We judge people based on how traditionally African American their facial features look, we penalize overweight defendants, we let unrelated factors like football games affect our decision making, and more fundamentally, we can't systematically update our priors in light of new evidence. All this means that we can gain a lot by partnering with AI, which can offset some of our flaws.[44]

We live in an imperfect world with no perfect solutions. If we allow the imperfection of new technology to dictate that it cannot be used because they feel unnatural, we are damning ourselves to stagnation.

Across the examples found in this chapter, the Social Luddite increases demand for their skills or abilities they previously invested in gaining, either as a means of improving their employment outlook or to gain social status. Even if they do not apply it to professional employment, expertise in wine or craft beer has conferred experts' status. Journalists don't like being forced to compete with anyone competent enough to get an account at a blogging website. Athletes don't like the idea of part of their role or importance being displaced by a dork with a spreadsheet. For most of the arts and humanities, we should expect the best of whatever interests us to be a recent creation, not something from a few decades or a few millennia ago.

Common themes emerge regarding Social Luddism upon collecting these stories, anecdotes, and ideas. One is to be suspicious when people claim expertise but are unwilling to put that expertise to any tangible test. For progress to take place, new ideas must be able to compete against entrenched interests. Even when entrenched interests do not seek legislation to protect themselves, they can use words and social suasion to prevent their knowledge or experience from being put to the test—whether that means experimentally, intellectually, through market competition, or some combination of all three. Viewing progress in these terms parallels the mechanisms of biological evolution, the growth of scientific knowledge, and entrepreneurship in the market economy.[45] For progress to take place, we must not allow the conventional or Social Luddite to stand in the way.

My discussion of Social Luddism makes it clear that those claiming expertise are self-interested and somewhat noxious, and "expertise" often preys upon ecological irrationality. Yet the first part of this book almost took it for granted that experts are correct, and expertise is a good thing. Remember free trade? Remember childhood vaccination? It would be self-serving of me if I claimed that economic experts deserve your deference but wine experts do not, and left it at that. The following chapter, therefore, puts into focus when to trust experts, as in the case of childhood vaccination, and when not to trust experts, as in the case wine expertise, and is unable to come to any comfortable conclusion.

NOTES

1. Joseph Schumpeter, *The Theory of Economic Development* (Cambridge: Harvard University Press, 1934).

2. Joseph Schumpeter, *Business Cycles: A Theoretical, Historical, and Statistical Analysis*, Volume II (New York: McGraw-Hill, 1939), 1033.

3. A clear starting point for Neo-Luddism (and even ecological irrationality more broadly) is the work of Jean-Jacques Rousseau, but a work that is even more

explicit on these terms is Polanyi, *The Great Transformation*. However, Polanyi's rise in prominence is a somewhat recent development, as documented by Daniel Immerwahr, "Polanyi in the United States: Peter Drucker, Karl Polanyi, and the Midcentury Critique of Economic Society," *Journal of the History of Ideas* 70, no. 3 (July 2009): 445–466. For an example of "free market" Neo-Luddism, see Karl Hess, *Community Technology* (New York: Harper & Row, 1979). However, at this point in time, Polanyi is the figure who is most clearly echoed by those who are hostile to the institutions of modernity.

4. Ted Kaczynski, "Industrial Society and Its Future," *The Washington Post*, September 22, 1995, https://www.washingtonpost.com/wp-srv/national/longterm/unabomber/manifesto.text.htm.

5. The closest work to Social Luddism I am aware of (and it is quite distant) is the position of Tyler Cowen, *In Praise of Commercial Culture* (Cambridge: Harvard University Press, 1998), 181–210. There is also some overlap with sociologists of knowledge Berger and Luckmann on expertise, although my analysis concerns only a subset of experts. See Peter Berger and Thomas Luckmann, *The Social Construction of Reality: A Treatise in the Sociology of Knowledge* (New York: Anchor Books, 1996); c.f. Roger Koppl, *Expert Failure* (New York: Cambridge University Press, 2017), 33–37; Roger Koppl, "The Social Construction of Expertise," *Society* 47, no. 3 (May 2010): 220–226. I will address Koppl's position in greater detail in chapter 10.

6. Bruce Yandle, "Bootleggers and Baptists: The Education of a Regulatory Economist," *Regulation* 7, no. 3 (May/June 1983): 12–16.

7. See for example, Kip Viscusi et al., *Economics of Regulation and Antitrust*, 168–172.

8. For a literature review, see Karl Storchmann, "Wine Economics," *Journal of Wine Economics* 7, no. 1 (May 2012), 24–27.

9. Claudia Fritz, Joseph Curtin, Jacques Poitevineau, Palmer Morel-Samuels, and Fan-Chia Tao, "Player Preferences among New and Old Violins," *Proceedings of the National Academy of Sciences of the United States of America* 109, no. 3 (January 2012): 760–763.

10. John Bohannon, Robin Goldstein, and Alexis Herschkowitsch, "Can People Distinguish Pâté from Dog Food?" *Chance* 23, no. 2 (2010): 43–46.

11. This may not be true in each and every case, but broadly speaking, light beer is on average far more difficult to make and has the grudging respect of microbrewers. See *Mental Floss*, "Scientific Reasons to Respect Light Beer," October 31, 2012, http://mentalfloss.com/article/12940/scientific-reasons-respect-light-beer.

12. *Time*, "BREWING: The Beer That Won the West," February 11, 1974, http://content.time.com/time/magazine/article/0,9171,908509,00.html.

13. For wine experts and beer snobs in particular, Social Luddites appeal to more than ecological irrationality to fool people, namely by stroking the ego of their patrons. It should go without saying there is more than one way that people want to be fooled.

14. Cowen, *An Economist Gets Lunch*.

15. Tyler Cowen, *Creative Destruction: How Globalization is Changing the World's Cultures* (Princeton: Princeton University Press, 2002).

16. Tyler Cowen, "Is KOKS the Best Restaurant in the World?" *Marginal Revolution*, August 17, 2016, https://marginalrevolution.com/marginalrevolution/2016/08/koks.html.

17. Amy E. Boyle, "Ray Bradbury: Fahrenheit 451 Misinterpreted," *LA Weekly*, May 30, 2007, https://www.laweekly.com/news/ray-bradbury-fahrenheit-451-misinterpreted-2149125.

18. As quoted in Steven G. Medema, *The Hesitant Hand: Taming Self-Interest in the History of Economic Ideas* (Princeton: Princeton University Press, 2009), 141. These are two quotations collected by Medema which I spliced together.

19. Staci D. Kramer, "High-Profile Buyouts Won't Save the New York Times From Newsroom Layoffs: Memo," *The Washington Post*, April 15, 2008, http://www.washingtonpost.com/wp-dyn/content/article/2008/04/15/AR2008041502597_pf.html.

20. At timestamp 5:37 of Vsauce, "A Defense of Comic Sans," February 11, 2013, https://www.youtube.com/watch?v=GUCcObwIsOs.

21. Michael Lewis, *Moneyball: The Art of Winning and Unfair Game* (New York: Norton, 2003).

22. Books have also been written about the Tampa Bay Rays and the Pittsburgh Pirates taking similar approaches and exploiting market inefficiencies. See Jonah Keri, *The Extra 2%: How Wall Street Strategies Took a Major League Baseball Team from Worst to First* (New York: ESPN Books, 2011); Travis Sawchik, *Big Data Baseball: Math, Miracles, and the End of a 20-Year Losing Streak* (New York: Flatiron Books, 2015).

23. This is the perspective of Paul DePodesta, one of the central figures of *Moneyball*. See Lewis, *Moneyball*, 18; c.f. Tobias J. Moskowitz and L. Jon Wertheim, *Scorecasting: The Hidden Influence Behind How Sports Are Played and Games Are Won* (New York: Crown Archetype, 2011).

24. Stephen Shmanske, "Austrian Themes, Data, and Sports Economics," *Review of Austrian Economics* 20, no. 1 (March 2007): 11–24.

25. I should note that much of what was presented in *Moneyball* was wrong. Scouting and scouting expertise are immensely valuable, and research in baseball since has often concluded that baseball wisdom derided for decades by analysts ended up being correct. But the point is to favor processes by which differing perspectives are able to compete, not that applied econometrics is the solution to everything. A recent example of the conventional wisdom continuing to be proven true can be found in Dan Brooks, Harry Pavlidis, and Jonathan Judge, "Moving Beyond WOWY: A Mixed Approach to Measuring Catcher Framing," *Baseball Prospectus*, February 5, 2015, https://www.baseballprospectus.com/news/article/25514/moving-beyond-wowy-a-mixed-approach-to-measuring-catcher-framing/.

26. *ESPN.com*, "Jayson Werth Rails Against 'Super Nerds' That Are 'Killing the Game'," August 9, 2018, http://www.espn.com/mlb/story/_/id/24329670/jayson-werth-rails-super-nerds-killing-game.

27. Sonny Bunch, "Criticism is Conversation, Not an Assault on Your Identity," *The Washington Post*, May 8, 2019, https://www.washingtonpost.com/opinions/2019/05/08/criticism-is-conversation-not-an-assault-your-identity/?utm_term=.bbd a36051175.

28. Bill James, *The New Bill James Historical Baseball Abstract*, revised ed. (New York: The Free Press, 2003).

29. Meg Rowley, "Let Us Like Baseball," *Fangraphs*, August 2, 2018, https://www.fangraphs.com/blogs/let-us-like-baseball/.

30. James, *The New Bill James Historical Baseball Abstract*, 240–241.

31. Eric Gastfriend, "90% of All Scientists That Have Ever Lived Are Alive Today," *Future of Life Institute*, November 5, 2015, https://futureoflife.org/2015/11/05/90-of-all-the-scientists-that-ever-lived-are-alive-today/

32. For example, Marina Caitlin Watts, "WATCH ME IF YOU CAN: 25 Things You Probably Didn't Know About Citizen Kane," *The Cornell Daily Sun*, March 11, 2016, https://cornellsun.com/2016/03/11/watch-me-if-you-can-25-things-you-probably-didnt-know-about-citizen-kane/; many other examples of film buffs citing this fact can be found using a search engine.

33. Heterodoxies in social science often look backwards in their rivalry with the orthodoxy. One example making this argument explicitly is Peter J. Boettke, Christopher J. Coyne, and Peter T. Leeson, "Earw(h)ig: I Can't Hear You Because Your Ideas Are Old," *Cambridge Journal of Economics* 38, no. 3 (May 2014): 531–544. It is my contention that the new statements by the heterodoxy, or the modern secondary literature within the heterodoxy, are more useful statements than the historical primary literature, unless it is your intention to do explicitly historical work with the primary literature.

34. Steven Johnson, *Everything Bad is Good for You* (New York: Riverhead Books, 2005), 133–135.

35. Christopher W. Blackwell, "The Assembly," *Dēmos: Classical Athenian Democracy*, March 26, 2003, http://www.stoa.org/projects/demos/article_assembly?page=2&greekEncoding=UnicodeC.

36. E.D. Hirsch, *Cultural Literacy: What Every American Needs to Know* (Boston: Houghton Mifflin, 1987).

37. Phillipe Aghion, Benjamin F. Jones, and Charles I. Jones, "Artificial Intelligence and Economic Growth," in *The Economics of Artificial Intelligence: An Agenda*, ed. Ajay Agrawal, Joshua Gans, and Avi Doldfarb, 237–282 (Chicago: University of Chicago Press, 2019).

38. Daniel Kahneman, *Thinking, Fast and Slow* (New York: Farrar, Straus and Giroux, 2011), 222–233; 234–244; c.f. Eric Topol, *Deep Medicine: How Artificial Intelligence Can Make Healthcare Human Again* (New York: Basic Books, 2019).

39. William M. Grove, David H. Zald, Boyd S. Lebow, Beth E. Snitz, and Chad Nelson, "Clinical Versus Mechanistic Prediction: A Meta-Analysis," *Psychological Assessment* 12, no. 1 (March 2000): 19–30.

40. Ryan Poplin, Avinash V. Varadarajan, Katy Blumer, Yun Liu, Michael V. McConnell, Greg S. Corrado, Lily Peng, and Dale R. Webster, "Prediction of Cardiovascular Risk Factors from Retinal Fundus Photographs via Deep Learning," *Nature*

Biomedical Engineering 2, no. 3 (March 2018): 158–164. A more recent, perhaps even more impressive example is Vahe Tshitoyan, John Dagdelen, Leigh Weston, Alexander Dunn, Ziqin Rong, Olga Kononova, Kristin A. Persson, Gerbrand Ceder, and Anubhav Jain, "Unsupervised Word Embeddings Captured Latent Knowledge from Materials Science Literature," *Nature* 571 (2019): 95–98.

41. For a listing of the many, many instances of this appearing in media, see *tvtropes*, "A.I. Is a Crapshoot," accessed July 15, 2019, https://tvtropes.org/pmwiki/pmwiki.php/Main/AIIsACrapshoot.

42. Cathy O'Neil, *Weapons of Math Destruction: How Big Data Increases Inequality and Threatens Democracy* (New York: Crown, 2016).

43. Jerry Z. Muller, *The Tyranny of Metrics* (Princeton: Princeton University Press, 2018).

44. Caleb Watney, "Fairy Dust, Pandora's Box.... or a Hammer," *Cato Unbound*, August 9, 2017, https://www.cato-unbound.org/2017/08/09/caleb-watney/fairy-dust-pandoras-box-or-hammer.

45. C.f. Matt Ridley, *The Evolution of Everything: How Ideas Emerge* (New York: Harper, 2015); Karl Popper, *Objective Knowledge: An Evolutionary Approach* (Oxford: Clarendon Press, 1972); David A. Harper, *Entrepreneurship and the Market Process: An Enquiry into the Growth of Knowledge* (London: Routledge, 1996).

Chapter 10

Whither Expertise?

The starting point for modern research on the social value of expertise is found in the 2005 book by psychologist Philip Tetlock, *Expert Political Judgment*.[1] Tetlock established a first-of-its-kind tournament measuring whether expert pundits and academics have any ability to predict future events over long periods of time. The answer may be familiar to what you would expect from the last chapter. Experts have far less ability to predict than one would reasonably expect, by some measure no better than monkeys throwing darts at a dartboard. The common reading of Tetlock's work became a populist one—that all the flashy credentials and school learning by the experts didn't do much of anything, and that experts are no better than the putative man on the street.[2]

The problem is that the populist reading of Tetlock is wrong. While Tetlock's data gave reason for being skeptical about the predictive ability of the typical pundit, the experts still outperformed the man on the street.[3] In later retellings of *Expert Political Judgment*,[4] Tetlock places greater emphasis on his finding that specific kinds of experts—these not falling on partisan lines—perform better than others, and we can identify and understand the tactics they use to predict more accurately. The tactics have little to do with tacit populist wisdom or worldliness, but instead are about engaging in difficult, counterintuitive, and highly numerate modes of thought.[5] Tetlock's work, unfortunately, has hardly been integrated into highbrow political discourse. For example, although a common trope on social media among some public intellectuals is to mock excessive precision in predictions (e.g., "2.11%? You sure you don't mean 2.1095345?"), Tetlock has found that those who report their predictions more precisely provide more accurate forecasts.[6]

Moreover, the Social Luddite "experts" found in the previous chapter are not difficult targets. Much of the knowledge Social Luddites hold is intentionally obfuscated, because it doesn't actually exist—Social Luddites *hate* making predictions that have teeth. But there are fields, such as medicine, where the non-conspiratorial among us would expect experts can be generally trusted. Yet, even if we restrict ourselves to the more trustworthy fields, signs for alarm are everywhere. For instance, nutritional science is in utter shambles. Arguably, all theories of nutrition seem equally plausible at this point, including something resembling conventional nutrition advice, nihilism toward all nutritional research, and diets (like low carb diets) which imply that conventional nutrition advice is more often than not *bad* for your health.[7]

A motivating example: it would also be nice if medical doctors would get themselves to remember to, you know, wash their hands between seeing patients. The Center for Disease Control must send out periodic reminders[8] to these well-trained professional doctors to do something they should have learned by the time they entered preschool because many of them apparently still cannot be bothered to do so. Meanwhile, a huge number of patients are adversely affected by healthcare-associated infections (HAIs). The CDC estimated that in 2015, there were 6,87,000 infections caused by what people caught in the hospital, not what they arrived with. This lead to an estimated 72,000 deaths over the course of the year.[9] While only a fraction of these infections can be traced to medical professionals failing to wash their hands, the World Health Organization tells us,

> Hand hygiene contributes significantly to keeping patients safe. It is a simple, low-cost action to prevent the spread of many of the microbes that cause healthcare-associated infections (HAI). While hand hygiene is not the only measure to counter HAI, compliance with it alone can dramatically enhance patient safety, because there is much scientific evidence showing that microbes causing HAI are most frequently spread between patients on the hands of health-care workers.[10]

In chapter 4, we examined the implicit economic costs, in terms of the additional risks borne by their children, for parents who do not vaccinate them. Just as we did for vaccines, we can analyze the yearly costs medical professionals impose by killing patients (if not murder, this should be considered criminally negligent homicide) by not washing their hands. Unlike my analysis of vaccinations, I will only be focusing on actual deaths caused by HAIs, not changes in rates of infection.

Let us follow chapter 4 and use the EPA value for the statistical value of a human life ($9.4 million in 2019 dollars). Then we can make a trio of alternative assumptions to serve as upper, middle, and lower bounds for the cost of poor medical professional hand hygiene: (1) that *all* patients who died of

HAIs were the result of medical professionals failing to wash their hands, (2) that half died for that reason, and (3) that 1 percent died for that reason. The first assumption yields a value of $677 billion, the second a value of $338 billion, and the third a value of $6.8 billion. That is to say, reasonable lower and upper bounds for the economic cost of medical professionals being too lazy to wash their hands is $6.8 billion and $677 billion per year, respectively. By the way, the $677 billion figure is approximately 3 percent of the U.S. GDP.

One would think the medical establishment would have learned this lesson already. The nineteenth-century Hungarian physician, Ignaz Semmelweis, surmised that high rates of mortality from childbed fever at maternity clinics were due to medical students going straight from examining cadavers to delivering babies. The changes he instituted led to dramatic declines in death rates at his clinics. Following the proposal of his hypothesis, as thanks, the medical profession ostracized him, and Semmelweis died in a mental institution at age forty-seven.[11]

Outside of medicine, social science research is in disarray due to what is known as the Replication Crisis. As a result of a technical issue which lies somewhere between bad methodology, poorly designed institutional incentives, and fraud, large swaths of empirical research have been shown to be simply wrong, with the field of social psychology acting as patient zero for the crisis. Worse, many of these results had been publicized extensively through the boom a decade ago in popular nonfiction in behavioral economics and social psychology. For the foreseeable future, these false findings will be repeated by the "informed" public. The most important casualty of the Replication Crisis so far is *priming*, an experimental tool used across many social sciences (but especially social psychology) to test a variety of hypothesis. Priming posits that rather inconsequential cues in the environment can have a meaningful effect on behavior. It appears that priming isn't actually real. It is not yet well-understood how much the Replication Crisis will more broadly impact findings in the rest of the social sciences, including those of economics.[12] Whoops.

As experts, economists' hands are not clean either, so to speak. As argued by economic historians David M. Levy and Sandra Peart,[13] economists have historically fought efforts to make their positions transparent and open to public discussion. Levy and Peart's collection of historical episodes, which they emphatically separate from political beliefs of economists,[14] includes the late nineteenth-century intellectual infatuation with eugenics,[15] the papering over of failed predictions in introductory economics textbooks by simply changing the dates of the predictions,[16] and quashing the discussion of more robust methods for rating corporate bonds. Levy and Peart's position differs from my own in its scope and focus, but each of these episodes reflects economic experts behaving badly.

Those examples are closer to intellectual history than problems with contemporary economists, but a 2018 Initiative on Global Markets (IGM) poll of elite economists asked whether, through regulation, requiring a graduate degree in economics for all senior-level public policy positions in government would improve economic policy.[17] Overall, economists said, "yes." One could try to excuse this—I suspect that the response to the poll would be more strongly in the affirmative for other fields like law or medicine—but the optics are awful: economists decry occupational licenses for every profession except their own.

Among the most forceful critics of economic experts from within the economics profession is William Easterly, a development economist at New York University. Easterly spent much of his career at the World Bank, where he developed a research program critical of his own institution and others like it, such as the International Monetary Fund (IMF). A primary function of these institutions is to provide development aid, that is, grants and loans intended to give a hand up to developing countries. Easterly believes that the aid is often counterproductive. After receiving permission from the World Bank, he voiced his viewpoint in 2001's *The Elusive Quest for Growth*.[18] Following the book's publication and success, the World Bank forced Easterly out of his position. Easterly argues that what the global poor needs to succeed is both economic freedom and political rights, and that the development aid doled out by institutions or foreign governments serve mainly to entrench the kleptocrats in power. What "foreign aid" has too often amounted to is handing stacks of money to the same political leaders who are at fault for keeping the global poor poor. This line of research later culminated in *The Tyranny of Experts: Economists, Dictators, and the Forgotten Rights of the Poor* in 2014.[19]

Easterly's position on development aid is within the scholarly mainstream, although not at the center of it.[20] I agree with Easterly regarding development aid, but I am less sure about his judgments regarding experts. As he notes, the emergence of the development community, including the World Bank, coincided with the onset of the Cold War. Pro-West international institutions avoided antagonizing allies run by predatory governments who opposed the Soviets in the Cold War to keep them in the West's orbit. For that reason, the World Bank and the IMF policy did little to promote democracy. In the decades following their founding, these institutions also advocated for developing countries to employ heavy-handed state intervention as a means of achieving economic growth. Those interventions included various soft socialist policies like extensive public ownership and protectionist "import substitution," which have largely been discredited—if not then, then certainly since.

It is fair to characterize an expert who pairs an ambivalence toward predatory autocrats with advocacy of central planning as "tyrannical," as Easterly does. But does this characterization still apply today? *Worldwide Governance Indicators* (WGI), first mentioned in chapter 6, is a policy index published by the World Bank and used to advocate for a relatively sane set of government policies. In addition to sound economic policies, WGI also includes a dimension called "Voice and Accountability," which is, effectively, a measure of democracy. Taking this into account, today's experts at the World Bank and IMF seem to be pulling the institutions in a democratic, market-friendly direction.[21] The foreign aid may be counterproductive, but if the aid is to be given out, it is better to be given out in conjunction with advice using sound economic expertise rather than the alternative, no?[22]

So why single out the *experts* in this story? For a period—albeit an extended one—development economists had some bad ideas in their heads, and they made the world worse in pushing those ideas. But today, if institutions like the World Bank and the IMF are still doing more bad than good by implicitly or explicitly supporting autocrats, it's better to have that paired with good policy recommendations on free trade and protecting property rights. Economic expertise is superfluous to Easterly's story—the force of his argument for today falls and rises with whether aid props up predatory governments.

I also see my position as distinct from a recent statement on experts, *Expert Failure* by Roger Koppl. Koppl sees "populism and the rule of experts, at least in their more extreme forms, [as] equally inconsistent with pluralistic democracy."[23] Koppl wishes to subject experts to competition and to allow for pluralistic decision-making.[24] This is my preference as well, but much of which I tried to argue in earlier chapters was that, at the *meta*-level, *experts are in closer agreement with Koppl and myself on the issues of democracy, pluralism, and competition, than what the members of the public would choose pluralistically.* The baseline presumption ought to be that the typical bureaucrat agrees with the statement that Trade Is Good more than does the median voter, for example.[25]

Other issues are illustrated by Richard Thaler and Cass Sunstein in their influential 2008 book on the application of behavioral economics to public policy, *Nudge*.[26] Thaler and Sunstein, calling their position "libertarian paternalism," argue that defaults should be shifted and incentives framed such that more people end up doing what experts think they should do, even though they would still be, technically, "free to choose" whatever they want. "Libertarian paternalist" proposals include rearranging snacks at the checkout counter so that healthier options are easier to see, or changing the default choice for retirement savings to encourage workers to save more of their income.

As innocuous as this sounds, libertarian paternalism also offers another reason for caution: the aforementioned Replication Crisis has undermined much of the social psychology which serves as the intellectual backbone of behavioral economics. For instance, one of Thaler and Sunstein's strongest motivating examples for their approach was the work of Brian Wansink,[27] who later would exemplify practicing the worst of what was called into question by the Replication Crisis.[28] Even as Thaler and Sunstein worked hard and carefully to create a palatable application of the insertion of expert opinion into public policy, they were quickly betrayed by the bad behavior of experts.

Discussing Thaler and Sunstein also raises a deeper concern that I have avoided addressing so far in this book—what is the proper role of paternalism? Ecological irrationality expressed through political institutions is a problem, in part, because it imposes costs on others. That is one problem. But we also care about other people screwing up their own lives. Homeopathy matters and is bad not just because it may facilitate the spread of infectious disease and cause negative effects on third parties. We also don't want other people to be fooled by charlatans. That sentiment is still a kind of paternalism.

Politics tends to warp whatever you feed into it, regardless of your goals or the goodness of your intentions. There is good reason to believe that new excuses for intervening in people's lives will go south when [whichever political party you dislike more] gains power. This is true even for the softer touch of libertarian paternalism.[29] We need to tread lightly with paternalism. Yet there is a parallel between the approach of Thaler and Sunstein and the approach of Jason Brennan: epistocracy is paternalism for democracy.

Regarding experts, there are, ultimately, three problems we must confront, two concerning facts and one concerning our values. The first is that even our "good" experts who assist society in making better decisions are themselves human with their own particular interests. This corresponds to, essentially, the principal-agent problem in economics:[30] we cannot perfectly monitor who we hire and corroborate that they do what we are paying them to do. We cannot be sure, for instance, that every bit of advice our medical doctors give us is entirely with our interests in mind. How much can this problem be mitigated?

The second is, how can everyday people figure out which experts carry useful knowledge, and which experts are hucksters? To some extent, competition (Koppl's favored solution) would weed out hucksters. But Social Luddites specialize in fooling people in ways they want to be fooled; markets aren't going to weed them out if they are fulfilling a "real demand" for how people want to be fooled. One would need to compare Koppl's imperfect solution with how well government bureaucracies (e.g., the Center for Disease Control, the Federal Reserve) are themselves at distinguishing expertise from snake oil, and whether the (sometimes) higher stakes for bureaucrats can effectively incentivize them to make a better call.

The final question is one of balancing our values. We want to get decisions "right" in terms of some utilitarian calculus—we want substantive free trade and the kids to get vaccinated. But our values and institutions are premised on the importance of individual choice, pluralism, and freedom. If we place all the weight on getting the decisions "right," it is at the expense of living in the free society we want to live in.

Let's move onto something more tangible. An excellent example of an expert providing expertise while respecting others' autonomy is Brown University health economist Emily Oster and her pair of books on pregnancy and parenting, *Expecting Better*[31] and *Cribsheet*.[32] Health experts, doctors, and nutritionists generally appear actively hostile to the idea that anyone would place any value whatsoever on anything besides their health. Most of these experts feel the need to demand everyone must eliminate all minimal or speculative risks to their health, no matter how costly they are to eliminate.[33]

In contrast, Oster presents the costs and benefits of common pieces of health advice (e.g., must women eliminate *all* alcohol when they are pregnant?) fairly and cogently, whereas the conventional expert wishes to turn the volume up to eleven for any and all demands to prioritize health. Not to downplay the worthiness of Oster's work, but it should not have taken this long for an honest, clear explanation of scientific research that encourages people to make their own decisions to appear on store shelves. It speaks ill of the medical profession that its members are so unwilling to convey facts in this form.

In fields where there is no Oster, there currently isn't an effective way for the layperson to distinguish scientific fact from quackery among experts. The more numerate you are, the better equipped you are to tell the difference between science and snake oil. But becoming more numerate is costly. We are rationally ignorant in conducting the business of our own lives, not just in politics, after all.[34] But if you are willing to take the deep dive on both becoming numerate and reading sets of academic literatures, that is, of course, an option. The age of the internet has made it far easier to collect, catalogue, and analyze a large number of disparate facts than ever before. But the disposition to find doing such a thing to be enjoyable is limited to a small number of personality types.[35] Other communities online (such as "LessWrong") have themselves gone through this process of diving through literatures for you, but even reading these summaries is tedious for a layperson.

We can encourage experts to become clearer and more scrupulous in communicating the costs and benefits of the choices we make. And we can hope that the population becomes more numerate, and less susceptible to snake oil. But we must eventually confront when and where expertise is allowed to override pluralism. So far, I have explicitly limited examples of ecological irrationality to whether a given means was appropriate for attaining a stated end. If we take ecological irrationality into practical politics, we would start running into issues that are clearly value-laden, such as the teaching of evolution in public schools. The tension between the dual goals of reducing ecological irrationality and preserving pluralism is most obvious when we consider teaching evolution, or when we confront some of the more value-laden arguments made against childhood vaccination.

The fundamental tension between these social values runs parallel to what political philosopher Jacob T. Levy addresses in his recent book, *Rationalism, Pluralism, & Freedom*.[36] In Levy's telling, the liberal-rationalist viewpoint wishes to "free" people from practices they perceive to be oppressive or backwards, thereby coming into conflict with the liberal-pluralist. For example, the liberal-rationalist will wish to free people from private associations promulgating racist worldviews. Although the worldview of the liberal-rationalist does not necessarily coincide with the elimination of ecological irrationality, there is a striking resemblance between the issues raised by Levy and the dystopian-but-free societies discussed in chapter 6 in the context of anarcho-capitalism.

If we consider the practical conflicts between liberal-rationalists and liberal-pluralists today, we can note that there are already institutional barriers restricting what the liberal-rationalist is allowed to regulate. These restrictions may be instructive for thinking about when and where, in parallel, expert opinion may be prohibited from supplanting free choice. The most notable of these restrictions are legal rules that place limits on the ability of liberal-rationalists to regulate religious expression. I see this as more or less analogous to a rule that, at a bare minimum, expertise may not supplant free choice when the conflict is over values. An *is*, as David Hume told us, cannot inform us about an *ought*.

This dovetails rather neatly with the fact that childhood vaccination is currently an edge-case in public policy. Failing to vaccinate is an unambiguous public health issue and a genuine externality. It is also the clearest example of parents having objectively wrong beliefs, and expert opinion being objectively correct. Moreover, carve-outs for religious objections tend to be given a priority, consistent with the principle that expertise first gets to supplant free choice when the disagreement is over facts, rather than overriding values. It's possible that current law and jurisprudence on these issues in the United States is approximately correct, and the status quo actually already stumbled upon the least bad answer.

On the other hand, in the infamous Supreme Court decision in 1927, *Buck v. Bell*, the same legal argument which grants the government the ability to compel vaccinations was used to justify compelling sterilization for the purpose of eugenics. "The principle that sustains compulsory vaccination is broad enough to cover cutting the Fallopian tubes" is a direct quotation from the ruling written by Justice Oliver Wendell Holmes that is horrifying and has never been formally overturned. In another world, would our current jurisprudence allow for the re-imposition of eugenics? It is never desirable to have a situation where we must depend on having "the right people in charge" to avoid fascistic policy—we want our institutions robust enough that no one group of people can throw us in that direction.[37] This is a slippery slope, obviously, that the West already slid down once before.[38] Even for mandatory childhood vaccination, there are further ramifications of permitting an erosion of liberty, granting that we agree with the expert opinion on childhood vaccination with zero caveats.

The best we can hope for may involve *some* amount of paternalistic deferral to expert opinion and *some* amount of private ecological irrationality which persists. For some issues, certain decisions will inevitably be placed in the dirty hands of medical doctors or other experts. In other areas, people will continue doing counterproductive things like DIY, simply because there isn't a reasonable way of using public policy to prevent that kind of behavior.

Allow me to roughly formalize my statement here diagrammatically using figure 10.1. On the x-axis is how much power we place institutionally in the hands of experts. Areas near the origin correspond to a small amount of deferring to experts. The far right along the x-axis corresponds to experts largely running society. The y-axis represents the social consequences, overall, of imposing the various levels of expert power, with the "consequences" being inclusive of effects on pluralism, liberty, freedom, a sense of autonomy, and the value of choice. The curves, as I have drawn them, are *one* possibility, one where the costs and benefits of the imposition of expert opinion confer net benefits on some portions of the x-axis.

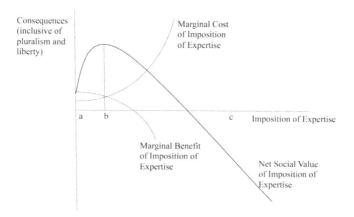

Figure 10.1   One Drawing of the Expertise Tradeoff. *Source*: Author.

The marginal benefit of deferring to experts is drawn such that the greatest benefit can be had via the first bit of authority we allow experts, with the value of this power diminishing with each additional unit of deference to experts. The "benefit" eventually goes negative, as there are areas where "expertise" will cause social harm (e.g., central planning of economies, which would appear around point *c*). The cost of deferring to experts (e.g., the principal-agent problem) starts at a low but positive position, and increases rapidly. The social optimum is where the marginal cost meets the marginal benefit, which is found at point *b*. This point, given the shape of these curves, is where society would be best off. This is indicated by the curve denoting the net social value of the imposition of expertise.

In the world described by this figure, there are certain things we could put in the hands of experts that would be beneficial, such as mandatory vaccines (or vaccines mandatory to attend a public school). The points between *a* and *b* are also where Thaler and Sunstein implicitly argue is the location of libertarian paternalist policies. It's possible that these curves do not describe the real world; if the marginal cost of imposing the expert will is always greater than the marginal benefit, then there is no space for the imposition of expertise. Alternatively, if you see the marginal benefits of expertise are greater than its marginal costs even at high levels of imposed expertise (or "expertise"), then you eventually take the position that all we need to do to rationalize society is to put the economy in the hands of central planners.[39]

To head off some concerns, let me make a few points about figure 10.1 clear. One, the difficulties involved with implementing expertise through governmental institutions should be thought of as being represented in the marginal cost and marginal benefit curves. Second, I believe it is reasonable to present marginal benefits as, on average, decreasing and marginal costs as, on average, increasing. This may be a very *rough* average, and it's easy to point to counterexamples to the average, but the world is not in so much disarray that the rough average should be expected to hold. If the issues which the state defers to experts on are instead essentially random, then the marginal cost and marginal benefit curves would be horizontal lines.

Finally, this discussion is not even meant to advocate that the state of the world we live in is as drawn in the figure, but to advocate that doing something like this is the proper framing of the question, Whither Expertise? When Koppl states[40] that "[a]ny attempt to impose a systematized body of knowledge on [society] will fail, and social cooperation be correspondingly thwarted" he neglects that there *are* situations, like childhood vaccination, where expert opinion diverges from views strongly held by members of the public, and those members of the public are simply wrong. The divergence of opinion between experts and members of the public is not because vaccine skeptics have some special knowledge of their individual circumstances, regardless of what they wish to believe.

We can recognize that experts, on average, have a better understanding of the world than nonexperts, and we may at times want to act on expertise. Doing so would be consistent with Brennan's epistocracy. If our current set of institutions gives greater weight to opinions of the elite and the informed, then our current political system already imperfectly reflects the issues I have raised. But it's possible that the costs and benefits actually imply that we should be moving away from, not toward epistocracy. Ultimately, grappling with the costs and benefits of expertise is the important question, and we shouldn't simply dial in on one side of the equation and leave it at that.

In the book's appendix, I will follow the spirit of this chapter by presenting and explaining the economic arguments *against trade*. I will tell you why I think they are wrong, but you can come to your own conclusion.

NOTES

1. Tetlock, *Expert Political Judgment.*
2. For example, Nassim Nicholas Taleb, *The Black Swan: The Impact of the Highly Improbable* (New York: Random House, 2007), 151–154.
3. Bryan Caplan, "Have the Experts Been Weighed, Measured, and Found Wanting?" *Critical Review* 19, no. 1 (2007): 81–91.
4. Philip Tetlock and Dan Gardner, *Superforecasting: The Art and Science of Prediction* (New York: Crown, 2015), 66–80.
5. Tetlock et al., *Superforecasting*, 105–192.
6. Tetlock et al., *Superforecasting*, 145–146.
7. On how little we know, see John P. A. Ioannidis, "The Challenge of Reforming Nutritional Epidemiological Research," *Journal of the American Medical Association* 320, no. 10 (September 2018): 969–970. Regarding the purported effectiveness of low carb diets, an important study funded by an institution seeking to find evidence in favor of them failed decisively. See Kevin D. Hall, Kong Y. Chen, Juen Guo, Yan Y Lam, Rudolph L. Leibel, Laurel E.S. Mayer, Marc Reitman, Michael Rosenbaum, Steven R. Smith, B. Timothy Walsh, and Eric Ravussin, "Energy Expenditure and Body Composition Changes after an Isocaloric Ketogenic Diet in Overweight and Obese Men," *The American Journal of Clinical Nutrition* 104, no. 2 (August 2016): 324–333.
8. CDC, "Clean Hands Count Campaign," last updated March 15, 2016, https://www.cdc.gov/handhygiene/campaign/index.html.
9. See CDC, "Data Portal," last updated October 5, 2018, https://www.cdc.gov/hai/data/portal/index.html; c.f. Shelley S. Magill, Erin O'Leary, Sarah J. Janelle, Deborah L. Thompson, Ghinwa Dumyati, Joelle Nadle, Lucy E. Wilson, Marion A. Kainer, Ruth Lynfield, Samantha Griessman, Susan M. Ray, Zintars Beldavs, Cindy Gross, Wendy Bamberg, Marla Sievers, Cathleen Concannon, Nicolai Buhr, Linn

Warnke, Meghan Maloney, Valerie Ocampo, Janet Brooks, Tolulope Oyewumi, Shamima Sharmin, Katherine Richards, Jean Rainbow, Monika Samper, Emily B. Hancock, Denise Leaptrot, Eileen Scalise, R. N., M. S. N., Farzana Badrun, Ruby Phelps, and Jonathan R. Edwards, "Changes in Prevalence of Health Care-Associated Infections in U.S. Hospitals," *New England Journal of Medicine* 379 (November 2018): 1732–1744.

10. WHO, "Clean Care is Safer Care," accessed July 1, 2019, http://www.who.int/gpsc/tools/faqs/evidence_hand_hygiene/en/.

11. Sherwin Nuland, *The Doctor's Plague: Germs, Childbed Fever, and the Strange Story of Ignaz Semmelweis* (New York: Great Discoveries, 2003).

12. Ioannidis et al., "The Power of Bias in Economics Research."

13. David M. Levy and Sandra J. Peart, *Escape from Democracy: The Role of Experts and the Public in Economic Policy* (Cambridge: Cambridge University Press, 2017).

14. Levy et al., *Escape from Democracy*, 46–67, 128–132.

15. Levy et al., *Escape from Democracy*, 89–109; see also Thomas C. Leonard, *Illiberal Reformers: Race, Eugenics, & American Economists in the Progressive Era* (Princeton: Princeton University Press, 2016).

16. Levy et al., *Escape from Democracy*, 110–136; see also Mark Skousen, "The Perseverance of Paul Samuelson's Economics," *Journal of Economic Perspectives* 11, no. 2 (Spring 1997): 137–152.

17. IGM Forum, "Occupational Licensing for Economists," April 17, 2018, http://www.igmchicago.org/surveys/occupational-licensing-for-economists.

18. William Easterly, *The Elusive Quest for Growth: Economists' Adventures and Misadventures in the Tropics* (Cambridge, MA: MIT Press, 2001).

19. Easterly, *The Tyranny of Experts*.

20. The scholarly mainstream on the topic is outlined by Easterly on the right, Paul Collier at the center, and Jeffrey Sachs on the left. See Paul Collier, *The Bottom Billion: Why the Poorest Countries are Failing and What Can Be Done About It* (New York: Oxford University Press, 2007); Jeffrey Sachs, "The Case for Aid," *Foreign Policy*, January 21, 2014, https://foreignpolicy.com/2014/01/21/the-case-for-aid/. For a more strident version of Easterly's argument, see Christopher Coyne, *Doing Bad by Doing Good: Why Humanitarian Action Fails* (Stanford: Stanford University Press, 2013).

21. Several papers have studied the effects of aid and membership in organizations like the World Bank on the quality of market institutions (i.e., economic freedom). For what it is worth, there is no consensus finding from the literature. See Robert Lawson, Ryan H. Murphy, and Benjamin Powell, "The Determinants of Economic Freedom: A Survey," *Working Paper* (Dallas: Southern Methodist University), https://papers.ssrn.com/sol3/papers.cfm?abstract_id=3266641.

22. My position is quite similar to Deaton, "On Tyrannical Experts and Expert Tyrants."

23. Koppl, *Expert Failure*, 6.

24. Koppl, *Expert Failure, passim*; 189–200.

25. Recall that if you take the intuition of the demand and supply of rationality seriously, it would imply that people whose decisions will actually impact society

will make themselves much more informed than someone without such an incentive. This would apply not only to politicians, but to the employees of the much-maligned "administrative state." Even as certain experts, including bureaucrats, may habitually act with horrific disregard for the welfare of others, they are still in a position to better appreciate the importance of the modern institutional environment.

26. Richard H. Thaler and Cass R. Sunstein, *Nudge: Improving Decisions About Health, Wealth, and Happiness*, revised ed. (New York: Penguin, 2009); c.f. Cass R. Sunstein, "Nudges vs. Shoves," *Harvard Law Review Forum* 127 (April 2014): 210–217.

27. Thaler and Sunstein, *Nudge*, 43–44.

28. Brian Resnik and Julia Belluz, "A Top Cornell Food Researcher Has Had 15 Studies Retracted. That's a Lot," *Vox*, October 24, 2018, https://www.vox.com/scien ce-and-health/2018/9/19/17879102/brian-wansink-cornell-food-brand-lab-retraction s-jama.

29. Mario J. Rizzo and Douglas Glen Whitman, "Little Brother is Watching You: New Paternalism on the Slippery Slopes," *University of Arizona Law Review* 51, no. 3 (2009): 685–739.

30. In addition to the narrowly defined principal-agent problem, see also Roger Koppl, "Experts and Information Choice," *Advances in Austrian Economics* 17 (2012): 171–202.

31. Emily Oster, *Expecting Better: Why the Conventional Pregnancy Wisdom is Wrong – And What You Really Need to Know* (New York: Penguin Press, 2013).

32. Emily Oster, *Cribsheet: A Data-Driven Guide to Better, More Relaxed Parenting, from Birth to Preschool* (New York: Penguin Press, 2019).

33. For the extent of this in public health in the UK alone, see Christopher Snowden, "2018: The Nanny State Year in Review," *Velvet Glove, Iron Fist*, December 30, 2018, https://velvetgloveironfist.blogspot.com/2018/12/2018-nanny-state-in-r eview.html?m=1.

34. If nothing else, in the sense of George Stigler, "The Economics of Information," *Journal of Political Economy* 69, no. 3 (June 1961): 213–225 or Herbert A. Simon, "Rational Choice and the Structure of the Environment," *Psychological Review* 63, no. 2 (March 1956): 129–138.

35. Tyler Cowen, *The Age of the Infovore: Succeeding in the Information Economy* (New York: Plume, 2010), 1–14.

36. Jacob T. Levy, *Rationalism, Pluralism, & Freedom* (Oxford: Oxford University Press, 2015).

37. Geoffrey Brennan and James Buchanan, *The Reason of Rules: Constitutional Political Economy* (Chicago: University of Chicago Press, 1985).

38. C.f. Mario J. Rizzo and Douglas Glen Whitman, "The Camel's Nose is in the Tent: Rules, Theories, and Slippery Slopes," *UCLA Law Review* 51, no. 2 (2003): 539–592.

39. Oskar Lange, "On the Economic Theory of Socialism I," *Review of Economic Studies* 4, no. 1 (October 1936): 189–201. Abba Lerner, "Theory and Practice in Socialist Economies," *Review of Economic Studies* 6, no. 1 (October 1938): 71–75.

40. Koppl, *Expert Failure*, 235.

Concluding Remarks

This book has wedded various intentionally provocative conclusions and narratives with what could be described as the most boring and conventional ideological presuppositions possible. For instance, that Trade Is Good. I have intentionally left it ambiguous whether I personally believe "Trade Is Good" means we should be merely breaking down trade barriers, as the developed world has slowly done over the last seventy years, or if I prefer the total deregulation of market forces. That ambiguity was purposeful, as in the current intellectual and political climate, the distinction is not particularly important; the appreciation of our modern institutions environment is what matters. The choice between the modern institutional environment and populism of any stripe is far more important than kicking up an internecine war.

The word "neoliberal," which has long been a pejorative and never used by the most strident defenders of market economies to describe themselves,[1] has recently resurfaced by some who seek to embrace it.[2] I would not necessarily characterize my own views as "neoliberal," but rhetorically, the ability to speak of one's self as a supporter of the institutions of modernity (while leaving it vague as to how far you are willing to go with it), is useful. If "neoliberal" is the term to adopt for someone who supports pluralism, the rule of law, science, markets, and all that, so be it.

While I have taken strongly countercultural positions in the course of this book, such as that "buy local" is conspicuous consumption, doing it yourself is a waste of time and effort, or social cohesion is frequently a bad thing, I do not wish for my message to be construed as falling on partisan lines. In the preface of the book, I mentioned several works across the political spectrum which voice optimism for what our modern institutional environment has accomplished. But these works each have their own point of view; *Enlightenment Now*, for instance, places a fair amount of emphasis on Pinker's New

Atheism. Jonah Goldberg's *Suicide of the West*, which I did not mention then but often comes very close to my core argument, is inseparable from Goldberg's neoconservatism. I hope to have conveyed a more conciliatory, big tent attitude along these specific lines, as where I have been controversial, I have been controversial enough. Whether you have agreed with me I suspect is rather unrelated to your surface-level political or religious affiliation.

Well, what now? With all that's been said, I can speculate and give a bit of structure to why I think ecological irrationality is more apparent in some places than in others. Early on, I described raw intelligence as being useful for reducing it. And Caplan's terminological choice of "rational irrationality" was meant to convey that people will engage in less of it when it is more costly for them. Besides those two points, I have three sets of reasons why I think ecological irrationality differs across time and space. While these thoughts build on previous chapters, they are more speculative than my earlier claims.

The first is simply whether ecological irrationality is *salient*. In the private sphere, we see it most widespread in the food we eat or the brand of a car we get into each morning. But the world we live in already tries to help us get around its salience. Across many industries and cultures, different trade practices have arisen to make the market part of "markets" less salient. This intentional—if unstated—obfuscation of markets facilitates transactions when ecological irrationality is more salient or markets are taboo. The most widespread example of this is the frequent circumvention of usury laws or religious proscriptions on usury through various trade practices. There is a small literature on the use of obfuscation in markets, sometimes associated with sociologist Gabriel Rossman, which amounts to instances of removing the salience of markets from social interactions.[3]

Conversely, markets are themselves capable of obfuscating the act of cooperating with foreigners or others not in the ingroup. Milton Friedman, echoing the *I, Pencil* story by Leonard Read, proselytizes, "Literally thousands of people cooperated to make this pencil. People who don't speak the same language, who practice different religions, who might hate one another if they ever met."[4] The anonymity of markets allows the xenophobe to, implicitly, cooperate with the foreigner. Yet the very purpose of what Elizabeth Currid-Halkett calls "conspicuous production" is, perniciously, to weaken this form of useful obfuscation. That is to say, a demand to know how your apple was sourced is an attack on the ability of human society to cooperate at the global scale, far more than it is a means of checking the excesses of global capitalism.

Besides salience, the second mechanism I suggest is an extension to the logic of the demand curve for irrationality. Irrationality is a luxury: first, in the sense that irrationality is something that you can't afford to engage in if you are on the cusp of starvation, and secondly, in the sense that as income increases, people will spend a higher percentage of their income on irrationality, just as they will spend more on fancy dinners and travel. We would expect, then, that all else equal, higher incomes buy more ecological irrationality. One tangible example of this would be that, even though intelligence and knowledge are positively linked to childhood vaccination, low vaccination rate areas are clustered in relatively wealthy and educated areas of the United States. I would suggest, very speculatively, that the failure to vaccinate in those wealthy and educated areas may represent a very weird, and very modern, form of status competition.

Finally, certain traditions and civil religions may mitigate ecological irrationality by instituting a form of faith or quasi-faith in concepts like property or market competition.[5] Examples of this would include Max Weber's *The Protestant Ethic* and aspects of America's civil religion. A faith or quasi-faith is sturdier than members of society fooling themselves with obfuscation, and we would expect groups with these kinds of traditions to be more successful than those without them. Still, since faith or quasi-faith in these traditions neither conforms to our instincts or ability to consciously reason, they are mechanisms that are susceptible to incursion.

Rather, we can hope that something sturdier can reduce ecological irrationality. The best we can hope for may be that education promoting an analytical, numerate understanding of the world will reduce ecological irrationality, though saying so is only to echo previous claims by Pinker and Caplan.[6] Or, in chapter 7, I argued that *bridging* (but not necessarily *bonding*) social capital reduces ecological irrationality, but either way, no one has any good idea of how to invest in social capital,[7] especially now that *Pokémon Go* is no longer popular. Ultimately, I do not have any complete explanation for how ecological irrationality varies across cultures and people, or the best path toward reducing it. The only answers I do have are the incomplete answers of salience, income, tradition and norms, education, intelligence, and social capital.

Let me restate the two narratives that ran through the course of this book. In the first, I described the meaning and historical setting of Bryan Caplan's "rational irrationality." In exploring the psychological underpinnings of "rational irrationality," I put forth that Caplan's model is better thought of as situations where our evolved modes of thinking are poor for functioning within our institutional environment. If we are sufficiently incentivized, humans are capable of performing the difficult, careful reasoning required for working in this environment, but in many cases, we are not.

Caplan's emphasis was on democratic decision-making, as there is no immediate reason for moving beyond your natural ways of thinking when you vote. But we can observe the natural ways of thinking arising elsewhere,

where it is actually costly. I explicitly linked it to the failure to vaccinate children, which corresponds implicitly to costing thousands of dollars per child given how parents would behave in other contexts. You see similar effects all across society, whether that is in the continued existence of the U.S. automobile industry, the buy local movement, do-it-yourself, or homeopathic medicine. Because these irrationalities relate to our difficulties in navigating the modern institutional environment, I proposed renaming Caplan's phenomenon "ecological irrationality."

I identified two explicit proposals for curbing ecological irrationality, epistocracy (rule by expert), most closely associated with Jason Brennan, and futarchy (vote on values, bet on beliefs), most closely associated with Robin Hanson. There are merits to both approaches, but I do not give either a full-throated endorsement. Epistocracy is presented as in conflict with democracy, when it is only in conflict with an ideologically defined version of democracy (mob democracy) that does not presently exist in the world. Epistocracy could be pursued with incremental changes to our political institutions. Futarchy circumvents some of the problems of epistocracy using prediction markets instead of informed opinion, but it is reasonable to ask for more intermediate steps demonstrating the effectiveness of prediction markets before drastically changing our political institutions. I consider two other more radical changes to political institutions, anarcho-capitalism (shifting all functions of government to the market) and a version of autocratic governance which is argued elsewhere to incentivize good policy. I conclude they are still weaker solutions than are epistocracy or futarchy.

The second narrative was more impressionistic and serialized, first conceptualizing ecological irrationality in terms of status signaling, discussing its implications for social capital and the do-it-yourself movement, and developing a new category of rent-seeking behavior. In each of these, ecological irrationality implies, directly or indirectly, that superficially praiseworthy behavior is selfish, or that seemingly pro-social behavior has anti-social ramifications. Within educated society, which includes nearly any reader of this book, what actually connotes status is the opposite of what is thought of as conspicuous consumption. Conventional conspicuous consumption is now associated with low status people who happen to have money. Social capital at high levels may contribute to ecological irrationality, and we have good reason to think bonding social capital, counterintuitively, can harm institutional quality. The intuition behind the "do-it-yourself" movement doesn't make any damned sense from an economic standpoint. And Social Luddites, exemplified by the wine expert, prey on what our brains wish to be true over what is actually true for their own selfish benefit. But at the same time, expert opinion is on average smarter than mass opinion, so it is difficult to say exactly where that leaves us. As long as we value pluralism in the modern world, it will remain ambiguous how much power to put in the hands of even an altruistic, informed expert.

Following these two narratives are a few points I wish to suggest as a few possible takeaways from the book. The first is concerned with how to interpret the legacy of *The Myth of the Rational Voter*. Recall that, within intellectual history, Caplan intended the book as the appropriate response to Donald Wittman's *The Myth of Democratic Failure*, who carried economic assumptions about rationality and equilibrium to their logical conclusion. *The Myth of the Rational Voter* gave clear rationales as to why there should be an asymmetry between rationality in markets and politics; contra Wittman—voters *are* extremely stupid. What I tried to do is to show that this asymmetry isn't exactly as Caplan presented it, with consumers willing to engage in markets in quite a bit of the same form of irrationality Caplan describes regarding voters. There are various reasons for thinking of political actors as behaving *more* rationally than voters want. If the role of the public sphere were to be dramatically reduced, and areas like law, justice, and financial or trade regulation were to be placed under the purview of markets, it isn't actually clear that this would reduce the level of expressed ecological irrationality. The correct interpretation of ecological irrationality isn't a complete endorsement of free markets. Rather, it is complicated and ambiguous.

I also am not confident in what would occur under either epistocracy or futarchy should they be put into place successfully. Whichever society that enacts them would likely see the elimination of various limitations on markets that no knowledgeable person favors, such as trade barriers, occupational licensure, or exclusionary zoning. But I don't think anyone should be surprised if these sets of political institutions increase the size of the welfare state (though it would be far more effectively administrated), shift to more inflationary monetary regimes, or enact certain regulations, like significant capital requirements for financial institutions. In these cases, on these margins, expert opinion would be leading us *away* from free market policies. I would be willing to bet that at least one of those three would take place in both epistocracy and futarchy, for what it is worth.

Second, my framing of social capital has the potential to offer a more fruitful paradigm for future research or public policy analysis. My slightly idiosyncratic definitions of bonding and bridging social capital is more conducive to thinking of social capital through a cultural lens, with clearer linkages to the character and quality of institutions, as well as to the broader history of political development. In my framework, bridging social capital is either always or almost always a good thing for a society to have more of, while bonding social capital is important at low levels but can be detrimental if it gets too high. There is a level of bonding social capital that is most consistent with modern institutions, at which ecological irrationality is minimized. Of course, it may be desirable to have more bonding social capital than that because social capital is good for other reasons, but that does not take away from the underlying point.

Lastly, chapters 5 and 8–10 attempted to elaborate on how ubiquitous rent-seeking really is even in a free society, but that it often invisibly occurs through the social realm. When advocates of free markets get sloppy in informal discussions, they sometimes speak as if rent-seeking is something that can only ever happen through the government.[8] And from the opposing direction, when Veblenian critics of markets attack conspicuous consumption, it is generally restricted to crass consumerism that they find distasteful. In reality, status signaling of various forms apparently takes up the preponderance of leisure time of anyone upper-middle class or higher in the West, not just the social climbers. Or to put it another way, we are all social climbers, it's just that some of us are less obvious about it than others are.

Putting policies in place that would actually curtail rent-seeking in the social realm are sharply counterintuitive. For instance, if someone signals low status by eating a well-done steak, and that provides a positive status externality for everyone else, should we subsidize eating steak well-done? If such a policy were ever to be seriously considered as a policy, that very consideration would be a sign that the status games had already moved on. And if a science fiction scenario were to arise where all of our actions, whether commercial or not, were perfectly taxed or subsidized in such a way that would frustrate all attempts at status signaling, I wonder if that, by peeling away a very deep component of human nature, it would actually cause serious problems for the human psyche.

The next time you are in your local gastropub marveling over the cheese that has suddenly become fashionable, which (if it is any good) will be on sale in the dairy section of Walmart within three years at half the price, take a second to think about how very complicated the commercial world is in its relentless churn, simultaneously doing things like lifting the most destitute out of poverty (that is, when we allow it to), and granting you the opportunity to try this cheese before anyone else so you can impress your friends. Your consumer demand, which you earned while probably working in a tiny niche occupation that didn't exist ten years ago, could be used on pretty much anything. You chose to buy the cheese. The market does whatever you want it to, and if you ask it to turn the gun on the institutions of modernity, including itself, it will do so with a smile and a coupon for repeat customers. Just ask yourself, whether markets against modernity is what you really want.

NOTES

1. Phillip Magness, "What Does 'Neoliberalism' Really Mean?" *Reason* (January 2019), https://reason.com/2018/12/30/what-does-neoliberalism-really/.

2. Sam Bowman, "I'm a Neoliberal. Maybe You Are Too," *Medium*, August 5, 2016, https://medium.com/@s8mb/im-a-neoliberal-maybe-you-are-too-b809a2a588d6.

3. Gabriel Rossman, "Obfuscatory Relational Work and Disreputable Exchange," *Sociological Theory* 32, no. 1 (March 2014): 43–63; Daniel Fridman and Alex Luscombe, "Gift-Giving, Disreputable Exchange, and the Management of Donations in a Police Department," *Social Forces* 96, no. 2 (December 2017): 507–528; Oliver Schilke and Gabriel Rossman, "It's Only Wrong If It's Transactional: Moral Perceptions of Obfuscated Exchange," *American Sociological Review* 83, no. 6 (December 2018): 1079–1107.

4. This exact language appears in *Free to Choose*, "The Power of the Market," episode 1, directed by Graham Massey, written by Milton Friedman. PBS, 1980.

5. In this particular instance, a "Hayekian" reading of what I am describing is correct. See F. A. Hayek, *Law, Legislation, and Liberty*, revised ed. (New York: Routledge, 2013), 486–507.

6. Pinker, *The Blank Slate*, 235–236; Caplan, *The Myth of the Rational Voter*, 197–199. Pinker, however, has since backtracked on the point, as in Pinker, *Enlightenment Now*, 355–356.

7. The most recent empirical finding has been that war increases social capital. It does not seem advisable to start wars for the sake of increasing social capital, and in any case, it seems more likely to be increasing bonding social capital, not bridging social capital. See Michal Bauer, Christopher Blattman, Julie Chytilova, Joseph Henrich, Edward Miguel, and Tamar Mitts, "Can War Foster Cooperation?" *Journal of Economic Perspectives* 30, no. 3 (Summer 2016), 249–274; Colin O'Reilly, "Can War Foster Institutional Change?" *Working Paper* (Omaha: Creighton University, 2018), https://papers.ssrn.com/sol3/papers.cfm?abstract_id=3197719.

8. For example, Sanford Ikeda, "Rent-Seeking: A Primer," Foundation for Economic Education, November 1, 2003, https://fee.org/articles/rent-seeking-a-primer/; c.f., Thomas J. DiLorenzo, "Property Rights, Information Costs, and the Economics of Rent Seeking," *Journal of Institutional and Theoretical Economics* 144, no. 2 (April 1988): 318–332.

Appendix

Trade is Bad?

In chapter 10, I alluded to one partial solution to the problem of bad experts—to improve the numeracy and knowledge of the public at large, so that the public can have a better sense of what is snake oil. I started this book by giving the intuition for why Trade Is Good. But you have heard the case for Trade Is Bad dozens of times. What is the best version of those arguments? How does that relate to the points I posed earlier? My preference is for decisions to be made pluralistically, and if we can have both rationalism and pluralism, we should try for that. With that in mind, I want to convey that expert opinion has considered the economic arguments for Trade Is Bad at some length. There may be some amount of reason to put an asterisk next to Trade Is Good, but the fundamental intuition for Trade Is Good remains: it is a kind of technology. The asterisks just aren't all that important.

The first argument I have discussed already—technological employment. Improved agricultural techniques mean we can use less labor on farms to get the same output, faster and more reliable information technology means offices need fewer support staff, and an overseas factory that produces more cheaply means we can use the labor previously employed in the local factories elsewhere in the economy. All three of those statements follow the same underlying economic logic. For all of modern history, with the exception of severe downturns in business cycle, markets have been able to reemploy workers who have become unemployed for technological reasons. Now, just because something has always been so does not mean it must continue to be so—in the same sense, we don't "know" that the sun will rise tomorrow—but an economy unable to find new jobs for those pushed into unemployment by trade would be a historical aberration. The version of the technological unemployment argument that may have some intellectual weight to it is about artificial intelligence and automation,[1] not trade, simply because one can speculate that the magnitude of the effects of artificial intelligence may be enormous.[2]

Some very recent research has found that the rise of China was exceptional, and had a tangible, lasting impact along the lines of technological unemployment, although it is easy to overstate or misstate the case.[3] Anecdotally, it is also easy to link such a story to, for example, the recent upward trends in the mortality rates of whites in the United States.[4] But the current best guess is that the massive surge in competition from China led to a net *redistribution*, not *reduction*, in jobs, from employment in low income areas of the United States to more service sector jobs in the high income areas of the United States.[5] This reduction is in conjunction, of course, with a larger size of the pie overall, because Trade Is Good. Furthermore, the aforementioned recent research on the effect of China's rise on the changing composition of employment in the United States showed that the effects ceased by 2007. There is no trade-related event as disruptive as the rise of China anywhere on the global horizon.

The second argument is that free trade could reduce the total amount of spending in a region and prevent the employment for everyone who wants a job at the going wage rate. This economic problem fits the "man on the street" intuition for why Trade Is Bad. Think of a business owner crying out that, without a secure level of demand for production, the owner will be unable to afford employing the firm's employees. Without income from those jobs, there won't be as much demand at the local supermarket and restaurants, meaning there will be cascading effects on others as well. The way this process is described is similar in many respects to descriptions of the low point of a business cycle.

The reason why business cycle downturns and the hypothesized negative effects of foreign competition have the same feeling is that they would operate through the same mechanism. According to most textbook presentations of business cycles and employment, labor markets function most smoothly when nominal prices—especially wages—slowly and steadily move upwards.[6] If the total dollar spending in an economy falls, either prices (and wages) need to fall or production (and jobs) needs to decrease. One way for spending to fall, again according to most textbook treatments, is for a region to import more goods than it exports. That is one of the small grains of truth for Trade Is Bad.

It is a measly grain of truth for a few reasons, however. One is that it is impossible to paint a complete picture of imports and exports of goods without also talking about the import and export of financial assets. If a region imports something, it needs to export something else. If it isn't exporting a good in exchange, it is exporting a financial asset. The wedge between how much an economy imports and exports goods is just the mirror image of how much it imports and exports financial assets. The wedge between how much a region imports and exports financial assets is also, equivalently, the wedge between how much a region is saving and how much a region is investing. (For recent figures for the United States written in plain English, see *Plumbing America's Balance of Trade*, freely available online, by Daniel Griswold.[7])

The United States, which has far more investment than it originates savings, needs to get the additional savings to fund the investment from somewhere. That somewhere is the rest of the world. The persistent wedge between how much the United States imports and exports is caused, primarily, by the persistence of the United States in saving less than what is invested in the United States. Various proposals to eliminate the wedge between imports and exports typically do not address this; for instance, banning steel imports will do far more to change the *composition* of what gets imported than to decrease the size of the wedge between exports and imports.[8] Since, we presumably don't want to reduce investment in the United States, the fastest way to eliminate the deficit, if that is what you really want to do, is to encourage the public to save more.

The other problem is, if you wish to ensure that an appropriate level of spending is happening in a country, manipulating rules governing trade is an incredibly awkward, blunt way to do that. There are already tools for managing this. What you will see in an introductory macroeconomics textbook are two tools, monetary policy and fiscal policy. Monetary policy is the relatively obvious solution to the problem of "there isn't enough spending and inflation in an economy," whereby the central bank prints more money. Fiscal policy (i.e., new government spending or tax cuts) acts as a standby to force more spending into an economy at times when it is believed that the central bank printing more money won't actually increase spending. Economists disagree over whether monetary or fiscal policy is what should be emphasized, and some disagree over whether "not enough spending" is even an important source of unemployment in the first place. Fine tuning the level of spending with trade policy, of all things, instead of conventional systems of management, is convoluted at best.

The most intellectually defensible rationale for Trade Is Bad is a concept known as industrial policy. The argument works like this. It is very hard to get a critical mass of potential employees with technical skills and abilities agglomerated into a single area. When any given company invests in the skills of its employee, it is also helping its future competitors by creating a new potential employee with that same set of skills. Think of an employer in Silicon Valley training a new programmer, for example. We see clusters of economic productivity, like Hollywood, that seem to exist not because of any policy or geographic characteristic, but because the firms clustering there feed off one another and create conditions conducive for the industry as a whole.

Within development economics, some economists have argued that using the tools of industrial policy, including tariffs, will help create these clusters of economic activity. (Some of these economists were also part of the earlier generation of bad experts William Easterly took aim at.) Many of the early development success stories in the second half of the twentieth century, mostly in East Asia, used these methods in nurturing their infant industries.[9] The problem, though, is that there are plenty of other countries that tried to grow their economies this way and failed. When industrial policy works, it works, and when it doesn't, it doesn't. In its initial phases, it is difficult to distinguish industrial policy from crony capitalism. Paul Krugman, who won a Nobel Prize for developing models of international trade to explain how these mechanisms and similar mechanisms could work, actually *fought* against their application in public policy, because models with circumstances where Trade is Bad function mostly as academic curiosities.

How might industrial policy and its theoretical mechanism (economics jargon: "increasing returns to scale") apply to countries that are already developed? First, where industrial policy seems to work, it is in the developing world where clusters of skills are not already present. Large stocks of technical skills for building automobiles were already present in Michigan when they first came into competition with foreign manufacturers, and those stocks of skills are still largely there. Industrial policy requires economic planners to somehow divine which industries a region may be able to compete in on the global marketplace. In the twenty-first century in Michigan, it's clear that, even with those skills present, Michigan competes only weakly in the global marketplace. Second, when the general concept of "industrial policy" is decomposed into different sets of policies, protectionism doesn't even look like what is driving the positive results; the other aspects of industrial policy are.[10]

Industrial policy falls under a class of policies that could solve particular market failures associated with increasing returns to scale. I can offer three suggestions that make more sense for developed countries than industrial policy, if you think increasing returns to scale is an important issue in developed economies. The first would be a regulation banning non-compete clauses in labor contracts.[11] Such a regulation is present in California and it is a plausible explanation for the entrepreneurial vigor found in Silicon Valley. The second recognizes that the places in the United States featuring the most economic prosperity today tend to have had large investments in technical universities decades ago;[12] for instance, the presence of Carnegie Mellon is an explanation as to why Pittsburgh has succeeded in recent decades where other Rust Belt cities have failed. Third, I mentioned in chapter 6 the possibility of creating special economic zones. These zones have streamlined regulatory environments that encourage new startups working in close proximity to one another.[13] Increasing the scope and presence of these economic zones could help a region reinvigorate its economy. All this is to say, if your diagnosis for developed economies is the need for a thriving cluster of development, there are a number of off-the-shelf policy proposals you could advocate for instead of trying to make industrial policy work in the developed world.

One non-economic argument against trade that is worth acknowledging is climate change. It is easy to draw connections between increasing levels of trade and carbon emissions. But this can be misleading. What is driving findings arguing this isn't that more container ships moving around the world emit more carbon—recall, per-unit carbon footprints of goods are often remarkably counterintuitive—but that *wealthier people have larger carbon footprints*. The imagery of busy shipping routes clogged with clouds of black smoke emitted by container ships is a distraction from the fact that climate change is being used as an excuse to stop economic growth. There are many off-the-shelf public policies that would prevent climate change without stopping economic growth in its tracks. And while these public policies have proved to be difficult to enact globally, so would be shutting off economic growth by ending global trade. If you wish to see an appropriate response to climate change, I would suggest the work of William Nordhaus,[14] who shared the Nobel Memorial Prize in economics in 2018 for this work.

Arguments against free trade take many forms, and are often intertwined non-economic rationales (like culture or national defense). But the best of the economic arguments will make use of some version of what I have described above, since all three economic arguments have some grain of truth. Persistent job losses as conceived of as technological unemployment are conceivable in some sense, but the marketplace has historically always found new employment for those who have lost their jobs (even if the job may be seen as undesirable). Moreover, technological unemployment is almost synonymous with economic growth. It also could be the case that more imports than exports will lead to less aggregate spending for a region, but there are ways we know of for addressing the problem of too little spending in an economy, like simply printing money. Trade deficits are better thought of as caused by a country's total investment exceeding its total savings, even if that sounds counterintuitive. Lastly, a minority of economists has seen a role for industrial policy in the story of economic development, but these narratives and models do not really apply to developed countries, and there are other tools in the toolbox for creating more agglomeration, if that is what is needed. The relationship between trade and climate change is worth acknowledging, but the relationship is not what it appears and there are far more effective and logical means of achieving the goal of preserving the climate.

I have given the reasons why I still think that Trade Is Good, but there is no reason not to acknowledge the grains of truth for Trade Is Bad. There are various issues at the margins that are up for debate. For instance, in the nineteenth century when the United States *was* a developing country, some of the periods of most vigorous growth temporally coincided with higher tariff rates[15]—though here, it is unclear what that tells us, since the growth in that period took place in the service sector, not manufacturing.[16] These questions at the margins, if pursued honestly and fervently, quickly get into the weeds of deep dives into history, arguing over how to apply statistical analyses, or making different assumptions in a mathematical model. And none of these questions at the margins casts doubt on the fundamental logic of Trade Is Good, which is a logic not appreciated by the "man on the street." I am not sure that these preceding paragraphs would convince an antagonistic reader, but I hope to have portrayed the issues fairly.

NOTES

1. Darrell M. West, *The Future of Work: Robots, AI, and Automation* (Washington, D.C.: The Brookings Institution, 2018); Steve Lohr, "Are Robots Coming for Your Job? Eventually, Yes," *The New York Times*, September 21, 2018, https://www.nytimes.com/2018/09/21/technology/artificial-intelligence-jobs.html.

2. Robin Hanson, *The Age of Em: Work, Love, and Life when Robots Rule the Earth* (New York: Oxford University Press, 2016).

3. David Autor, David Dorn, and Gordon H. Hanson, "The China Shock: Learning from Labor-Market Adjustment to Large Changes in Trade," *Annual Review of Economics* 8 (October 2016): 205–240.

4. Anne Case and Angus Deaton, "Rising Morbidity and Mortality in Midlife among White non-Hispanic Americans in the 21st Century," *Proceedings of the National Academy of Sciences of the United States of America* 112, no. 49 (December 2015): 15078–15083.

5. Nicholas Bloom, Kyle Handley, Andre Kurmann, and Philip Luck, "The Impact of Chinese Trade on U.S. Employment: The Good, The Bad, and The Debatable," *Working Paper* (Stanford: Stanford University, 2019), https://nbloom.peopl e.stanford.edu/sites/g/files/sbiybj4746/f/bhkl_posted_draft.pdf.

6. See Truman F. Bewley, *Why Wages Don't Fall during a Recession* (Cambridge, MA: Harvard University Press, 2002); George A. Akerlof, George L. Perry, and William T. Dickens, "The Macroeconomics of Low Inflation," *Brookings Papers on Economic Activity* 1 (1996): 1–76.

7. Daniel Griswold, *Plumbing America's Balance of Trade* (Arlington, VA: Mercatus Center, 2017), https://www.mercatus.org/system/files/mercatus-griswold-bala nce-of-trade-v1.pdf.

8. Joseph Gagnon, "We Know What Causes Trade Deficits," *Trade and Investment Policy Watch*, April 7, 2017, https://piie.com/blogs/trade-investment-polic y-watch/we-know-what-causes-trade-deficits. See also, C. Fred Bergsten and Joseph

Gagnon, *Currency Conflict and Trade Policy: a New Strategy for the United States* (Washington, DC: Peterson Institute for International Economics, 2017).

9. One such narrative can be found in Paul W. Kuznets, "An East Asian Model of Economic Development: Japan, Taiwan, and South Korea," *Economic Development and Cultural Change* 36, no. 3 (April 1988): S11–S43.

10. Ann Harris and Andres Rodriguez-Clare, "Trade, Foreign Investment, and Industrial Policy for Developing Countries," in *Handbook of Development Economics*, volume 5, ed. Dani Rodrick and Mark Rosenzweig (Oxford, UK: North-Holland, 2010), 4039–4214.

11. Steven Greenhouse, "Noncompete Clauses Increasingly Pop Up in Array of Jobs," *New York Times*, June 8, 2014, https://www.nytimes.com/2014/06/09/busin ess/noncompete-clauses-increasingly-pop-up-in-array-of-jobs.html.

12. Regarding the incredible importance of education for regional outcomes, see Nicola Gennaioli, Rafael La Porta, Florencio Lopez-De-Silanes, and Andrei Shleifer, "Human Capital and Regional Development," *Quarterly Journal of Economics* 128, no. 1 (February 2013): 105–164. For a broader elaboration of this and related ideas, written for the layperson, see Glaeser, *The Triumph of the City*.

13. Bell, *Your Next Government?*

14. William Nordhaus, *The Climate Casino: Risk, Uncertainty, and Economics for a Warming World* (New Haven: Yale University Press, 2013).

15. Ha-Joon Chang, *Kicking Away the Ladder: Development Strategy in Historical Perspective* (London: Anthem, 2002).

16. Douglas Irwin, "Review of *Kicking Away the Ladder: Development Strategy in Historical Perspective*," EH.net, April, 2004, https://eh.net/book_reviews/ki cking-away-the-ladder-development-strategy-in-historical-perspective/; Stephen B. Broadberry, "How Did the United States and Germany Overtake Britain? A Sectoral Analysis of Comparative Productivity Levels, 1870–1990," *The Journal of Economic History* 58, no. 2 (June 1998): 375–407.

Bibliography

Acemoglu, Daron, Tristan Reed, and James A. Robinson. "Chiefs: Economic Development and Elite Control of Civil Society in Sierra Leone." *Journal of Political Economy* 122, no. 2 (April 2014): 319–368.

Aghion, Phillippe, Yann Algan, Pierre Cahuc, and Andrei Shleifer. "Regulation and Distrust." *Quarterly Journal of Economics* 125, no. 3 (August 2010): 1015–1049.

Aghion, Phillipe, Benjamin F. Jones, and Charles I. Jones. "Artificial Intelligence and Economic Growth." In *The Economics of Artificial Intelligence: An Agenda*, edited by Ajay Agrawal, Joshua Gans, and Avi Doldfarb, 237–282. Chicago: University of Chicago Press, 2019.

Akerlof, George A., George L. Perry, and William T. Dickens. "The Macroeconomics of Low Inflation." *Brookings Papers on Economic Activity* 1 (1996): 1–76.

Al-Najjar, Nabil L. and Jonathan Weinstein. "The Ambiguity Aversion Literature: A Critical Assessment." *Economics and Philosophy* 25, no. 3 (November 2009): 249–284.

Alesina, Alberto, Edward Glaeser, and Bruce Sacerdote. "Why Doesn't the United States Have a European-Style Welfare State?" *Brookings Papers on Economic Activity* 2 (2001): 187–277.

Alesina, Alberto, Armando Miano, and Stefanie Stantcheva. "Immigration and Redistribution." *NBER Working Paper* no. 24733. Cambridge: National Bureau of Economic Research, 2018.

Aligica, Paul and Vlad Tarko. "Polycentricity: From Polanyi to Ostrom, and Beyond." *Governance: An International Journal of Policy, Administration, and Institutions* 25, no. 2 (2012): 237–262.

Alternative Fuels Data Center. "Average Per-Passenger Fuel Economy of Various Travel Modes." Last updated November, 2018. https://afdc.energy.gov/data/10311.

Amadae, S.M. and Bruce Bueno de Mesquita. "The Rochester School: The Origins of Positive Political Theory." *Annual Review of Political Science* 2 (June 1999): 269–295.

Anderson, Benedict. *Imagined Communities: Reflections on the Origin and Spread of Nationalism*. New York: Verso, 1983.

Anderson, Terry L. and Peter J. Hill. *The Not So Wild, Wild West: Property Rights on the Frontier*. Stanford: Stanford University Press, 2004.

Antoci, Angelo, Fabio Sabatini, and Mauro Sodini. "Economic Growth, Technological Progress, and Social Capital: The Inverted U Hypothesis." *Metroeconomica* 64, no. 3 (July 2013): 401–431.

Ariely, Dan, Anat Bracha, and Stephen Meier. "Doing Good or Doing Well? Image Motivation and Monetary Incentives in Behaving Prosocially." *American Economic Review* 99, no. 1 (March 2009): 544–555.

Arnhart, Larry. "The Evolution of Darwinian Liberalism." *Journal of Bioeconomics* 17, no. 1 (April 2015): 3–15.

Atran, Scott. "Folk Biology and the Anthropology of Sciences: Cognitive Universals and Cultural Particulars." *Behavioral and Brain Sciences* 2, no. 4 (August 1998)1: 547–609.

Autor, David, David Dorn, and Gordon H. Hanson. "The China Shock: Learning from Labor-Market Adjustment to Large Changes in Trade." *Annual Review of Economics* 8 (October 2016): 205–240.

Banfield, Edward. *The Moral Basis of a Backwards Society*. New York: The Free Press, 1958.

Banzhaf, H. Spencer. "The Cold War Origins of the Value of Statistical Life." *Journal of Economic Perspectives* 28, no. 4 (Fall 2004): 213–226.

Barshad, Amos. "Yankees Suck! Yankees Suck! The Twisted, True Story of the Drug-Addled, Beer-Guzzling Hardcore Punks Who Made the Most Popular T-Shirts in Boston History." *Grantland*, September 1, 2015. http://grantland.com/features/yankees-suck-t-shirts-boston-red-sox/.

Bauer, Michal, Christopher Blattman, Julie Chytilova, Joseph Henrich, Edward Miguel, and Tamar Mitts. "Can War Foster Cooperation?" *Journal of Economic Perspectives* 30, no. 3 (Summer 2016): 249–274.

BBC. "Apology after Japanese Train Departs 20 Seconds Early." November 16, 2017. https://www.bbc.com/news/world-asia-42009839.

Beaven, Colin. *No Impact Man: The Adventures of a Guilty Liberal Who Attempts to Save Our Planet, and the Discoveries He Makes About Himself and Our Way of Life in the Process*. New York: Farrar, Strauss and Giroux, 2009.

Becker, Gary S. *The Economics of Discrimination*. Chicago: University of Chicago Press, 1957.

Becker, Gary S. "A Theory of the Allocation of Time." *The Economic Journal* 75, no. 299 (September 1965): 493–517.

Becker, Gary S. *The Economic Approach to Human Behavior*. Chicago: University of Chicago Press, 1976.

Becker, Gary S. "A Theory of Competition among Pressure Groups for Political Influence." *Quarterly Journal of Economics* 98, no. 3 (August 1983): 371–400.

Becker, Gary S. "Public Policies, Pressure Groups, and Dead Weight Costs." *Journal of Public Economics* 28, no. 3 (December 1985): 329–347.

Becker, Gary S. *A Treatise on the Family*. Cambridge: Harvard University Press, 1993.

Beggren, Niclas and Christian Bjornskov. "The Market-Promoting and Market-Preserving Role of Social Trust in Reforms of Policies and Institutions." *Southern Economic Journal* 84, no. 1 (July 2017): 3–25.

Bell, Daniel. *The Cultural Contradictions of Capitalism*. New York: Basic Books, 1976.

Bell, Tom W. *Your Next Government? From the Nation State to Stateless Nations*. Cambridge: Cambridge University Press, 2017.

Belluz, Julia. "Americans Spend Billions on Homeopathy. The Best Evidence Say They Are Wasting Their Money." *Vox*, March 11, 2015. https://www.vox.com/2015/3/11/8190427/homeopathy.

Bennett, Daniel, Hugo Faria, James Gwartney, and Daniel Morales. "Economic Institutions and Comparative Economic Development: A Post-Colonial Perspective." *World Development* 96 (August 2017): 503–519.

Bennett, Stephen E. and Jeffrey Friedman. "The Irrelevance of Economic Theory to Understanding Economic Ignorance." *Critical Review* 20, no. 3 (2008): 195–258.

Benson, Bruce. "The Mythology of Holdout as a Justification for Eminent Domain and Public Provision of Roads." *The Independent Review* 10, no. 2 (Fall 2005): 165–194.

Beretti, Antoine, Charles Figuieres, and Cilles Grolleau. "Using Money to Motivate Both 'Saints' and 'Sinners': A Field Experiment on Motivational Crowding-Out." *Kyklos* 66, no. 1 (February 2013): 64–77.

Berger, Joel. "Are Luxury Brand Labels and 'Green' Labels Costly Signals of Social Status? An Extended Replication." *PLOS ONE* 12, no. 2 (February 7, 2017): e0170216.

Berger, Peter and Thomas Luckmann. *The Social Construction of Reality: A Treatise in the Sociology of Knowledge*. New York: Anchor Books, 1996.

Bergsten, C. Fred and Joseph Gagnon. *Currency Conflict and Trade Policy: A New Strategy for the United States*. Washington, DC: Peterson Institute for International Economics, 2017.

Berman, Sheri. "Civil Society and the Collapse of the Weimar Republic." *World Politics* 49, no. 3 (April 1997): 401–429.

Bewley, Truman F. *Why Wages Don't Fall during a Recession*. Cambridge, MA: Harvard University Press, 2002.

Bisinella, Valentina, Paola Federica Albizzati, Thomas Freuergaard, and Anders Damgaard. "Life Cycle Assessment of Grocery Carrier Bags." *Environmental Project* no. 1985. Copenhagen: Danish Environmental Protection Agency, 2018.

Biskup, Martin J., Seth Kaplan, Jill C. Bradley-Geist, and Ashley A. Membere. "Just How Miserable is Work? A Meta-Analysis Comparing Work and Non-Work Affect." *PLOS One* 14, no. 3 (March 2019): e0212594.

Biswas-Diener, Robert. "The Subjective Well-Being of Small Societies." In *Handbook of Well-Being*, edited by Ed Deiner, Shigehiro Oishi, and Luis Tray, 1–11. Salt Lake City: DEF Publishers, 2018.

Blackwell, Christopher W. "The Assembly." *Dēmos: Classical Athenian Democracy*, March 26, 2003. http://www.stoa.org/projects/demos/article_assembly?page=2&greekEncoding=UnicodeC.

Blanchard, Troy C. and Todd L. Matthews. "The Configuration of Local Economic Power and Civic Participation in the Global Economy." *Social Forces* 84, no. 4 (June 2006): 2241–2257.

Blanchard, Troy C., Charles Tolbert, and Carson Mencken. "The Health and Wealth of U.S. Counties: How the Small Business Environment Impacts Alternative Measures of Development." *Cambridge Journal of Regions, Economy, and Society* 5, no. 1 (March 2012): 149–162.

Blinder, Alan S. "Offshoring: The Next Industrial Revolution?" *Foreign Affairs* 85, no. 2 (March 2006): 113–128.

Bloom, Nicholas, Kyle Handley, Andre Kurmann, and Philip Luck. "The Impact of Chinese Trade on U.S. Employment: The Good, the Bad, and the Debatable." Working paper. Stanford: Stanford University, 2019. https://nbloom.people.sta nford.edu/sites/g/files/sbiybj4746/f/bhkl_posted_draft.pdf.

Boettke, Peter and Rosolino Candela. "Rational Choice as If the Choosers Were Human." In *Handbook of Behavioral Economics and Smart Decision-Making: Rational Decision within the Bounds of Reason*, edited by Morris Altman, 68–85. Northampton: Edward Elgar, 2017.

Boettke, Peter J., Christopher J. Coyne, and Peter T. Leeson. "Earw(h)ig: I Can't Hear You Because Your Ideas Are Old." *Cambridge Journal of Economics* 38, no. 3 (May 2014): 531–544.

Boettke, Peter and Alain Marciano. "The Past, Present, and Future of Virginia Political Economy." *Public Choice* 163, no. 1 (April 2015): 53–65.

Bohannon, John, Robin Goldstein, and Alexis Herschkowitsch. "Can People Distinguish Pâté from Dog Food?" *Chance* 23, no. 2 (2010): 43–46.

Bolick, Clint. *Grassroots Tyranny: The Limits of Federalism*. Washington, DC: Cato Institute, 1993.

Borcan, Oana, Ola Olsson, and Louis Putterman. "State History and Economic Development: Evidence from Six Millennia." *Journal of Economic Growth* 23, no. 1 (March 2018): 1–40.

Bourdieu, Pierre. *Distinction: A Social Critique of the Judgement of Taste*. Cambridge: Harvard University Press, 1984.

Bowles, Samuel and Herbert Gintis. "Social Capital and Community Governance." *The Economic Journal* 112 (November 2002): F419–F436.

Bowman, Sam. "I'm a Neoliberal. Maybe You Are Too." *Medium*, August 5, 2016. https://medium.com/@s8mb/im-a-neoliberal-maybe-you-are-too-b809a2a588d6.

Boyle, Amy E. "Ray Bradbury: Fahrenheit 451 Misinterpreted." *LA Weekly*, May 30, 2007. https://www.laweekly.com/news/ray-bradbury-fahrenheit-451-misinterpret ed-2149125.

Brandt Urs Steiner, and Gert Tinggaard Svendsen. "How Robust is the Welfare State When Facing Open Borders? An Evolutionary Game-Theoretic Model." *Public Choice* 178, no. 1–2 (January 2019): 179–195.

Brennan, Geoffrey and James M. Buchanan. *The Power to Tax: Analytical Foundations of a Fiscal Constitution*. Cambridge: Cambridge University Press, 1980.

Brennan, Geoffrey and James M. Buchanan. *The Reason of Rules: Constitutional Political Economy*. Chicago: University of Chicago Press, 1985.

Brennan, Geoffrey and Loren Lomasky. *Democracy and Decision: The Pure Theory of Electoral Preference*. Cambridge: Cambridge University Press, 1993.

Brennan, Jason. *Against Democracy*. Princeton: Princeton University Press, 2016.

Brennan, Jason and Peter Jaworski. *Markets without Limits*. New York: Routledge, 2015.

Brewer, Marilynn B. "The Psychology of Prejudice: Ingroup Love or Outgroup Hate?" *Journal of Social Issues* 55, no. 3 (1999): 429–444.

Broadberry, Stephen B. "How Did the United States and Germany Overtake Britain? A Sectoral Analysis of Comparative Productivity Levels, 1870–1990." *The Journal of Economic History* 58, no. 2 (June 1998): 375–407.

Brooks, Dan, Harry Pavlidis, and Jonathan Judge. "Moving Beyond WOWY: A Mixed Approach to Measuring Catcher Framing." *Baseball Prospectus*, February 5, 2015. https://www.baseballprospectus.com/news/article/25514/moving-beyond-wowy-a-mixed-approach-to-measuring-catcher-framing/.

Brooks, David. *Bobos in Paradise: The New Upper Class and How They Got There*. New York: Simon & Schuster, 2000.

Brown, Donald E. *Human Universals*. New York: McGraw-Hill, 1991.

Buchanan, James M. and Roger Congleton. *Politics by Principle, Not Interest: Towards Nondiscriminatory Democracy*. Cambridge: Cambridge University Press, 1998.

Buchanan, James M. and Gordon Tullock. *The Calculus of Consent*. Ann Arbor: University of Michigan Press, 1962.

Bunch, Sonny. "Criticism is Conversation, Not an Assault on Your Identity." *The Washington Post*, May 8, 2019. https://www.washingtonpost.com/opinions/2019/05/08/criticism-is-conversation-not-an-assault-your-identity/?utm_term=.bbda36051175.

Bureau of Labor Statistics. "Consumer Price Index for All Urban Consumers (CPI-U): U.S. City Average, by Expenditure Category)." Last updated June 12, 2019. https://www.bls.gov/news.release/cpi.t01.htm.

Cameron, Judy and W. David Pierce. "Reinforcement, Reward, and Intrinsic Motivation: A Meta-Analysis." *Review of Educational Research* 64, no. 3 (September 1994): 363–423.

Caplan, Bryan. "Rational Irrationality: A Framework for the Neoclassical-Behavioral Debate." *Eastern Economic Journal* 26, no. 2 (Spring 2000): 191–211.

Caplan, Bryan. "Systematically Biased Beliefs about Economics: Robust Evidence of Judgmental Anomalies from the Survey of Americans and Economists on the Economy." *The Economic Journal* 112, no. 479 (April 2002): 433–458.

Caplan, Bryan. "From Friedman to Wittman: The Transformation of Chicago Political Economy." *Econ Journal Watch* 2, no. 1 (April 2005): 1–21.

Caplan, Bryan. "Have the Experts Been Weighed, Measured, and Found Wanting?" *Critical Review* 19, no. 1 (2007): 81–91.

Caplan, Bryan. *The Myth of the Rational Voter*. Princeton: Princeton University Press, 2007.

Caplan, Bryan. "Reply to My Critics." *Critical Review* 20, no. 3 (2008): 377–413.

Caplan, Bryan. "Persuasion, Slack, and Traps: How Can Economists Change the World?" *Public Choice* 142, no. 1 (January 2010): 1–8.

Caplan, Bryan. "Market Failure: The Case of Organic Food." *Econlog*, May 21, 2012, https://www.econlib.org/archives/2012/05/market_failure_6.html.

Caplan, Bryan. "The Logic of Gilensian Activism." *Econlog*, September 15, 2014. https://www.econlib.org/archives/2014/09/gilens_page_and.html.

Caplan, Bryan. *The Case against Education: Why the Education System Is a Waste of Time and Money*. Princeton: Princeton University Press, 2018.

Caplan, Bryan. "Week 12: Dictatorship." Accessed June 29, 2019. http://econfaculty.gmu.edu/bcaplan/e854/pc11.htm.

Caplan, Bryan and Stephen C. Miller. "Intelligence Makes People Think More Like Economists: Evidence from the General Social Survey." *Intelligence* 38, no. 6 (November–December 2010): 636–647.

Caplan, Bryan and Stephen C. Miller. "Positive versus Normative Economics: What's the Connection? Evidence from the *Survey of Americans and Economists on the Economy* and the *General Social Survey*." *Public Choice* 150, no. 1 (January 2012): 241–261.

Carden, Art. "Inputs and Institutions as Conservative Elements." *Review of Austrian Economics* 22, no. 1 (September 2009): 1–19.

Carden, Art, Charles Courtemanche, and Jeremy Meiners. "Does Wal-Mart Reduce Social Capital?" *Public Choice* 138, no. 1–2 (January 2009): 109–136.

Carl, Noah. "Cognitive Ability and Political Beliefs in the United States." *Personality and Individual Differences* 83 (September 2015): 245–248.

Caro, Robert. *The Power Broker: Robert Moses and the Fall of New York*. New York: Knopf, 1974.

Caro, Robert. *The Means of Ascent*. New York: Knopf, 1990.

Case, Anne and Angus Deaton. "Rising Morbidity and Mortality in Midlife among White non-Hispanic Americans in the 21st Century." *Proceedings of the National Academy of Sciences of the United States of America* 112, no. 49 (December 2015): 15078–15083.

Cassette, Aurelie and Sonia Paty. "Fiscal Decentralization and the Size of Government: A European Country Empirical Analysis." *Public Choice* 143, no. 1–2 (2010): 173–189.

Cavanagh, David. "I Can See the Monsters." Q Magazine (October 2000): 94–104.

CDC. "Invasive Pneumococcal Disease in Children 5 Years after Conjugate Vaccine Introduction – Eight States, 1998–2005." *MMWR* 57, no. 6 (February 15, 2008): 144–148.

CDC. "Summary of Notifiable Diseases – United States, 2008." *MMWR* 57, no. 54 (June 25, 2010).

CDC. "Clean Hands Count Campaign." (2018). Last updated March 15, 2016. https://www.cdc.gov/handhygiene/campaign/index.html.

CDC. "Data Portal." Last updated October 5, 2018. https://www.cdc.gov/hai/data/portal/index.html.

Chamlee-Wright, Emily and Virgil H. Storr. "Social Capital, Lobbying, and Community-Based Interest Groups." *Public Choice* 149, no. 1–2 (October 2011): 167–185.

Chang, Ha-Joon. *Kicking Away the Ladder: Development Strategy in Historical Perspective*. London: Anthem, 2002.

Cheung, Steven N.S. "The Transaction Cost Paradigm." *Economic Inquiry* 36 (October 1998): 514–521.

Chi, Kelly Rai, James MacGregor, and Richard King. *Fair Miles: Recharting the Food Miles Map.* London: IIED, 2009.

Chiappe, Dan and Kevin MacDonald. "The Evolution of Doman-General Mechanisms in Intelligence and Learning." *The Journal of General Psychology* 132, no. 1 (January 2005): 5–40.

Claar, Victor and Colleen Haight. "Fair Trade Coffee: Correspondence." *Journal of Economic Perspectives* 29, no. 1 (Winter 2015): 215–216.

Claridge, Tristan. "Explanations of Different Levels of Social Capital." *Social Capital Research & Training*, January 28, 2018. https://www.socialcapitalresearch.com/levels-of-social-capital/.

Clark, Alexander M. and Matthew T.G. Clark. "Pokémon Go and Research: Qualitative, Mixed Methods Research, and the Supercomplexity of Interventions." *International Journal of Qualitative Methods* 15, no. 1 (December 2016): 1–3.

Clark, J. R. and Dwight Lee. "Econ 101 Morality: The Amiable, the Mundane, and the Market." *Econ Journal Watch* 14, no. 1 (January 2017): 61–76.

Clausing, Kimberly. *Open: The Progressive Case for Free Trade, Immigration, and Global Capital.* Cambridge: Harvard University Press, 2019.

Clemens, Michael, Claudio Montenegro, and Lant Pritchett. "The Place Premium: Bounding the Price Equivalent of Migration Barriers." *Review of Economics and Statistics* 101, no. 2 (May 2019): 201–213.

Coase, Ronald H. "The Nature of the Firm." *Economica* 4, no. 16 (November 1937): 386–405.

Coleman, James. "Social Capital and the Creation of Human Capital." *American Journal of Sociology* 94 (1988, Supplement): S95–S120.

Collier, Paul. *The Bottom Billion: Why the Poorest Countries are Failing and What Can Be Done About It.* New York: Oxford University Press, 2007.

Collier, Paul. *Wars, Guns, and Votes: Democracy in Dangerous Places.* New York: HarperCollins, 2010.

Confer, Jaime C. Judith A. Easton, Diana S. Fleischman, Cari D. Goetz, David M. G. Lewis, Carin Perilloux, and David M. Buss. "Evolutionary Psychology: Controversies, Questions, Prospects, and Limitations." *American Psychologist* 65, no. 2 (February–March 2010): 110–126.

Conn, Steven. "Business Schools Have No Business in the University." *The Chronical of Higher Education*, February 20, 2018. https://www.chronicle.com/article/Business-Schools-Have-No/242563.

Consumer Reports. "Which Car Brands Make the Best Vehicles." Last updated February 21, 2019. https://www.consumerreports.org/cars-driving/which-car-brands-make-the-best-vehicles/.

Cornell, Saul and Justin Florence. "The Right to Bear Arms in the Era of the Fourteenth Amendment: Gun Rights or Gun Regulation." *Santa Clara Law Review* 50, no. 4 (2010): 1043–1071.

Cosmides, Leda and John Tooby. "Cognitive Adaptations for Social Exchange." In *The Adapted Mind: Evolutionary Psychology and the Generation of Culture*, edited by Jerome H. Barkow, Leda Cosmides, and John Tooby, 163–228. New York: Oxford University Press, 1992.

Cowen, Tyler. *In Praise of Commercial Culture*. Cambridge: Harvard University Press, 1998.

Cowen, Tyler. *Creative Destruction: How Globalization is Changing the World's Cultures*. Princeton: Princeton University Press, 2002.

Cowen, Tyler. *Discover Your Inner Economist: Use Incentives to Fall in Love, Survive Your Next Meeting, and Motivate Your Dentist*. New York: Plume, 2008.

Cowen, Tyler. *The Age of the Infovore: Succeeding in the Information Economy*. New York: Plume, 2010.

Cowen, Tyler. *An Economist Gets Lunch: New Rules for Everyday Foodies*. New York: Dutton Adult, 2012.

Cowen, Tyler. "Is KOKS the Best Restaurant in the World?" *Marginal Revolution*, August 17, 2016. https://marginalrevolution.com/marginalrevolution/2016/08/koks.html.

Cowen, Tyler. *Stubborn Attachments*. San Francisco: Stripe Press, 2018.

Cowen, Tyler. *Big Business: A Love Letter to an American Anti-Hero*. New York: St. Martin's Press, 2019.

Coyne, Christopher. *Doing Bad by Doing Good: Why Humanitarian Action Fails*. Stanford: Stanford University Press, 2013.

Crain, Caleb. "The Case Against Democracy." *The New Yorker*, October 31, 2016. https://www.newyorker.com/magazine/2016/11/07/the-case-against-democracy.

Currid-Halkett, Elizabeth. *The Sum of Small Things: A Theory of the Aspirational Class*. Princeton: Princeton University Press, 2017.

Darby, Kim Marvin T. Battle, Stan Ernst, and Brian Roe. "Decomposing Local: A Conjoint Analysis of Locally Produced Foods." *American Journal of Agricultural Economics* 90, no. 2 (May 2008): 476–486.

Darwin, Charles. *The Descent of Man, and the Selection in Relation to Sex*. London: John Murray, 1871.

Davis, Matthew M., Mitesh S. Patel, and Achamyeleh Gebremariam. "Decline in Varicella-Related Hospitalizations and Expenditures for Children and Adults after Introduction of Varicella Vaccine in the United States." *Pediatrics* 114, no. 3 (September 2004): 786–792.

Davis, Zuri. "Is This the Summer of Snitches?" *Reason*, June 30, 2018. https://reason.com/blog/2018/06/30/burrito-bob-police-bart-san-francisco.

Dawson, John W. "Causality in the Freedom-Growth Relationship." *European Journal of Political Economy* 19, no. 3 (September 2003): 479–495.

De Haan, Jakob and Jan-Egbert Sturm. "Does More Democracy Lead to Greater Economic Freedom? New Evidence for Developing Countries." *European Journal of Political Economy* 19, no. 3 (September 2003): 547–563.

Deaton, Angus. "On Tyrannical Experts and Expert Tyrants." *Review of Austrian Economics* 28, no. 4 (December 2015):407–412.

Den Uyl, Douglas J. and Douglas B. Rasmussen. "The Myth of Atomism." *The Review of Metaphysics* 59, no. 4 (June 2006): 841–868.

DenBleyker, Rob. [no title.] *Cyanide and Happiness* no. 2932, September 22, 2012. http://explosm.net/comics/2932.

Desrochers, Pierre and Hiroko Shimizu. *The Locavore's Dilemma: In Praise of the 10,000-Mile Diet.* New York: Public Affairs, 2012.

DiLorenzo, Thomas J. "Property Rights, Information Costs, and the Economics of Rent Seeking." *Journal of Institutional and Theoretical Economics* 144, no. 2 (April 1988): 318–332.

Dixit, Avinash. *Lawlessness and Economics: Alternative Modes of Governance.* Princeton: Princeton University Press, 2004.

Doherty, Brian. *Radicals for Capitalism: A Freewheeling History of the Modern American Libertarian Movement.* New York: Public Affairs, 2007.

Dragusanu, Raluca and Nathan Nunn. "The Effects of Fair Trade Certification: Evidence from Coffee Producers in Costa Rica." *NBER Working Paper* no. 24260. Cambridge: National Bureau for Economic Research, June 2019.

Dreher, Rod. *Crunchy Cons: How Birkenstocked Burkeans, Gun-Loving Organic Gardeners, Evangelical Free-Range Farmers, Hip Homeschooling Mamas, Right-Wing Nature Lovers, and Their Diverse Tribe of Countercultural Conservatives Plan to Save America (or at least the Republican Party).* New York: Crown, 2006.

Easterly, William. *The Elusive Quest for Growth: Economists' Adventures and Misadventures in the Tropics.* Cambridge, MA: MIT Press, 2001.

Easterly, William. *The Tyranny of Experts: Economists, Dictators, and the Forgotten Rights of the Poor.* New York: Basic Books, 2014.

Easterly, William and Ross Levine. "Tropics, Germs, and Crops: How Endowments Influence Economic Development." *Journal of Monetary Economics* 50, no. 1 (January 2003): 3–39.

Echebarria, Carmen and Jose M. Barrutia. "Limits of Social Capital as a Driver of Innovation: An Empirical Analysis in the Context of European Regions." *Regional Studies* 47, no. 7 (2013): 1001–1017.

Edwards, Chris. "The Sugar Racket." *Cato Institute Tax & Budget Bulletin* no. 46 (June 2007). https://object.cato.org/sites/cato.org/files/pubs/pdf/tbb_0607_46.pdf.

Egan, Timothy. "The Disgust Election." *New York Times*, October 23, 2014. https://www.nytimes.com/2014/10/24/opinion/the-disgust-election.html.

Ellefson, Lindsey. "After Defeat, Japan's World Cup Team Leaves behind Spotlessly Clean Locker Room and a 'Thank You' Note." *CNN*, July 3, 2018. https://www.cnn.com/2018/07/03/football/japan-belgium-russia-thank-you-locker-room-trnd/index.html.

Elster, Jon. "Economic Order and Social Norms." *Journal of Institutional and Theoretical Economics* 144, no. 2 (April 1998): 357–366.

Elster, Jon and Helene Landemore. "Ideology and Dystopia." *Critical Review* 20, no. 3 (2008): 273–289.

Emergent Order. "EconPop – The Economics of WALL-E." June 6, 2014. https://www.youtube.com/watch?v=g9Og4qkn67o.

Erdmann, Kevin. *Shut Out: How a Housing Shortage Caused the Great Recessions and Crippled Our Economy.* Lanham: Rowman & Littlefield, 2019.

ESPN.com. "Jayson Werth Rails Against 'Super Nerds' That Are 'Killing the Game.'" August 9, 2018. http://www.espn.com/mlb/story/_/id/24329670/jayson-werth-rails-super-nerds-killing-game.

Evans, Anthony J. and Jeffrey Friedman. "'Search' vs. 'Browse': A Theory of Error Grounded in Radical (Not Rational) Ignorance." *Critical Review* 23, no. 1–2 (2011): 73–104.

Fadyen, M. Ann and Albert A. Canella Jr. "Social Capital and Knowledge Creation: Diminishing Returns of the Number and Strength of Exchange." *The Academy of Management Journal* 47, no. 5 (October 2004): 735–746.

Fama, Eugene and Richard Thaler. "Are Markets Efficient?" *Chicago Booth Review*, June 30, 2016. http://review.chicagobooth.edu/economics/2016/video/are-markets-efficient.

Fernbach, Philip M., Nicholas Light, Sydney E. Scott, Yoel Inbar, and Paul Rozin. "Extreme Opponents of Genetically Modified Foods Know the Least But Think They Know the Most." *Nature Human Behaviour*, 3 (January 2019): 251–256.

Feyer, James. "Trade and Income – Exploiting Time Series in Geography." *NBER Working Paper* no. 14910, Cambridge: National Bureau for Economic Research, 2009.

Fiske, Alan P. "The Four Elementary Forms of Sociality: Framework for a Unified Theory of Social Relations." *Psychological Review* 99, no. 4 (October 1992): 689–723.

Fiske, Alan P. and Philip E. Tetlock. "Taboo Trade-offs: Reactions to Transactions that Transgress the Spheres of Justice." *Political Psychology* 18, no. 2 (June 1997): 255–297.

Florida, Richard. *The Rise of the Creative Class*. New York: Basic Books, 2002.

Frank, Robert. *The Darwin Economy: Liberty, Competition, and the Common Good*. Princeton: Princeton University Press, 2011.

Frank, Robert. "The Progressive Consumption Tax: A Win-Win Solution for Reducing American Income Inequality." *Slate*, December 7, 2011. https://slate.com/business/2011/12/the-progressive-consumption-tax-a-win-win-solution-for-reducing-american-economic-inequality.html.

Free to Choose. "The Power of the Market," episode 1. Directed by Graham Massey. Written by Milton Friedman. PBS, 1980.

Frey, Bruno S. and Felix Oberholzer-Gee. "The Cost of Price Incentives: An Empirical Analysis of Motivation Crowding-Out." *American Economic Review* 87, no. 4 (September 1997): 746–755.

Fridman, Daniel and Alex Luscombe. "Gift-Giving, Disreputable Exchange, and the Management of Donations in a Police Department." *Social Forces* 96, no. 2 (December 2017): 507–528.

Friedman, David D. "Private Creation and Enforcement of Law – A Historical Case." *Journal of Legal Studies* 8, no. 2 (March 1979): 399–415.

Friedman, David D. *Price Theory: An Intermediate Text*. Cincinnati: South-Western Publishing Co., 1996.

Friedman, Patri and Brad Taylor. "Seasteading: Competitive Governments on the Ocean." *Kyklos* 65, no. 2 (May 2012): 218–235.

Fritz, Claudia, Joseph Curtin, Jacques Poitevineau, Palmer Morel-Samuels, and Fan-Chia Tao. "Player Preferences among New and Old Violins." *Proceedings of the National Academy of Sciences of the United States of America* 109, no. 3 (January 2012): 760–763.

Fukuyama, Francis. *Trust: The Social Virtues and the Creation of Prosperity*. New York: The Free Press, 1995.

Fukuyama, Francis. *The Origins of Political Order: From Prehuman Times to the French Revolution*. New York: Farrar, Straus and Giroux, 2011.

Fussell, Paul. *Class: A Guide through the American System*. New York: Simon and Schuster, 1983.

Gagnon, Joseph. "We Know What Causes Trade Deficits." *Trade and Investment Policy Watch*, April 7, 2017. https://piie.com/blogs/trade-investment-policy-watch/we-know-what-causes-trade-deficits.

Galarraga, Ibon and Anil Markandya. "Economic Techniques to Estimate the Demand for Sustainable Products: A Case Study for Fair Trade and Organic Coffee in the United Kingdom." *Economia Agaria y Recursos Naturales* 4, no. 7 (2004): 109–134.

Galor, Oded and David N. Weil. "From Malthusian Stagnation to Modern Growth." *American Economic Review* 89, no. 2: 150–154.

Ganzach Yoav. "Intelligence and the Rationality of Political Preferences." *Intelligence* 69 (July–August 2018): 59–70.

Gastfriend, Eric. "90% of All Scientists That Have Ever Lived Are Alive Today." *Future of Life Institute*, November 5, 2015. https://futureoflife.org/2015/11/05/90-of-all-the-scientists-that-ever-lived-are-alive-today/.

Gelman, Andrew, Nate Silver, and Aaron Edlin. "What is the Probability Your Vote Will Make a Difference?" *Economic Inquiry* 50, no. 2 (April 2012): 321–326.

Gennaioli, Nicola, Rafael La Porta, Florencio Lopez-De-Silanes, and Andrei Shleifer. "Human Capital and Regional Development." *Quarterly Journal of Economics* 128, no. 1 (February 2013): 105–164.

Gentner, Dedre and Keith J. Holyoak. "Reasoning and Learning by Analogy: Introduction." *American Psychologist* 52, no. 1 (January 1997): 32–34.

George, Andy. "How to Make a $1500 Sandwich in Only 6 Months." *How To Make Everything*, September 15, 2015. https://www.youtube.com/watch?v=URvWSsAgtJE.

Gigerenzer, Gerd. *Rationality for Mortals: How People Cope with Uncertainty*. Oxford: Oxford University Press, 2010.

Gigerenzer, Gerd. "The Bias Bias in Economics." *Review of Behavioral Economics* 5, no. 3–4 (2018): 303–336.

Gigerenzer, Gerd and Henry Brighton. "Homo Heuristicus: Why Biased Minds Make Better Inferences." *Topics in Cognitive Science* 1, no. 1 (January 2009): 107–143.

Gigerenzer, Gerd and Daniel G. Goldstein. "Reasoning the Fast and Frugal Way: Models of Bounded Rationality." *Psychological Review* 103, no. 4 (October 1996): 650–659.

Gigerenzer Gerd, Peter M. Todd, and the ABC Research Group. *Simple Heuristics that Make Us Smart*. Oxford: Oxford University Press, 2000.

Gilens, Martin. *Affluence and Influence: Economic Inequality and Political Power*. Princeton: Princeton University Press, 2012.

Glaeser, Edward. "The Locavore's Dilemma: Urban Farms Do More Harm than Good to the Environment." *Boston.com*, June 16, 2011. http://archive.boston.com/bostonglobe/editorial_opinion/oped/articles/2011/06/16/the_locavores_dilemma/.

Glaeser, Edward. *The Triumph of the City: How Our Greatest Invention Makes Us Richer, Smarter, Greener, Healthier, and Happier.* New York: Penguin, 2011.

Glaeser, Edward and Joseph Gyourko, "The Economic Implications of Housing Supply." *Journal of Economic Perspectives* 32, no. 1 (Winter 2018): 3–30.

Glanz, Jason M., David L. McClure, and David J. Magid. "Parental Refusal of Varicella Vaccination and the Associated Risk of Varicella Infection in Children." *Archives of Pediatrics & Adolescent Medicine* 164, no. 1 (January 2010): 66–70.

Glanz, Jason M., David L. McClure, David J. Magid, Matthew F. Daley, Eric K. France, Daniel A. Salmon, and Simon J. Hambridge. "Parental Refusal of Pertussis Vaccination is Associated with an Increased Risk of Pertussis Infection in Children." *Pediatrics* 123, no. 6 (June 2009): 1446–1451.

Glanz, Jason M., David L. McClure, Sean T. O'Leary, Komal J. Narwaney, David J. Magid, Matthew F. Daley, and Simon J. Hambridge. "Parental Decline of Pneumococcal Vaccination and Risk of Pneumococcal Related Disease in Children." *Vaccine* 29, no. 5 (January 29, 2011): 994–999.

Goetz, Stephen J. and Anil Rupasingha. "Wal-Mart and Social Capital." *American Journal of Agricultural Economics* 88, no. 5 (December 2006): 1296–1303.

Goldberg, Jonah. *Suicide of the West: How the Rebirth of Tribalism, Populism, Nationalism, and Identity Politics is Destroying American Democracy.* New York: Crown Forum, 2018.

Goodwin, Barry K., Michele C. Marra, and Nicholas E. Piggott. "The Cost of a GMO-Free Market Basket of Food in the United States." *AgBioForum* 19, no. 1 (2016): 25–33.

GRA, Incorporated. *Economic Values for FAA Investment and Regulatory Decisions, A Guide.* FAA Office of Aviation Policy and Plans, U.S. Federal Aviation Administration. Washington, DC, 2007.

Granovetter, Mark S. "The Strength of Weak Ties." *American Journal of Sociology* 78, no. 6 (1973): 1360–1380.

Gray, M. Nolan. "How Should We Interpret Jane Jacobs?" *Market Urbanism*, June 30, 2018. https://marketurbanism.com/2018/07/30/how-should-we-interpret-jane-jacobs/.

Greenhouse, Steven. "Noncompete Clauses Increasingly Pop Up in Array of Jobs." *New York Times*, June 8, 2014. https://www.nytimes.com/2014/06/09/business/noncompete-clauses-increasingly-pop-up-in-array-of-jobs.html.

Greenwood, Robin, Andrei Shleifer, and Yang You. "Bubbles for Fama." *Journal of Financial Economics* 131, no. 1 (January 2019): 20–43.

Griggs, Brandon. "Living While Black." *CNN*, December 28, 2018. https://www.cnn.com/2018/12/20/us/living-while-black-police-calls-trnd/index.html.

Griskevicius, Vladas, Joshua M. Tybur, Jill Sundie, Robert B. Cialdini, Geoffrey F. Miller, and Douglas T. Kenrick. "Blatant Benevolence and Conspicuous Consumption: When Romantic Moves Elicit Strategic Costly Signals." *Journal of Personality and Social Psychology* 93, no. 1 (July 2007): 85–102.

Griskevicius, Vladas, Joshua M. Tybur, and Bran Van Bergh. "Going Green to Be Seen: Status, Reputation, and Conspicuous Conservation." *Journal of Personality and Social Psychology* 98, no. 3 (March 2010): 392–404.

Griswold, Daniel. *Plumbing America's Balance of Trade*. Arlington, VA: Mercatus Center, 2017. https://www.mercatus.org/system/files/mercatus-griswold-balance-of-trade-v1.pdf.

Grove, William M., David H. Zald, Boyd S. Lebow, Beth E. Snitz, and Chad Nelson. "Clinical Versus Mechanistic Prediction: A Meta-Analysis." *Psychological Assessment* 12, no. 1 (March 2000): 19–30.

Gwartney, James, Randall Holcombe, and Robert Lawson. "Institutions and the Impact of Investment on Growth." *Kyklos* 59, no. 2 (May 2006): 255–273.

Gwartney, James, Robert Lawson, Joshua Hall, and Ryan H. Murphy. *Economic Freedom of the World*. Vancouver: Fraser Institute, 2018.

Haidt, Jonathan. *The Righteous Mind: Why Good People Are Divided by Politics and Religion*. New York: Pantheon, 2012.

Hall, Kevin D., Kong Y. Chen, Juen Guo, Yan Y Lam, Rudolph L. Leibel, Laurel E.S. Mayer, Marc Reitman, Michael Rosenbaum, Steven R. Smith, B. Timothy Walsh, and Eric Ravussin. "Energy Expenditure and Body Composition Changes after an Isocaloric Ketogenic Diet in Overweight and Obese Men." *The American Journal of Clinical Nutrition* 104, no. 2 (August 2016): 324–333.

Hansen, Gary D. and Edward C. Prescott. "Malthus to Solow." *American Economic Review* 92, no. 4 (September 2002): 1205–1217.

Hanson, Robin. "Shall We Vote on Values, But Bet on Beliefs?" *Journal of Political Philosophy* 21, no. 2 (June 2013): 151–178.

Hanson, Robin. *The Age of Em: Work, Love, and Life when Robots Rule the Earth*. New York: Oxford University Press, 2016.

Hardy, Charlie L. and Mark Van Vugt. "Nice Guys Finish Last: The Competitive Altruism Hypothesis." *Personality and Social Psychological Bulletin* 32, no. 10 (October 2006): 1402–1413.

Harford, Tim. *Adapt: Why Success Always Starts with Failure*. New York: Picador, 2011.

Hargreaves Heap, Shaun P. "Social Capital and Snake Oil." *Review of Austrian Economics* 21, no. 2–3 (September 2008): 199–207.

Hargreaves Heap, Shaun P. and Daniel John Zizzo. "The Value of Groups." *American Economic Review* 99, no. 1 (March 2009): 295–323.

Harper, David A. *Entrepreneurship and the Market Process: An Enquiry into the Growth of Knowledge*. London: Routledge, 1996.

Harris, Ann, and Andres Rodriguez-Clare. "Trade, Foreign Investment, and Industrial Policy for Developing Countries." In *Handbook of Development Economics*, volume 5, edited by Dani Rodrick and Mark Rosenzweig, 4039–4214. Oxford, UK: North-Holland, 2010.

Harris, Sam. *The Moral Landscape: How Science Can Determine Human Values*. New York: Free Press, 2010.

Hayek, F.A. "The Atavism of Social Justice." In *New Studies in Politics, Philosophy, and Economics*, 57–68. New York: Routledge, 1978.

Hayek, F.A. *Law, Legislation, and Liberty*, revised edition. New York: Routledge, 2013.

Heinlein, Robert. *Time Enough for Love*, reissue edition. New York: Ace, 1988.

Hendrickson, Mark. "U2's Bono Courageously Embraces Capitalism." *Forbes*, November 8, 2013. https://www.forbes.com/sites/markhendrickson/2013/11/08/u2s-bono-courageously-embraces-capitalism/#5225baa7575a.

Hess, Karl. *Community Technology*. New York: Harper & Row, 1979.

Hill, Holly A. Laurie D. Elams-Evans, David Yankey, James A. Singleton, and Yoojae Kang. "Vaccination Coverage Among Children Aged 19–35 Months – United States, 2017." *Morbidity and Mortality Weekly Report* 67, no. 40 (October 12, 2018): 1123–1128.

Hinnfors, Jonas, Andrea Spehar, and Gregg Bucken-Knapp. "The Missing Factor: Why Social Democracy Can Lead to Restrictive Immigration Policy." *Journal of European Public Policy* 19, no. 4 (2012): 585–603.

Hirata, Keiko and Mark Warschauer. *Japan: The Paradox of Harmony*. New Haven: Yale University Press, 2014.

Hirsch, E.D. *Cultural Literacy: What Every American Needs to Know*. Boston: Houghton Mifflin, 1987.

Hodgson, Geoffrey. *Economics and Utopia*. London: Routledge, 1998.

Hoppe, Hans-Hermann. "The Case for Free Trade and Immigration Restrictions." *Journal of Libertarian Studies* 13, no. 2 (Summer 1998): 221–233.

Hoppe, Hans-Hermann. *Democracy – The God That Failed: The Economics and Politics of Monarchy, Democracy, and Natural Order*. New York: Routledge, 2001.

Horwitz, Steve. "The Calling: In Defense of Complex, Global, Fast Living." *FFF Articles*, May 2, 2013. https://www.fff.org/explore-freedom/article/the-calling-in-defense-of-complex-global-fast-living/.

Hou, Kewei, Chen Xue, and Lu Zhang. "Replicating Anomalies." *The Review of Financial Studies*. Forthcoming.

Hsieh, Chang-Tai, Erik Hurst, Charles I. Jones, and Peter Klenow. "The Allocation of Talent and U.S. Economic Growth." *NBER Working Paper*, no. 18693. Cambridge: National Bureau of Economic Research, 2013.

Hseih, Chang-Tai and Enrico Moretti. "Housing Constraints and Spatial Misallocation." *American Economic Journal: Macroeconomics* 11, no. 2 (April 2019): 1–39.

Huemer, Michael. *The Problem of Political Authority: An Examination of the Right to Coerce and Duty to Obey*. New York: Palgrave Macmillan, 2012.

Hunt, Alistair and Ramon Arigoni Ortiz. "Review of Revealed Preference Studies on Children's Environmental Health." Report prepared for OECD Project on the "Valuation of Environment-Related Health Impacts, with a Particular Focus on Children." Unpublished manuscript, Bath: University of Bath, 2006. http://www.researchgate.net/profile/Ramon_Ortiz/publication/267220759_Review_of_Revealed_Preferences_Studies_on_Children's_Environmental_Health/links/544fca980cf201441e934e6f.pdf.

IGM Forum. "Occupational Licensing for Economists." April 17, 2018. http://www.igmchicago.org/surveys/occupational-licensing-for-economists.

Ikeda, Sanford. "Rent-Seeking: A Primer." Foundation for Economic Education, November 1, 2003. https://fee.org/articles/rent-seeking-a-primer/.

Illing, Sean. "Epistocracy: A Political Theorist's Case for Letting Only the Informed Vote." *Vox*, November 9, 2018. https://www.vox.com/2018/7/23/17581394/against-democracy-book-epistocracy-jason-brennan.

Immerwahr, Daniel. "Polanyi in the United States: Peter Drucker, Karl Polanyi, and the Midcentury Critique of Economic Society." *Journal of the History of Ideas* 70, no. 3 (July 2009): 445–466.

Ingram, James C. *International Economics*, 2nd ed. New York: Wiley and Sons, 1986.

International Monetary Fund. *Annual Report on Exchange Arrangements and Exchange Restrictions*. Washington, DC: International Monetary Fund, 2015.

Ioannidis, John P. A. "The Challenge of Reforming Nutritional Epidemiological Research." *Journal of the American Medical Association* 320, no. 10 (September 2018): 969–970.

Ioannidis, John P.A., T.D. Stanley, and Hristos Doucouliagos. "The Power of Bias in Economics Research." *The Economic Journal* 127, no. 605 (October 2017): F236-F265.

Irwin, Douglas. "Review of *Kicking Away the Ladder: Development Strategy in Historical Perspective*." EH.net, April, 2004. https://eh.net/book_reviews/kicking -away-the-ladder-development-strategy-in-historical-perspective/.

Irwin, Douglas. "Does Trade Reform Promote Economic Growth? A Review of Recent Evidence." *NBER Working Paper* no. 25927. Cambridge: National Bureau of Economic Research, 2019.

Jacobs, Jane. *The Death and Life of Great American Cities*. New York: Vintage, 1961.

Jackson, Jeremy Art Carden, and Ryan A. Compton. "Economic Freedom and Social Capital." *Applied Economics* 54 (2015): 5853–5867.

James, Bill. *The New Bill James Historical Baseball Abstract*. Revised edition. New York: The Free Press, 2003.

Johar, J.S and M. Joseph Sirgy. "Value-Expressive versus Utilitarian Advertising Appeals: When and Why to Use Which Approach." *Journal of Advertising* 20, no. 3 (1991): 23–33.

Johnson, Steven. *Everything Bad Is Good for You*. New York: Riverhead Books, 2005.

Jones, Bradley. "Support for Free Trade Agreements Rebounds Modestly, but Wide Partisan Differences Remain." *Factank*, April 25, 2017. http://www.pewresear ch.org/fact-tank/2017/04/25/support-for-free-trade-agreements-rebounds-mode stly-but-wide-partisan-differences-remain/.

Kaczynski, Ted. "Industrial Society and Its Future." *The Washington Post*, September 22, 1995. https://www.washingtonpost.com/wp-srv/national/longterm/unabomber/ manifesto.text.htm.

Kahneman, Daniel. *Thinking, Fast and Slow*. New York: Farrar, Straus and Giroux, 2011.

Keen, Steve. *Debunking Economics: The Naked Emperor of the Social Sciences*. New York: St. Martin's Press, 2002.

Kenrick, Douglas T. and Vladas Griskevicius. *The Rational Animal: How Evolution Made Us Smarter Than We Think*. New York: Basic Books, 2013.

Kerekes, Carrie B. and Claudia R. Williamson. "Discovering Law: Hayekian Competition in Medieval Iceland." *Griffith Law Review* 21, no. 2 (2012): 432–447.

Keri, Jonah. *The Extra 2%: How Wall Street Strategies Took a Major League Baseball Team from Worst to First*. New York: ESPN Books, 2011.

Khan, Razib. "Do Liberals Oppose Genetically Modified Organisms More Than Con-servatives?" *Gene Expression*, June 11, 2013. http://blogs.discovermagazine.com/gnxp/2013/06/do-liberals-oppose-genetically-modified-organisms-more-than-conservatives/#.WUBZVty1uM9.

Kim, Seon-Woong, Jayson L. Lusk, and B. Wade Brorsen. "'Look at Me, I'm Buying Organic': The Effect of Social Pressure on Organic Food Purchases." *Journal of Agricultural and Resource Economics* 43, no. 3 (2018): 364–387.

Klein, Daniel B. "The People's Romance: Why People Love Government (As Much as They Do)." *The Independent Review* 10, no. 1 (Summer 2005): 5–37.

Klein, Daniel B. "The Ideological Migration of Economics Laureates: Introduction and Overview." *Econ Journal Watch* 10, no. 3 (September 2013): 218–239.

Klein, Daniel B. and Charlotta Stern. "Professors and their Politics: The Policy Views of Social Scientists." *Critical Review* 17, no. 3–4 (2005): 257–303.

Knack, Stephen and Philip Keefer. "Institutions and Economic Performance: Cross-Country Tests Using Alternative Institutional Measures." *Economics & Politics* 7, no. 3 (November 1995): 207–227.

Koppl, Roger. "The Social Construction of Expertise." *Society* 47, no. 3 (May 2010): 220–226.

Koppl, Roger. "Experts and Information Choice." *Advances in Austrian Economics* 17 (2012): 171–202.

Koppl, Roger. *Expert Failure*. New York: Cambridge University Press, 2017.

Kramer, Staci D. "High-Profile Buyouts Won't Save the New York Times From Newsroom Layoffs: Memo." *The Washington Post*, April 15, 2008. http://www.washingtonpost.com/wp-dyn/content/article/2008/04/15/AR2008041502597_pf.html.

Krikorian. Mark. "Immigration + Welfare = Bad News." *National Review*, August 8, 2012. https://www.nationalreview.com/corner/immigration-welfare-bad-news-mark-krikorian/.

Krueger, Anne O. "The Political Economy of the Rent-Seeking Society." *American Economic Review* 64, no. 3 (June 1974): 291–303.

Krugman, Paul. *Pop Internationalism*. Cambridge: MIT Press, 1996.

Kuznets, Paul W. "An East Asian Model of Economic Development: Japan, Taiwan, and South Korea." *Economic Development and Cultural Change* 36, no. 3 (April 1988): S11–S43.

Kwak, James. *Economism: Bad Economics and the Rise of Inequality*. New York: Pantheon, 2017.

La Porta, Rafael, Florencio Lopez-de-Silanes, and Andre Shleifer. "The Economic Consequences of Legal Origins." *Journal of Economic Literature* 46, no. 2 (June 2008): 285–322.

Lander, Christian. "Christian Lander: 'Stuff White People Like' | Talks at Google." *Talks at Google*, July 17, 2008. https://www.youtube.com/watch?v=KfRgjW4hFcU.

Lander, Christian. *Stuff White People Like*. New York: Random House, 2008.

Lander, Christian. *Whiter Shades of Pale*. New York: Random House, 2010.

Lange, Oskar. "On the Economic Theory of Socialism I." *Review of Economic Studies* 4, no. 1 (October 1936): 189–201.

Lawson, Robert A. and Walter Block. "Government Decentralization and Economic Freedom." *Asian Economic Review* 38, no. 3 (1996): 421–434.

Lawson, Robert, Ryan H. Murphy, and Benjamin Powell. "The Determinants of Economic Freedom: A Survey." Working Paper. Dallas: Southern Methodist University. https://papers.ssrn.com/sol3/papers.cfm?abstract_id=3266641.

Leeson, Peter T. "Better Off Stateless: Somalia Before and After Government Collapse." *Journal of Comparative Economics* 35, no. 4 (December 2007): 689–710.

Leeson, Peter T. *Anarchy Unbound: Why Self-Governance Works Better Than You Think.* Cambridge: Cambridge University Press, 2014.

Leeson Peter T. and Jacob W. Russ. "Witch Trials." *The Economic Journal* 128, no. 613 (August 2018): 2066–2105.

Leibrecht, Markus and Hans Pitlik. "Social Trust, Institutional and Political Constraints on the Executive and Deregulation of Markets." *European Journal of Political Economy* 39 (September 2015): 249–268.

Leonard, Thomas C. *Illiberal Reformers: Race, Eugenics, & American Economists in the Progressive Era.* Princeton: Princeton University Press, 2016.

Lerner, Abba. "Theory and Practice in Socialist Economies." *Review of Economic Studies* 6, no. 1 (October 1938): 71–75.

Levy, David M. and Sandra J. Peart. "'Almost Wholly Negative': The Ford Foundation's Appraisal of the Virginia School." Working paper, Fairfax: George Mason University, 2014. https://papers.ssrn.com/sol3/papers.cfm?abstract_id=2485695.

Levy, David M. and Sandra J. Peart. *Escape from Democracy: The Role of Experts and the Public in Economic Policy.* Cambridge: Cambridge University Press, 2017.

Levy, Jacob T. *Rationalism, Pluralism, & Freedom.* Oxford: Oxford University Press, 2015.

Lewis, Michael. *Moneyball: The Art of Winning and Unfair Game.* New York: Norton, 2003.

Lindbergh, Ben. "Sabermetrics is Killing Bad Dugout Decisions." *Fivethirtyeight*, January 14, 2016. https://fivethirtyeight.com/features/sabermetrics-is-killing-bad-dugout-decisions/.

Lindsey, Brink. *The Age of Abundance: How Prosperity Transformed America's Politics and Culture.* New York: HarperCollins, 2007.

Lohr, Steve. "Are Robots Coming for Your Job? Eventually, Yes." *The New York Times*, September 21, 2018. https://www.nytimes.com/2018/09/21/technology/artificial-intelligence-jobs.html.

Lomasky, Loren. "Swing and a Myth: A Review of Caplan's 'The Myth of the Rational Voter.'" *Public Choice* 135, no. 3–4 (June 2008): 469–484.

Lopez-Guerra, Claudio. *Democracy and Disenfranchisement: The Morality of Electoral Exclusions.* New York: Oxford University Press, 2011.

Loureiro, Maria L. and Justus Lotade. "Do Fair Trade and Eco-Labels in Coffee Wake Up the Consumer Conscience?" *Ecological Economics* 53, no. 1 (April 2005): 129–138.

Loury, Glenn C. "A Dynamic Theory of Racial Income Differences." In *Women, Minorities, and Employment*, edited by Phyllis A. Wallace and Annette M. LaMond, 153–188. Lexington: Lexington Books, 1977.

Ludeke, Steven G. and Stig H. R. Rasmussen. "Different Political Systems Suppress or Facilitate the Impact of Intelligence on How You Vote: A Comparison of the U.S. and Denmark." *Intelligence* 70 (September–October 2018): 1–6.

Lundstrom, Susanna. "The Effect of Democracy on Different Categories of Economic Freedom." *European Journal of Political Economy* 21, no. 4 (December 2005): 967–980.

Lusk, Jayson L. and F. Norwood Bailey. "The Locavore's Dilemma: Why Pineapples Shouldn't be Grown in North Dakota." *Library of Economics and Liberty*, January 3, 2011. http://www.econlib.org/library/Columns/y2011/LuskNorwoodlocavore.html.

Lutter, Mark. "Pokémon Coming Together: The Revival of American Civic Culture." *The Daily Caller*, July 11, 2016. https://dailycaller.com/2016/07/11/pokemon-coming-together-the-revival-of-american-civic-culture/.

Machan, Tibor. "Liberalism and Atomistic Individualism." *Journal of Value Inquiry* 34, no. 2–3 (September 2000): 227–247.

Mackie, Gerry. "Rational Ignorance and Beyond." In *Collective Wisdom: Principles and Mechanisms*, edited by Helene Landmore and Jon Elster, 290–319. Cambridge, UK: Cambridge University Press, 2012.

Magill, Shelley S., Erin O'Leary, Sarah J. Janelle, Deborah L. Thompson, Ghinwa Dumyati, Joelle Nadle, Lucy E. Wilson, Marion A. Kainer, Ruth Lynfield, Samantha Griessman, Susan M. Ray, Zintars Beldavs, Cindy Gross, Wendy Bamberg, Marla Sievers, Cathleen Concannon, Nicolai Buhr, Linn Warnke, Meghan Maloney, Valerie Ocampo, Janet Brooks, Tolulope Oyewumi, Shamima Sharmin, Katherine Richards, Jean Rainbow, Monika Samper, Emily B. Hancock, Denise Leaptrot, Eileen Scalise, R.N., M.S.N., Farzana Badrun, Ruby Phelps, and Jonathan R. Edwards. "Changes in Prevalence of Health Care-Associated Infections in U.S. Hospitals." *New England Journal of Medicine* 379 (November 2018): 1732–1744.

Magness, Phillip. "What Does 'Neoliberalism' Really Mean?" *Reason,* January 2019. https://reason.com/2018/12/30/what-does-neoliberalism-really/.

Malkiel, Burton. *A Random Walk Down Wall Street: The Time-Tested Strategy for Successful Investing.* 11th ed. New York: W.W. Norton & Company, 2016.

Marquet, Oriol, Claudia Alberico, Deepti Adlakha, and J. Aaron Hipp. "Examining Motivations to Play Pokémon Go and Their Influence on Perceived Outcomes and Physical Activity." *JMIR Serious Games* 5, no. 4 (October–December 2017): e21.

Marris, Emma. "Hipsters Who Hunt." *Slate*, December 5, 2012. http://www.slate.com/articles/health_and_science/science/2012/12/hunting_by_liberal_urban_locavores_is_a_trend_good_for_the_environment.html.

McCloskey, Deirdre. *Bourgeois Dignity: Why Economics Cannot Explain the Modern World*. Chicago: University of Chicago Press, 2010.

McGinty, Jo Craven. "Why the Government Puts a Dollar Value on Life." *Wall Street Journal*, March 25, 2016. https://www.wsj.com/articles/why-the-government-puts-a-dollar-value-on-life-1458911310.

McKenzie, Richard B. *Predictably Rational? In Search of Defenses for Rational Behavior in Economics*. Berlin: Springer, 2010.

McWilliams, James E. *Just Food: Where Locavores Get it Wrong and How We Can Eat Truly Responsibly.* New York: Little, Brown and Company, 2009.

McWilliams, James E. "The Butcher Next Door." *Slate*, June 6, 2012. http://www .slate.com/articles/life/food/2012/06/diy_animal_slaughter_urban_hipsters_think_ it_s_a_good_idea_it_isn_t_.html.

Medema, Steven G. *The Hesitant Hand: Taming Self-Interest in the History of Economic Ideas.* Princeton: Princeton University Press, 2009.

Mellers, Barbara, Philip Tetlock, and Hal R. Arkes. "Forecasting Tournaments, Epistemic Humility, and Attitude Depolarization." *Cognition* 188 (July 2019): 19–26.

Mendenhall, Allen. *Literature and Liberty: Essays in Libertarian Literary Criticism.* Lanham, MD: Lexington Books, 2014.

Mental Floss. "Scientific Reasons to Respect Light Beer." October 31, 2012. http:// mentalfloss.com/article/12940/scientific-reasons-respect-light-beer.

Miller, Geoffrey. *The Mating Mind: How Sexual Choice Shaped the Evolution of Human Nature.* New York: Doubleday, 2000.

Miller, Geoffrey. *Spent: Sex, Evolution, and Consumer Behavior.* New York: Viking, 2009.

Miller, Stephen C. "Economic Bias and Ideology: Evidence from the General Social Survey." *Journal of Private Enterprise* 25, no. 1 (Fall 2009): 31–49.

Mises, Ludwig von, *Human Action: A Treatise on Economics.* New Haven: Yale University Press, 1949.

Mitchell, William C. "Chicago Political Economy: A Public Choice Perspective." *Public Choice* 63, no. 3 (December 1989): 283–292.

Mochon, Daniel, Michael I. Norton, and Dan Ariely. "Bolstering and Restoring Feelings of Competence via the IKEA Effect." *International Journal of Research in Marketing* 29, no. 4 (December 2012): 363–369.

Molina-Morales, F. Xavier and M. Teresa Martinez-Fernandez. "Too Much Love in the Neighborhood Can Hurt: How an Excess of Intensity and Trust in Relationships May Produce Negative Effects on Firms." *Strategic Management Journal* 30, no. 9 (September 2009): 1013–1023.

Morris, Charles R. "We Were Pirates, Too." *Foreign Policy*, December 6, 2012. https ://foreignpolicy.com/2012/12/06/we-were-pirates-too/.

Moskowitz Tobias J. and L. Jon Wertheim. *Scorecasting: The Hidden Influence Behind How Sports Are Played and Games Are Won.* New York: Crown Archetype, 2011.

Muir, David, "Reporter's Notebook: Inside a Chinese Factory Town." *ABC News*, November 10, 2010. http://abcnews.go.com/Business/chinas-booming-factory-t owns-specialize-zippers-umbrellas-santa/story?id=12150627.

Muller, Jerry Z. *The Tyranny of Metrics.* Princeton: Princeton University Press, 2018.

Munger, Michael C. "They Clapped: Can Price-Gouging Laws Prohibit Scarcity?" *Library of Economics and Liberty*, January 8, 2007. https://www.econlib.org/librar y/Columns/y2007/Mungergouging.html.

Munger, Michael C. *The Thing Itself: Essays on Academics and the State.* Mungerella Publishing, 2015.

Munger, Michael C. *Tomorrow 3.0: Transaction Costs and the Sharing Economy.* Cambridge: Cambridge University Press, 2018.

Murphy, Ryan H. "Heterogeneous Moral Views in the Stateless Society." *Libertarian Papers* 7, no. 1 (2015): 39–54.

Murphy. Ryan H. "Rational Irrationality across Institutional Contexts." *Journal des Economistes et des Etudes Humaines* 21, no. 1–2 (December 2015): 321–335.

Murphy, Ryan H. "What Do Recent Trends in *Economic Freedom of the World* Really Tell Us?" *Economic Affairs* 35, no. 1 (February 2015): 138–150.

Murphy, Ryan H. "Kissing Babies to Signal You Are Not a Psychopath." *Journal of Neuroscience, Psychology, and Economics* 9, no. 3–4 (2016): 217–225.

Murphy, Ryan H. *The New Aristocrats: A Cultural and Economic Analysis of the New Status Signaling.* Briefing Paper, London: Adam Smith Institute, 2016.

Murphy, Ryan H. "The Willingness-to-Pay for Caplanian Irrationality." *Rationality and Society* 28, no. 1 (2016): 52–82.

Murphy, Ryan H. "The Diseconomies of Do-It-Yourself." *The Independent Review* 22, no. 2 (Fall 2017): 245–255.

Murphy, Ryan H. "Corporations as the Outgroup?" Working paper. Dallas: Southern Methodist University, 2018. https://papers.ssrn.com/sol3/papers.cfm?abstract_id=3279828.

Murphy, Ryan H. "Imperfect Democracy and Economic Freedom." *Journal of Public Finance and Public Choice* 33, no. 2 (October 2018): 197–224.

Murphy, Ryan H. "The Perils of Buying Social Capital Locally." *Journal of Private Enterprise* 33, no. 2 (Summer 2018): 67–81.

Murphy, Ryan H. "Governance and the Dimensions of Autocracy." *Constitutional Political Economy* 30, no. 2 (June 2019): 131–148.

Murphy, Ryan H. "Putting a Price on the Large Personal Cost of Failing to Vaccinate." *InsideSources*, April 25, 2019. https://www.insidesources.com/putting-a-price-on-the-large-personal-cost-of-failing-to-vaccinate/.

Murphy, Ryan H. "The Rationality of Literal Tide Pod Consumption." *Journal of Bioeconomics* 21, no. 2 (July 2019): 111–122.

Murray, Charles. *Coming Apart: The State of White America, 1960–2010.* New York: Crown Forum, 2012.

Nevins, Joseph. "Kicking the Habit: Air Travel in the Time of Climate Change." *YES!*, December 13, 2010. https://www.yesmagazine.org/planet/kicking-the-habit-air-travel-in-a-time-of-climate-change.

Nilsson, Arthur, Arvid Erlandsson, and Daniel Vastfjall. "The Complex Relation Between Receptivity to Pseudo-Profound Bullshit and Political Ideology." *Personality and Social Psychology Bulletin*, forthcoming.

Nordhaus, William. *The Climate Casino: Risk, Uncertainty, and Economics for a Warming World.* New Haven: Yale University Press, 2013.

North, Douglass C. "Institutions, Transaction Costs and Economic Growth." *Economic Inquiry* 25, no. 3 (July 1987): 419–428.

North, Douglass C. *Institutions, Institutional Change, and Economic Performance.* Cambridge: Cambridge University Press, 1990.

Norton, Michael I., Daneil Mochon, and Dan Ariely. "The IKEA Effect: When Labor Leads to Love." *Journal of Consumer Psychology* 22, no. 3 (July 2012): 453–460.

Nowrasteh, Alex. "Karl Polanyi's Battle with Economic History." *Libertarianism. org*, September 12, 2013. https://www.libertarianism.org/blog/karl-polanyis-battl e-economic-history.

Nowrasteh, Alex. "The Fiscal Impact of Immigration." In *The Economics of Immigration: Market-Based Approaches, Social Science, and Public Policy*, edited by Benjamin Powell, 38–69. New York: Oxford University Press, 2015.

Nozick, Robert. *Anarchy, State, and Utopia*. New York: Basic Books, 1974.

Nuland, Sherwin. *The Doctor's Plague: Germs, Childbed Fever, and the Strange Story of Ignaz Semmelweis*. New York: Great Discoveries, 2003.

Offit, Paul. *Deadly Choices: How the Anti-Vaccine Movement Threatens Us All*. New York: Basic Books, 2011.

Ohman, Arne and Susan Mineka. "Fears, Phobias, and Preparedness: Toward an Evolved Module of Fear and Fear Learning." *Psychological Review* 108, no. 3 (July 2001): 483–522.

Ohman, Arne and Susan Mineka. "The Malicious Serpent: Snakes as Prototypical Stimulus for an Evolved Module of Fear." *Current Directions in Psychological Science* 12, no. 1 (February 2003): 5–9.

Olson, Mancur. *The Logic of Collective Action: Public Goods and the Theory of Groups*. Cambridge: Harvard University Press, 1965.

Olson, Mancur. *Power and Prosperity: Outgrowing Communist and Capitalist Dictatorships*. Oxford: Oxford University Press, 2000.

O'Neil, Cathy. *Weapons of Math Destruction: How Big Data Increases Inequality and Threatens Democracy*. New York: Crown, 2016.

O'Reilly, Colin. "Can War Foster Institutional Change?" Working Paper. Omaha: Creighton University, 2018. https://papers.ssrn.com/sol3/papers.cfm?abstract_i d=3197719.

Osman, Suleiman. *The Invention of Brownstone Brooklyn: Gentrification and the Search for Authenticity in Postwar New York*. New York: Oxford University Press, 2011.

Oster, Emily. *Expecting Better: Why the Conventional Pregnancy Wisdom is Wrong – And What You Really Need to Know*. New York: Penguin Press, 2013.

Oster, Emily. *Cribsheet: A Data-Driven Guide to Better, More Relaxed Parenting, from Birth to Preschool*. New York: Penguin Press, 2019.

Ostrom, Elinor. *Governing the Commons: The Evolution of Institutions for Collective Action*. New York: Cambridge University Press, 1990.

Ozimek, Adam. "Dear Homesteaders, Self-Reliance is a Delusion." *Forbes*, July 29, 2017. https://www.forbes.com/sites/modeledbehavior/2017/07/29/the-delusion-o f-self-reliant-off-the-grid-living/#c126e4c343d2.

Pacione, Michael. "Local Exchange Trading Systems as a Response to the Globalisation of Capitalism." *Urban Studies* 34, no. 8 (October 1997): 1179–1199.

Park, Kristen and Miguel I. Gomez. "Do Price Premiums Exist for Local Products?" *Journal of Food Distribution Research* 43, no. 1 (March 2012): 145–152.

Peltzman, Sam. "Toward a More General Theory of Regulation." *Journal of Law & Economics* 19, no. 2 (August 1976): 211–240.

Pennington, Mark. *Robust Political Economy: Classical Liberalism and the Future of Public Policy*. Northampton: Edward Elgar, 2011.

Peyser, Thomas. "Capitalist Vistas: Walt Whitman and Spontaneous Order." In *Literature and the Economics of Liberty: Spontaneous Order in Culture*, edited by Paul A. Cantor and Stephen Cox, 263–292. Auburn, AL: Ludwig von Mises Institute, 2009.

Pinker, Steven. *The Language Instinct: How Minds Create Language*. New York: W. Morrow, 1994.

Pinker, Steven. *The Blank Slate: The Modern Denial of Human Nature*. New York: Penguin, 2002.

Pinker, Steven. *The Better Angels of Our Nature: Why Violence Has Declined*. New York: Viking, 2011.

Pinker, Steven. *Enlightenment Now: The Case for Reason, Science, Humanism, and Progress*. New York: Viking, 2018.

Pinker, Steven and Paul Bloom. "Natural Language and Natural Selection." *Behavioral and Brain Sciences* 13, no. 4 (December 1990): 707–727.

Plott, Elaina. "Marco Rubio's Billion Dollar Sugar Addiction." *National Review*, November 13, 2015. http://www.nationalreview.com/article/427001/marco-rubi os-billion-dollar-sugar-addiction-elaina-plott.

Poland, Gregory A. and Robert M. Jacobson. "Understanding Those Who Do Not Understand: A Brief Review of the Anti-Vaccine Movement." *Vaccine* 19, no. 17–19 (March 21, 2001): 2440–2445.

Polanyi, Karl. *The Great Transformation*. New York: Farrar & Rinehart, 1944.

Pollan, Michael. *The Omnivore's Dilemma: A Natural History of Four Meals*. New York: Penguin, 2006.

Poplin, Ryan. Avinash V. Varadarajan, Katy Blumer, Yun Liu, Michael V. McConnell, Greg S. Corrado, Lily Peng, and Dale R. Webster. "Prediction of Cardiovascular Risk Factors from Retinal Fundus Photographs via Deep Learning." *Nature Biomedical Engineering* 2, no. 3 (March 2018): 158–164.

Popper, Karl. *Objective Knowledge: An Evolutionary Approach*. Oxford: Clarendon Press, 1972.

Portes, Alejandro. "Social Capital: Its Origins and Applications in Modern Sociology." *Annual Review of Sociology* 24 (August 1998): 1–24.

Portes, Alejandro and Patricia Landolt. "Downsides of Social Capital." *American Prospect* 26 (May–June 1996): 18–26.

Posner, Eric A. and E. Glen Weyl. *Radical Markets: Uprooting Capitalism and Democracy for a Just Society*. Princeton: Princeton University Press, 2018.

Posner, Richard. *Economic Analysis of Law*, 2nd ed. Boston: Little-Brown, 1977.

Potter, Andrew. *The Authenticity Hoax: How We Get Lost Finding Ourselves*. New York: HarperCollins, 2010.

Powell, Benjamin. "A Taste for Protectionism: Coca-Cola in the Classroom." *Journal of Private Enterprise* 23, no. 1 (Fall 2007): 154–158.

Powell, Benjamin, editor. *The Economics of Immigration: Market-Based Approaches, Social Science, and Public Policy*. Oxford: Oxford University Press, 2015.

Powell, Benjamin, Ryan Ford, and Alex Nowrasteh. "Somalia After State Collapse: Chaos or Improvement?" *Journal of Economic Behavior & Organization* 67, no. 3–4 (September 2008): 657–670.

Prevost, Lisa. *Snob Zones: Fear, Prejudice, and Real Estate*. Boston: Beacon Press, 2013.

Prokop, Andrew. "Why the Electoral College is the Absolute Worst, Explained." *Vox*, December 19, 2016. https://www.vox.com/policy-and-politics/2016/11/7/12315 574/electoral-college-explained-presidential-elections-2016.

Putnam, Robert. *Making Democracy Work: Civic Traditions in Modern Italy*. Princeton: Princeton University Press, 1993.

Putnam, Robert. *Bowling Alone*. New York: Simon & Schuster, 2000.

Putnam, Robert. "*E Pluribus Unum*: Diversity and Community in the Twenty-first Century." *Scandinavian Journal of Political Studies* 30, no. 2 (June 2007): 137–174.

Quiggan, John. *Zombie Economics: How Dead Ideas Still Walk among Us*. Princeton: Princeton University Press, 2010.

Ramachandran, Vilayanur S. and Baland Jalal. "The Evolutionary Theory of Psychology and Jealousy." *Frontiers in Psychology* 8 (2017): 1619.

Read, Leonard. *I, Pencil*. Irvington-on-Hudson: Foundation for Economic Education, 1958.

Reder, Melvin W. "Chicago Economics: Permanence and Change." *Journal of Economic Literature* 20, no. 1 (March 1982): 1–38.

Resnik, Brian and Julia Belluz. "A Top Cornell Food Researcher Has Had 15 Studies Retracted. That's a Lot." *Vox*, October 24, 2018. https://www.vox.com/scien ce-and-health/2018/9/19/17879102/brian-wansink-cornell-food-brand-lab-retra ctions-jama.

Ridley, Matt. *The Red Queen: Sex and the Evolution of Human Nature*. New York: MacMillan, 1994.

Ridley, Matt. *The Origins of Virtue: Human Instincts and the Evolution of Cooperation*. New York: Penguin, 1996.

Ridley, Matt. *The Rational Optimist: How Prosperity Evolves*. New York: Harper-Collins, 2010.

Ridley, Matt. *The Evolution of Everything: How Ideas Emerge*. New York: Harper, 2015.

Rizzo, Mario J. and Douglas Glen Whitman. "The Camel's Nose is in the Tent: Rules, Theories, and Slippery Slopes." *UCLA Law Review* 51, no. 2 (2003): 539–592.

Rizzo, Mario J. and Douglas Glen Whitman. "Little Brother is Watching You: New Paternalism on the Slippery Slopes." *University of Arizona Law Review* 51, no. 3 (2009): 685–739.

Roberts, Gilbert. "Competitive Altruism: From Reciprocity to the Handicap Principle." *Proceedings of the Royal Society of London B* 265 (March 1998): 427–431.

Robertson, D.H. *Control of Industry*. London: Nisbet & Co. Ltd., 1923.

Robin, Vicki. *Blessing the Hands that Feed Us: What Eating Closer to Home Can Teach Us about Food, Community, and Our Place on Earth*. New York: Viking, 2014.

Rode, Martin and James Gwartney. "Does Democratization Facilitate Economic Liberalization?" *European Journal of Political Economy* 28, no. 4 (December 2012): 607–619.

Rognlie, Matt. "Deciphering the Fall and Rise in Net Capital Share: Accumulation or Scarcity?" *Brookings Papers in Economic Activity* (Spring 2015): 1–54.

Romer, Paul. "Technologies, Rules, and Progress: The Case for Charter Cities." *Center for Global Development Essay*. Washington, D.C.: Center for Global Development, 2010. https://www.cgdev.org/publication/technologies-rules-and-progress-case-charter-cfgities.

Rosling, Hans. *Factfulness: Ten Reasons We're Wrong About the World – and Why Things Are Better Than You Think*. New York: Flatiron Books, 2018.

Rossman, Gabriel. "Obfuscatory Relational Work and Disreputable Exchange." *Sociological Theory* 32, no. 1 (March 2014): 43–63.

Rothstein, Bo. *Social Traps and the Problem of Trust*. Cambridge: Cambridge University Press, 2005.

Rowley, Charles K. and Daniel Houser. "The Life and Times of Gordon Tullock." *Public Choice* 152, no. 1 (July 2012): 3–27.

Rowley, Meg. "Let Us Like Baseball." *Fangraphs*, August 2, 2018. https://www.fangraphs.com/blogs/let-us-like-baseball/.

Rubin, Paul H. *Darwinian Politics: The Evolutionary Origin of Freedom*. Piscataway: Rutgers University Press, 2002.

Rubin, Paul H. "Folk Economics." *Southern Economic Journal* 70, no. 1 (July 2003): 157–171.

Saade, R. Lira and S. Montes Hernandez. "Cucurbits (*Cucurbita* spp.)." In *Neglected Crops: 1492 from a Different Perspective*, edited by J.E. Hernandez Bermejo and J. Leon, 67–68. Rome: Food and Agriculture of the United Nations, 1994.

Sachs, Jeffrey. "The Case for Aid." *Foreign Policy*, January 21, 2014. https://foreignpolicy.com/2014/01/21/the-case-for-aid/.

Salter, Alexander W. "Sovereignty as Exchange of Political Property Rights." *Public Choice* 165, no. 1–2 (October 2015): 79–96.

Salter, Alexander W. "Political Property Rights and Governance Outcomes: A Theory of the Corporate Polity." *Journal of Private Enterprise* 31, no. 4 (Winter 2016): 1–20.

Salter Alexander W. and Abigail Hall. "Calculating Bandits: Quasi-Corporate Governance and Institutional Selection in Autocracies." *Advances in Austrian Economics* 19 (2015): 193–213.

Satyanath, Shanker, Nico Voigtlander, and Hans-Joachim Voth. "Bowling for Fascism: Social Capital and the Rise of the Nazi Party." *Journal of Political Economy* 125, no. 2 (April 2017): 478–526.

Sawchik, Travis. *Big Data Baseball: Math, Miracles, and the End of a 20-Year Losing Streak*. New York: Flatiron Books, 2015.

Schelling, Thomas C. "Dynamic Models of Segregation." *Journal of Mathematical Sociology* 1, no. 2 (1971): 143–186.

Schilke, Oliver and Gabriel Rossman. "It's Only Wrong If It's Transactional: Moral Perceptions of Obfuscated Exchange." *American Sociological Review* 83, no. 6 (December 2018): 1079–1107.

Schlossberg, Tatiana. "Flying is Bad for the Planet. You Can Make it Better." *The New York Times*, June 27, 2017. https://www.nytimes.com/2017/07/27/climate/airplane-pollution-global-warming.html.

Schlottmann, Christopher and Jeff Sobo. *Foods, Animals, and the Environment: An Ethical Approach.* New York: Routledge, 2018.

Schollenberg, Linda. "Estimating the Hedonic Price for Fair Trade in Sweden." *British Food Journal* 114, no. 3 (2012): 428–446.

Schumpeter, Joseph. *The Theory of Economic Development.* Cambridge: Harvard University Press, 1934.

Schumpeter, Joseph. *Business Cycles: A Theoretical, Historical, and Statistical Analysis.* Volume II. New York: McGraw-Hill, 1939.

Schwab, Klaus, editor. *The Global Competitiveness Report 2015–2016.* Geneva: World Economic Forum, 2015.

Seabright, Paul. *The Company of Strangers: A Natural History of Economic Life.* 2nd Edition. Princeton: Princeton University Press, 2010.

Sexton, Steven. "Does Local Production Improve Environmental and Health Outcomes?" *Agricultural and Resource Economics Update* 13, no. 2 (November–December 2009): 5–8.

Sexton Steven and Alison Sexton. "Conspicuous Conservation: The Prius Halo and Willingness to Pay for Environmental Bona Fides." *Journal of Environmental Economics and Management* 67, no. 3 (May 2014): 303–317.

Shanks, David R., Miguel A. Vadillo, Benjamin Riedel, Ashley Clymo, Sinita Govind, Nisha Hickin, Amanda J.F. Tamman, and Lawa M.C. Puhlmann. "Romance, Risk, and Replication: Can Consumer Choices and Risk-Taking Be Primed by Mating Motives?" *Journal of Experimental Psychology: General* 144, no. 6 (December 2015): e142–e158.

Shenkman, Rick. *Political Animals: How Our Stone-Age Brain Gets in the Way of Smart Politics.* New York, Basic Books, 2016.

Shmanske, Stephen. "Austrian Themes, Data, and Sports Economics." *Review of Austrian Economics* 20, no. 1 (March 2007): 11–24.

Shoag, Daniel and Stan Veuger. "Shops and the City: Evidence on Local Externalities and Local Government Policies from Big-Box Bankruptcies." *Review of Economics and Statistics* 100, no. 3 (July 2018): 440–453.

Simler, Kevin and Robin Hanson. *The Elephant in the Brain: Hidden Motives in Everyday Life.* New York: Oxford University Press, 2018.

Simon, Herbert A. "A Behavioral Model of Rational Choice." *Quarterly Journal of Economics* 69, no. 1 (February 1955): 99–118.

Simon, Herbert A. "Rational Choice and the Structure of the Environment." *Psychological Review* 63, no. 2 (March 1956): 129–138.

Singer, Peter. *The Expanding Circle: Ethics and Sociobiology.* New York: Farrar, Straus and Giroux, 1981.

Singer, Peter. *A Darwinian Left.* New Haven: Yale University Press, 2000.

Singh, Maanvi. "How Snobbery Helped Take the Spice Out of European Cooking." *NPR*, March 26, 2015. https://www.npr.org/sections/thesalt/2015/03/26/394339284/how-snobbery-helped-take-the-spice-out-of-european-cooking.

Skousen, Mark. "The Perseverance of Paul Samuelson's *Economics*." *Journal of Economic Perspectives* 11, no. 2 (Spring 1997): 137–152.

Smaldino, Paul E. and Joshua M. Epstein. "Social Conformity despite Preferences for Distinctiveness." *Royal Society Open Science* 2 (March 2015): 140437.

Smith, Vernon L. "Constructivist and Ecological Rationality in Economics." *American Economic Review* 93, no. 3 (June 2003): 465–508.

Snowden, Christopher. "2018: The Nanny State Year in Review." *Velvet Glove, Iron Fist*, December 30, 2018. https://velvetgloveironfist.blogspot.com/2018/12/2018-nanny-state-in-review.html?m=1.

Somin, Ilya. *Democracy and Political Ignorance: Why Smaller Government is Smarter*. Stanford: Stanford University Press, 2013.

Somin, Ilya. "Over 80 Percent of Americans Support Mandatory Labels on Food Containing DNA." *The Washington Post*, January 17, 2015. https://www.washingtonpost.com/news/volokh-conspiracy/wp/2015/01/17/over-80-percent-of-americans-support-mandatory-labels-on-foods-containing-dna/?utm_term=.aa4c8126ee4e.

Sowell, Thomas. *Migrations and Cultures*. New York: Basic Books, 1996.

Spiller, Pablo T. "Politicians, Interest Groups, and Regulators: A Multiple-Principals Agency Theory of Regulation, or 'Let Them Be Bribed.'" *Journal of Law & Economics* 33, no. 1 (April 1990): 65–101.

Spitznagel, Mark and Nassim Nicholas Taleb. "Another 'Too Big to Fail' System in G.M.O.s." *The New York Times*, July 13, 2015. https://www.nytimes.com/2015/07/14/business/dealbook/another-too-big-to-fail-system-in-gmos.html.

Stansel, Dean. "Interjurisdictional Competition and Local Government Spending in U.S. Metropolitan Areas." *Public Finance Review* 34, no. 2 (March 2006): 173–194.

Starmans, Christina, Mark Shaskin, and Paul Bloom. "Why People Prefer Unequal Societies." *Nature Human Behaviour* 1, no 0082 (April 2017).

Stigler, George. "The Economics of Information." *Journal of Political Economy* 69, no. 3 (June 1961): 213–225.

Stigler, George. "The Theory of Economic Regulation." *The Bell Journal of Economics and Management Science* 2, no. 1 (Spring 1971): 3–21.

Storchmann, Karl. "Wine Economics." *Journal of Wine Economics* 7, no. 1 (May 2012): 24–27.

Stringham, Edward P. *Private Governance: Creating Oder in Economic and Social Life*. Oxford: Oxford University Press, 2015.

Stromberg, Joseph. "Kale, Brussels Sprouts, Cauliflower, and Cabbage Are All Varieties of the Same Magical Species." *Vox*, February 10, 2015. https://www.vox.com/xpress/2014/8/6/5974989/kale-cauliflower-cabbage-broccoli-same-plant.

Sumner, Scott. "Nominal GDP Futures Targeting." *Journal of Financial Stability* 17 (April 2015): 65–75.

Sumner, Scott. "Don't be Early in Bubble Predictions." *Econlog*, August 9, 2017. https://www.econlib.org/archives/2017/08/dont_be_early_i.html.

Sumner, Scott. "How Do We Evaluate Robert Shiller's Forecast?" *Econlog*, September 13, 2017, https://www.econlib.org/archives/2017/09/how_do_we_evalu.html.

Sundie, Jill M., Douglas T. Kenrick, Vladas Griskevicius, Joshua M. Tybur, Kathleen D. Vohs, and Daniel J. Bear. "Peacocks, Porsches, and Thorstein Veblen: Conspicuous Consumption as a Sexual Signaling Mechanism." *Journal of Personality and Social Psychology* 100, no. 4 (April 2011): 664–680.

Sunstein, Cass R. "Nudges vs. Shoves." *Harvard Law Review Forum* 127 (April 2014): 210–217.

Tabuchi, Hiroko. "Layoffs Taboo, Japan Workers Are Sent to the Boredom Room." *New York Times*, August 16, 2013. https://www.nytimes.com/2013/08/17/business/global/layoffs-illegal-japan-workers-are-sent-to-the-boredom-room.html.

Taleb, Nassim Nicholas. *The Black Swan: The Impact of the Highly Improbable.* New York: Random House, 2007.

Tango, Tom M., Mitchel G. Lichtman, and Andrew E. Dolphin. *The Book: Playing the Percentages in Baseball.* Dulles, VA: Potomac Books, 2007.

Tarko, Vlad. *Elinor Ostrom: An Intellectual Biography.* London: Rowman & Littlefield, 2016.

Taylor, Brad. "Rational Irrationality as Dual Process Theory." In *Exit and Voice: Papers from a Revisionist Public Choice Perspective*, 40–57. PhD diss., Canberra, Australia: Australian National University, 2014.

Taylor, Brad and Eric Crampton. "Anarchy, Preferences, and Robust Political Economy." Working Paper. Toowoomba: University of Southern Queensland, 2009. https://papers.ssrn.com/sol3/papers.cfm?abstract_id=1340779.

Tetlock, Philip. *Expert Political Judgment: How Good Is It? How Can We Know?* Princeton: Princeton University Press, 2005.

Tetlock, Philip and Dan Gardner. *Superforecasting: The Art and Science of Prediction.* New York: Crown, 2015.

Thaler, Richard H. and Cass R. Sunstein. *Nudge: Improving Decisions About Health, Wealth, and Happiness.* Revised edition. New York: Penguin, 2009.

Thornton, Paul. "Nextdoor, Where Every Neighborhood is Under Siege." *Los Angeles Times*, May 5, 2018. http://www.latimes.com/la-ol-opinion-newsletter-nextdoor-20180505-htmlstory.html#

Thwaites, Thomas. *The Toaster Project: Or a Heroic Attempt to Build a Simple Electric Appliance from Scratch.* New York, NY: Princeton Architectural Press, 2011.

Time. "BREWING: The Beer That Won the West." February 11, 1974. http://content.time.com/time/magazine/article/0,9171,908509,00.html.

Tocqueville, Alexis de. *Democracy in America.* Edited by Eduardo Nolla. Translated by James T. Schneider. Indianapolis: Liberty Fund, 2012.

Topol, Eric. *Deep Medicine: How Artificial Intelligence Can Make Healthcare Human Again.* New York: Basic Books, 2019.

Touboul, Jonathan. "The Hipster Effect: When Anti-Conformists All Look the Same." arXiv:1410.8001 (February 2019).

The Townshend. "About." Accessed June 27, 2019. http://www.thetownshend.com/about.

"The Townshend – Quincy (Phantom Gourmet)." Phantom Gourmet. May 2, 2016. https://www.youtube.com/watch?v=qNy6dFPxk3w.

Tshitoyan, Vahe, John Dagdelen, Leigh Weston, Alexander Dunn, Ziqin Rong, Olga Kononova, Kristin A. Persson, Gerbrand Ceder, and Anubhav Jain. "Unsupervised Word Embeddings Captured Latent Knowledge from Materials Science Literature." *Nature* 571 (2019): 95–98.

Tullock, Gordon. "The Welfare Costs of Tariffs, Monopolies and Theft." *Western Economic Journal* 5, no. 3 (June 1967): 224–232.

Tuschman, Avi. *Our Political Nature: The Evolutionary Origins of What Divides Us.* Amherst: Prometheus Books, 2013.

tvtropes. "A.I. Is a Crapshoot." Accessed July 15, 2019. https://tvtropes.org/pmwiki/pmwiki.php/Main/AIIsACrapshoot.

tvtropes. "Bourgeois Bohemian." Accessed June 28, 2019. https://tvtropes.org/pmwiki/pmwiki.php/Main/BourgeoisBohemian.

United States Department of Agriculture. "Organic Market Overview." Last updated April 4, 2017. https://www.ers.usda.gov/topics/natural-resources-environment/organic-agriculture/organic-market-overview.aspx.

United States Environmental Protection Agency. "Morality Risk Valuation." Accessed June 27, 2019. https://www.epa.gov/environmental-economics/mortality-risk-valuation.

Vavreck, Lynn. "A Measure of Identity: Are You Wedded to Your Party?" *The New York Times*, January 31, 2017. https://www.nytimes.com/2017/01/31/upshot/are-you-married-to-your-party.html.

Viscusi, W. Kip, John M. Vernon, and Joseph E. Harrington, Jr. *The Economics of Regulation and Antitrust*, 4th ed. Cambridge, MA: MIT Press, 2006.

Voigt, Stefan. "Breaking with the Notion of Social Contract: Constitutions as Based on Spontaneously Arisen Institutions." *Constitutional Political Economy* 10 (October 1999): 283–300.

Volokh, Eugene. "The United States is Both a 'Republic' and a 'Democracy' – Because 'Democracy' is like 'Cash.'" *The Washington Post*, November 14, 2016. https://www.washingtonpost.com/news/volokh-conspiracy/wp/2016/11/14/the-united-states-is-both-a-republic-and-a-democracy-because-democracy-is-like-cash/?utm_term=.9771330defdb.

Vossen, Bas van der and Jason Brennan. *In Defense of Openness: Why Global Freedom Is the Humane Solution to Global Poverty.* New York: Oxford University Press, 2018.

Vsauce. "A Defense of Comic Sans." February 11, 2013. https://www.youtube.com/watch?v=GUCcObwIsOs.

Waldfogel, Joel. "The Deadweight Loss of Christmas." *American Economic Review* 83, no. 5 (December 1993): 1328–1336.

Watney, Caleb. "Fairy Dust, Pandora's Box … or a Hammer." *Cato Unbound*, August 9, 2017. https://www.cato-unbound.org/2017/08/09/caleb-watney/fairy-dust-pandoras-box-or-hammer.

Watts, Marina Caitlin. "WATCH ME IF YOU CAN: 25 Things You Probably Didn't Know About Citizen Kane." *The Cornell Daily Sun*, March 11, 2016. https://cornellsun.com/2016/03/11/watch-me-if-you-can-25-things-you-probably-didnt-know-about-citizen-kane/.

Weinersmith, Zach. "The Greatest Generation." *Saturday Morning Breakfast Cereal*, August 7, 2018. https://www.smbc-comics.com/comic/the-greatest-generation.

West, Darrell M. *The Future of Work: Robots, AI, and Automation.* Washington, DC: The Brookings Institution, 2018.

Whiting, Robert. *You Gotta Have Wa.* Second edition. New York: Vintage, 2009.

WHO. "Clean Care is Safer Care." Accessed July 1, 2019. http://www.who.int/gpsc/tools/faqs/evidence_hand_hygiene/en/.

Wiebe, Toban. "Evolutionary Psychology and Anti-Market Bias." *Mises Daily*, September 15, 2010. https://mises.org/library/evolutionary-psychology-and-antimarket-bias.

Wilcox, W. Bradford, Paul Taylor, and Chuck Donovan. "When Marriage Disappears: The Retreat from Marriage in Middle America." *Heritage Lectures* no. 1179 (2011).

Williamson, Claudia R. "Informal Institutions Rule: Institutional Arrangements and Economic Performance." *Public Choice* 139, no. 3–4 (June 2009): 371–387.

Williamson, Oliver E. *The Transaction Cost Economics Project: The Theory and Practice of the Governance of Contractual Relations.* Northampton: Edward Elgar, 2013.

Wilson, Lindsay. "The Carbon Foodprint of 4 Diets Compared." *Shrink That Footprint*, accessed June 28, 2019. http://shrinkthatfootprint.com/food-carbon-footprint-diet.

Wittman Donald. Why Democracies Produce Efficient Results." *Journal of Political Economy* 97, no. 6 (December 1989): 1395–1424.

Wittman, Donald. *The Myth of Democratic Failure: Why Political Institutions Are Efficient.* Chicago: University of Chicago Press, 1995.

Yandle, Bruce. "Bootleggers and Baptists: The Education of a Regulatory Economist." *Regulation* 7, no. 3 (May/June 1983): 12–16.

Yglesias, Matthew. *The Rent is Too Damn High: What to do about It, And Why It Matters More than You Think.* New York: Simon & Schuster, 2012.

Zakaria, Fareed. *The Future of Freedom: Illiberal Democracy At Home and Abroad.* New York: W.W. Norton & Company, 2003.

Index

About the Author

Ryan H. Murphy is a senior research fellow at the O'Neil Center for Global Markets and Freedom at SMU Cox School of Business. He is a co-author of the *Economic Freedom of the World* report and has published over fifty academic journal articles. He received his PhD in economics from Suffolk University in 2013.

Lightning Source UK Ltd.
Milton Keynes UK
UKHW011254140622
404417UK00001B/2